DOG WHISPERER

with *Cesar Millan*

THE ULTIMATE EPISODE GUIDE

✦ ✦ ✦

JIM MILIO and
MELISSA JO PELTIER

A FIRESIDE BOOK

PUBLISHED BY SIMON & SCHUSTER

NEW YORK   LONDON   TORONTO   SYDNEY

Disclaimer: Techniques presented on the *Dog Whisperer* programs and in this book are educational and informative in nature. For advice appropriate to your situation, please consult a professional.

Fireside
A Division of Simon & Schuster, Inc.
1230 Avenue of the Americas
New York, NY 10020

First Fireside trade paperback edition April 2008

FIRESIDE and colophon are registered trademarks of Simon & Schuster, Inc.

For information about special discounts for bulk purchases,
please contact Simon & Schuster Special Sales at 1-800-456-6798 or
business@simonandschuster.com.

Designed by Jan Pisciotta

Manufactured in the United States of America

10 9 8 7 6 5 4 3 2 1

Library of Congress Cataloging-in-Publication Data

Milio, Jim, and Melissa Jo Peltier.
    Dog whisperer with Cesar Millan : the ultimate episode guide / Jim Milio and Melissa Jo Peltier.
        p.   cm.
    "A Fireside Book."
    Includes index.
    1. Dog Whisperer with Cesar Millan (Television program).   2. Dogs—Behavior.
3. Dogs—Training.   4. Human-animal communication.   I. Title.
SF433.M555   2008
636.7'0887—dc22   2007042836

ISBN-13: 978-1-4165-6143-9
ISBN-10:   1-4165-6143-9

To Mark Hufnail,
Without whom nothing is possible.
Three out, three back.

ACKNOWLEDGMENTS

The authors wish to thank:

The entire staff and crew of the *Dog Whisperer* series (page 335) for their consistently outstanding work and true dedication to the show. You are truly "L.A.'s Finest."

SueAnn Fincke, the heart and soul of the series. Where would we be without you?

Bonnie Peterson and Catherine Stribling, for hanging in at MPH during thick and thin, and keeping us from falling into the abyss.

Sheila Emery and Kay Sumner, for signing up Cesar and bringing him to partner with us, and for everything you do to help make the show a success.

Nicholas Ellingsworth, for helping pull together everything we needed to make this book possible.

John Ford, for taking a giant leap of faith.

Loreen Ong, Michael Cascio, Steve Schiffman, Russell Howard, Chris Albert, Mike Beller, Colette Beaudry, Char Serwa, and the National Geographic Channel team, for helping make *Dog Whisperer with Cesar Millan* #1.

Stacey Candella and the staffs of Cesar Millan, Inc., and the Ilusion and Cesar Millan Foundation, for their tireless efforts on behalf of Cesar and Ilusion.

Cherise Paluso of the Dog Psychology Center, for her invaluable help and good humor, even when she's juggling ten balls at a time.

Finally, to Ilusion and Cesar Millan: It is an honor and a privilege to stand with you as colleagues, teachers, students, and above all, as friends.

Jim Milio wishes to thank Sonny and Alex, the two most important productions of his life.

Melissa Jo Peltier wishes to thank her husband, John Gray, for a lifetime of memories in only five years. Let the adventure continue . . .

CONTENTS

SEASON **TWO**
Introduction 109

SEASON THREE
Introduction 221

INTRODUCTION by Cesar Millan

When we created the Dog Whisperer show, I really wanted it to be exciting, entertaining, and informative. But most of all, I wanted the show to present to viewers a new way to relate to their dogs—a common-sense way. People in America are very intellectual, emotional, and spiritual, but they're not instinctual. I wanted to try to help bring instinct back. Instinct to me represents Mother Nature, and I know dogs are a window to Mother Nature.

There is a lot of great information out there about dog behavior and dog training, and there are many dedicated experts who have written brilliantly about the subject. But I believe I have something unique to offer, since I grew up in a different country and had the advantage of living with my grandfather, a very wise man who taught me, "Never work against Mother Nature." My first lessons about dogs did not come from human professors in a university; instead, dogs themselves taught me about dogs. What these "natural professors" taught me was that dogs' needs are very basic—exercise, discipline, and affection, in that order—but that many well-meaning dog owners don't know how to go about fulfilling these needs. I think one reason for the show's popularity is that people are thirsting for this kind of information because they want to become more in tune with their dogs.

The most rewarding part of the show for me has been watching people open up to the process and realize that it's not the dog—it's them. They begin to see themselves not as their name or their income or their job, but as the energy they are projecting toward all the other beings around them. I love being there when the lightbulb goes on and they finally realize that they are the source, they are the ones making the dog stable or unstable. That's when the transformation truly begins.

I would like our little show to be one part of a movement that helps people take responsibility for their own effect on everything around them. If we start with our dogs, then we can begin to look around and ask, "How can we use this concept of calm-assertive energy to transform our relationships with our mothers, our fathers, our husbands, our wives, and our children?" When you transform yourself, you transform everything around you. In this way, learning to understand and fulfill our dogs, and learning to access the calm-assertive energy within us, can lead us to change our way of being toward one another—and, I hope, the world.

The Genesis of
DOG WHISPERER with Cesar Millan

On September 25, 2002, the Los Angeles Times ran an article entitled "Redeeming Rover" that profiled dog behavior expert Cesar Millan and his miraculous transformations of badly behaved canines. That article resulted in scores of producers descending on Millan's Dog Psychology Center located near downtown Los Angeles to try to sign up the rights for a possible TV series.

Among that horde were Kay Sumner and Sheila Emery. Although Kay and Sheila didn't have the splashiest résumés in this elbowing pack of producers, Cesar got a good vibe and ultimately joined up with them. (Cesar later told us that his pack of forty dogs also had the best reaction to Kay and Sheila's energy.) Among the things Kay and Sheila promised Cesar was that he wouldn't have to change himself or the way he works with dogs for the television show they envisioned, a guarantee none of their competitors were willing to offer.

Sheila and Kay produced a five-minute demo video showing Cesar in action. Through her industry contacts, Kay managed to get preliminary interest in a Cesar-related show at two cable channels, Animal Planet and the relatively new National Geographic Channel.

Kay and Sheila needed network-approved production partners in order for a Cesar Millan series to receive serious consideration. Kay and Sheila both knew MPH Entertainment partner Jim Milio, so they brought the idea and video of Cesar to MPH. Jim and MPH partners Melissa Jo Peltier and Mark Hufnail were intrigued enough to want to meet with Cesar.

Not long afterward, Cesar, his wife and partner, Ilusion, and a very imposing pit bull named Daddy paid a visit to MPH's Burbank offices. Cesar talked passionately about the "power of energy" and how dogs that have been troubled for ten years or more can be completely turned around, sometimes in an afternoon. Cesar explained how Americans tend to treat their dogs as humans and detailed how that often creates problems for both the animals and their owners. There would be plenty of years to absorb the many details of his message—but on that day, it was Cesar's passion, his charisma and, most of all, his integrity that truly knocked everyone out.

Animal Planet had an interest in Cesar but didn't want to commit to anything beyond a single pilot episode. There was an entirely different attitude at the National Geographic Channel. Nat Geo's new executive vice president, John Ford, had worked with MPH on several other programs when he had headed the TLC cable network, and there was a lot of mutual respect there. The newly formed Cesar Millan production team put together a full series concept titled "Leader of the Pack" and MPH shot a second demo video. National Geographic stepped up and really rolled the dice, ordering an incredible *twenty-six* episodes, a daring gamble for a modern cable television network. John Ford and his group obviously saw in Cesar the same qualities that the producers did.

As preproduction began, the show's producers put ads in local newspapers seeking people who had serious dog behavior problems that they wanted to fix. Interested pet owners showed up at dog auditions, designed to determine which kinds of stories would work best for the show. Sheila, Kay, and Ilusion Millan spent many evenings meeting dog lovers and their problem pooches to make assessments. Because of Ilusion's extensive knowledge of Cesar's methods, she was quickly able to tell whether a dog's issues were a quick fix or something that would require more than one session with Cesar. There was one unexpected side effect of auditions: several dogs marked their territory all over the MPH offices so the producers added a new line item to the budget: "carpet cleaning for dog messes."

During preproduction, the creative team devised the basic format for every story. First, the canine would demonstrate its bad dog behavior. Next, Cesar would interview the owner(s), a process eventually dubbed "the consultation." Then Cesar would go to work, rehabilitating the dog and training the owner. After the hands-on Cesar session, there would be a follow-up interview with Cesar and the owner. It was also decided that every story would be filmed using two cameras—one to follow Cesar, the other to follow the dog and its owner. During this early phase, the name of the series was changed from *Leader of the Pack* to *Dog Whisperer with Cesar Millan*.

As the first day of shooting approached, the initial story being prepared featured a lovely young couple whose aggressive dog attacked people when they went out on walks. But after Sheila scouted the couple's downtown L.A. loft, she hurried back to report that the woman was apparently a part-time dominatrix who had a vast collection of S&M gear hanging on the walls. Thinking that the National Geographic Channel executives might not want to "Dare to Explore" this particular couple, the crew went to do a story about a young woman named Tina Madden and a tiny—but nasty—Chihuahua named NuNu. Out came the cameras, Cesar worked his magic: NuNu became a sweet, passive little Chihuahua, and Tina was filled with hope. Cesar had made a huge difference in their lives in fewer than three hours. The production team continued to tape stories throughout the summer in and around Southern California. As the shooting continued, everyone began to get the feeling that something special was happening, that Dog Whisperer was not just another television series.

Dog Whisperer with Cesar Millan launched into the sea of basic cable programming on September 13, 2004, at 6:30 p.m. EST. Because it did not start out as a prime-time series, there was no advertising to promote the show. Fortunately, as viewers found the series, they too were astounded at Cesar's uncanny ability. The show debuted to respectable ratings, but as subsequent episodes aired, word of mouth started building. A handful of newspaper articles along with Cesar's guest appearances on Good Morning America, the Tonight Show, and Oprah also provided a big boost to the series's popularity.

The show also attracted some controversy. In the world of dog training, there is a joke: the only thing two dog trainers can agree on is that they both don't like the methods of another trainer. Even though Cesar is not a dog trainer, there was a small but very vocal group in what is known as the "positive only" training arena who objected to Cesar's corrections of dogs and some of the other methods he used for rehabilitation. Before the show had even aired, there was a coordinated letter-writing campaign to National Geographic, even though most of the letter writers demanding that the show be canceled had not actually seen it. Fortunately, there was a much larger group of veterinarians, trainers, and other animal professionals—and, ultimately, the home audience—that wholeheartedly supported the show and could see from the footage that Cesar's methods worked and were not harmful or cruel to the dogs. Instead, many of these dogs—and their owners—have been transformed forever, often in the course of a few hours. The proof is on tape.

Then the positive viewer mail started flowing in. It's rare in the world of television to get responses like "Cesar, you changed my life!" "We TiVo every episode and invite our friends with bad dogs over to watch." "Cesar, I use your techniques on my kids and they work on them, too." "Cesar, I'm going to become a vet because of you." It was clear that the show struck a chord for dog lovers and, surprisingly, for people who didn't even own—or like—dogs.

The show's producers maintain that *Dog Whisperer* is the only *real* reality show on television. You can't convince these dogs to fake bizarre behaviors. In fact, most viewers don't realize that Cesar doesn't allow any retakes when he's rehabilitating a dog. ("They don't understand 'take two,'" he says.) Cesar usually knows nothing about the dogs or owners he is about to meet, and the crew truly never knows where Cesar—or the dogs—are going to go or what they're going to do next. Some skeptics have claimed that the show edits out "the bad parts" or that some of the cases have been heavily edited to show miracles occurring where allegedly nothing happened. The truth is that it's "the bad parts"—when Cesar is in the midst of a difficult case—that are usually the first things to go *into* an episode: That's what makes the show so fascinating to watch. Stories are edited to accommodate time constraints, but there is never an attempt to hide what Cesar did or how much time it took for him to correct a bad behavior. Often, there are onscreen references detailing how much time it took Cesar to achieve results. There is no need to "cheat" through editing, because Cesar is that absolute rarity in television—the real deal.

In the summer of 2005, National Geographic ordered a second season, expanding the individual episodes to an hour and requesting that the series be shot in HD (high-definition) video. In 2006, a third season of twenty episodes was ordered, allowing Cesar to leave his home turf of Southern California and go on the road to help dogs all across America. As this book goes to print, a fourth season of thirty-five episodes is already on the air.

In the meantime, Cesar Millan is becoming an international phenomenon. With the series now airing in more than twenty foreign countries, *Dog Whisperer* and Cesar are rapidly growing in popularity both in the United States and throughout the world.

Producing the *Dog Whisperer with Cesar Millan* television series has been intensely gratifying and rewarding, for both Cesar and the production team. There is a great spirit among the staff, and all involved continue to be amazed and inspired by the transformations of the dogs taking place right before their eyes.

It is our joyful mission to help Cesar spread his message about calm-assertive leadership and a privilege to continue his mission to make the world a better place . . . one dog at a time.

Season
ONE

The first season of "*Dog Whisperer*" consists of twenty-six half-hour epi-sodes. It was during this first season that the production team worked out the best way to film each story. During the early shoots, Cesar would arrive with the crew and wait while they filmed the dog's bad behavior. However, with Cesar in the area, sometimes the dogs would refuse to behave badly—they sensed a "pack leader" in the general vicinity and started to behave on their own! It was then decided that Cesar should arrive *after* the crew had videotaped the bad behavior and pre-interviewed the owners.

The series had an extremely low budget during the first season. Ilusion would put on Cesar's makeup as he sat on the curb—there was no money for a dressing room or motor home. The "catered" lunch was from Subway or Togo's or Quiznos, usually eaten at the owner's backyard table or on the same curb where Cesar got made up. Fortunately, all the owners graciously allowed the crew to use their bathrooms.

No one can actually recall how it was accomplished, but during the first season the crew usually shot two full stories in a ten- to twelve-hour day. That

meant arriving at the person's home, filming the bad dog behavior, filming the consultation with Cesar, filming Cesar working with the dog and owners, then filming separate follow-up interviews with the owners and Cesar.* After a half-hour lunch break, the crew traveled to the next location to repeat the entire process with another family.

_____

*The Dog Whisperer team attempted to contact all episode participants, but not all responded. Follow-ups are provided wherever they were available.

Chapter 1

Aggression Toward People

NuNu in Tina's arms.

Demon Chihuahua

(episode 101)

Name: NuNu

Breed: Chihuahua

Most house cats weigh more than NuNu, a four-pound Chihuahua. But what NuNu lacks in mass, he makes up for with a seriously bad attitude. NuNu is fiercely protective of his owner, Tina Madden, and in his first month at home, NuNu bit Tina's roommate, Barclay, six times, drawing blood more than once. But even Barclay doesn't want Tina to give nasty NuNu away. Tina also believes there's a reason why NuNu turned up in her life. "I think this dog chose me. I think I'm his person, and that's another reason I couldn't give him up."

When Cesar arrives and hears all about NuNu's hellish behavior, the dog tries to sneak past Cesar to get to Tina on the couch, but Cesar won't let NuNu

Follow-up 🐾 🐾 🐾

NuNu and Tina's case is the first ever filmed for *Dog Whisperer.* According to Tina, "I have to say that in 2004 I could have never dreamed that a little four-pound terror of a dog and Cesar Millan, a man I had never heard of, would change the course of my life forever. With Cesar's knowledge and my commitment to his rehabilitation, NuNu is a dog that most people would dream of having."

NuNu has also become something of a national celebrity, earning the title of America's favorite Chihuahua in an Insider TV poll, beating out infamous competitors like Paris Hilton's Tinkerbell and Britney Spears's Lucky.

Behind the scenes

In an unexpected turn of events, Tina now works as one of Cesar's assistants at the Dog Psychology Center, helping to rehabilitate other dogs. "This has truly been an experience of a lifetime," says Tina.

near her. "It is very important to let him know that the couch isn't going to belong to him anymore." After Tina hands NuNu over to Cesar, the demon Chihuahua goes ballistic in Cesar's lap, snapping, flailing, and trying to bite Cesar any way he can. "This is part of the dominance. If I back away right now, he wins."

"I didn't want a dog that does this to people," says a teary-eyed Tina, as NuNu lunges for Cesar's hand. Cesar doesn't flinch. "You've got to stand your ground and let him know that this behavior is unwanted by you. But if you run away, if you become nervous, then it's only going to intensify his unwanted behavior. And it's not that we're using force." Cesar gently holds NuNu down by his neck while waiting for the temper tantrum to dissipate.

Inside their apartment and on a walk, Cesar demonstrates how Tina and Barclay can reclaim the keys to their kingdom by acting in a new way toward NuNu—as his calm-assertive pack leaders. "When you see that he is getting into that zone, do not allow his brain to escalate too long." Cesar demonstrates how they can stop unwanted behavior as it begins by gently but firmly touching two fingers to NuNu's neck, like the bite that a mother dog would give her pup.

On their walk, Cesar shows Tina tips that will help make her a pack leader in NuNu's eyes. She needs to go out the door before NuNu and walk proudly with shoulders back and head held high, with NuNu walking beside her or right behind her.

Tina understands that to change NuNu, she has to change her own behavior first. "The most important thing I learned from Cesar is that I have to be more dominant with my dog rather than let my dog dominate me and everything that I do in my life. Sometimes you have to look inside yourself and change yourself, in order to change the creatures around you."

The Grooming Gremlin

Name: Josh

Breed: Maltese mix

Ronette Tomlinson is in a pickle. She dreams of the day she can take her dog Josh to the groomer and get him all spruced up. Unfortunately, this nine-month-old Maltese-poodle mix's tantrums and fearsome biting have worsened to the point that no groomer will go near him. Now Josh's fur is matted and knotted, with scraggly strands that droop over his eyes.

Cesar, Ronette, and Josh during their grooming session.

After he hears the basics from Ronette, Cesar explains, "In Josh's mind, you are his female—which is not healthy." Cesar tells Ronette that she and all the members of the family need to become Josh's pack leaders by being more dominant. "You're going to make sure that he follows rules, boundaries, and limitations."

Fortunately for Ronette, Cesar worked as a groomer and an assistant vet tech as a teenager in Mexico and spent his entire first year in America grooming dogs in San Diego. Just before the hairy showdown, Cesar takes Josh for a walk, which Cesar considers a vital bonding ritual between human and dog. Josh balks at first, but he soon relaxes. Back inside Ronette's house, however, the battle of wills continues. With one hand, Cesar holds Josh firmly by the neck, mimicking the bite of a more dominant dog. But every time Cesar brings a pair of shears near Josh's face, the maniacal Maltese lashes out violently. Josh even succeeds in biting Cesar a few times and draws blood. But Cesar soldiers on. "It's like a rattlesnake trying to strike you, but it's not going make me back away." Cesar makes a *"tsst"* sound whenever Josh misbehaves, so the dog makes a connection between the sound and the unwanted behavior.

When Cesar asks for a napkin so his blood won't get everywhere, he is surprised to learn that Ronette is a nurse. Cesar wants Ronette to use the same energy she uses with her patients whenever she deals with Josh and not just feel sorry for the poor lit-

Follow-up ❁ ❁ ❁

Ronette can groom and brush Josh anytime without a problem. She continues to work hard to stay Josh's calm-assertive pack leader.

Key Cesar Tip

Small dogs often use their teeth to dominate, because we let them get away with much more threatening or aggressive behavior than we would a larger dog. No matter how small and cute your dog is, biting or baring teeth is not an acceptable behavior.

tle rescued dog. Cesar's words hit home for Ronette. "The way I am in my profession is the way I have to be with Josh. I have to know that it's not that I don't love him but that I'm doing certain things for his own good. And I have to do it, and I have to be strong and confident about it."

As the session continues, Josh's resistance diminishes to the point where Cesar hands the scissors over to a stunned Ronette. "I never thought I would be actually trimming his hair. That was amazing."

Beware of Teddy

Name: Teddy

Breed: Labrador retriever

"*Teddy's got that* smile and that tail wag, and you think he's happy and fine. But Teddy kind of lures you in, then all of a sudden he will snap," says Steve Garelick. Steve's nine-year-old yellow Lab, Teddy, does look like an angel, but he bites like a hound from hell. He has attacked more than one stranger and has even bitten Steve's wife, Lisa.

Steve admits, "We basically live our lives where we keep Teddy separated from people and dogs. We have to post signs if we have a party making sure nobody goes out to the backyard when we're not watching." But the Garelicks fear the most for their two-and-a-half-year-old daughter, Sara. "I love Teddy, I love to pet him," chirps the adorable toddler. Steve says, "If he were ever aggressive toward Sara, we would definitely have to give him away."

During their initial consultation, Cesar is shocked to discover that Teddy's biting behavior has been going on for nine years, essentially since the day the Garelicks brought him home. Cesar tells them, "There are only two positions when you live with animals—the leader and the followers. You have been in the follower position." When Cesar tells them that he's ready to meet Teddy, Steve asks him, "Do you have a big, padded suit?"

Cesar carefully enters the Garelicks' backyard, carrying a tennis racket to use as a shield against Teddy's violent lunges. At first Teddy keeps running away, but Cesar advances on the dog no matter how many times Teddy tries to avoid him. After Cesar corners the dog at one end of the yard, he holds out the loop of Teddy's chain. After several moments of hesitation, Teddy lets Cesar slip the collar over his neck. "He became friendly. So I used that as an advantage, to let him know that I'm not here just to dominate him. I also want to walk with him. But I let him know that we were going to leave his home with him following me. I want *him* to play the follower position."

Steve and Lisa, both shocked to see their dog not lashing out at a stranger, accompany Cesar as they take a walk with Teddy around their neighborhood. When Cesar tells Teddy to sit, the dog does so immediately. Cesar tells the amazed couple, "Right now he trusts you, but he doesn't respect you. You guys need to be trained to recog-

Steve and Lisa confirm Cesar's belief that you *can* indeed teach an old dog new tricks. They both worked hard in taking the dominant role in their household, and Teddy's changed behavior has transformed him into the happy-go-lucky yellow Lab they always dreamed of.

Behind the scenes

While she was filming Teddy's bad behavior, the dog lunged at the crew's production assistant, trying to bite her. Fortunately, Teddy only punctured and tore her jeans. That video is used in the story.

nize energy and understand how important it is to be the leader."

But can Teddy still coexist safely with Sara? Steve recalls, "We prepared Teddy when the baby was coming. We introduced smells into the home, we brought in pampers and let him sniff those things before she was actually born, so that he knew there were going to be some changes in the house. The first night we brought Sara home, we had Teddy sleep in the same room with her. And he knew he wasn't going to be pushed aside for Sara, so that there was no jealousy."

Cesar concludes, "One thing that Steve and Lisa did right was they made sure Teddy was very submissive to Sara. So Sara from the beginning became the dominant one. If Steve and Lisa devote themselves to mastering control of Teddy, Sara will be the greatest pack leader ever."

One Last Chance

Name: Coach

Breed: boxer

Six-year-old Coach had fewer than twenty-four hours to live. Although boxers are teacher John Albert's favorite breed, Coach's aggressive behavior had brought the Albert family to the brink of a life-and-death decision.

In the beginning, Coach was great with the kids and was also an excellent watchdog. But recently, Coach's behavior has deteriorated into uncontrolled aggression toward the world outside the Alberts' yard. Coach began running full speed and then throwing his entire body at the side gate in an attempt to ward off "intruders."

The problems escalated when Coach escaped and threatened a male neighbor. According to John's wife, Stella, "He was considering suing us for

Cesar and Coach.

everything we had, and he pulled a pocket knife on Coach and was prepared to kill him in the street if he came any closer." Desperate for some kind of help, the Alberts called their dog trainer and vet for advice. John recalls, "We talked to a lot of people about it. The impression we got was that this was a behavior that couldn't be fixed, and that he would eventually harm our children and turn on us." These experts recommended that the Alberts euthanize Coach immediately.

The Alberts made the painful decision to put Coach to sleep. The memory of that day still brings tears to Stella's eyes. "My son Cade wanted to keep some of his fur and he wanted us to bring Coach his blanket so Coach smell him before he died—so he could die in Cade's blanket."

Then, in a twist of fate, the night before Coach was supposed to be put to sleep, Stella was reading their local newspaper. "I saw a tiny little ad that said if you have problems with your dog, give us a call." The ad had been placed by *Dog Whisperer* producers searching for stories for the TV series, yet to air its first episode.

Coach is now a perfect dog and the Alberts are thrilled to have him as an important part of their family. Instead of the trauma of having his dog put down, Cade now walks to school with his pet every day, with Coach carrying Cade's books in his backpack. According to John, "Cesar's done more for us than just teach us how to walk a dog. He saved our dog's life."

Coach gets a last-minute stay of execution when Cesar responds to the call. Cesar believes that many dogs are put to death unnecessarily, due to a simple lack of information.

As Cesar moves to open the door to the backyard where Coach awaits, the boxer begins barking. Once Cesar steps outside, Coach seems to calm down quickly. Cesar observes Coach's body language and realizes almost instantly what the problem is. "The way he's behaving around me right now is very calm and submissive. This is not a dangerous dog. This is a dog that is bored. He needs a challenge."

Cesar is shocked that the situation had escalated to this point. "When I was invited to come to this home, I pictured this horrendous dog. This is somebody who was on death row. I'm blown away that there was actually a decision to put him down—not only from neighbors but also from doctors. They didn't come and really evaluate Coach's psychological state of mind."

Cesar wants to help the Alberts deal with Coach's territorial behavior by utilizing his exercise, discipline, and affection formula. Since Stella admits they had been afraid to walk Coach and have kept him in the backyard all the time, Cesar insists that the family start Coach on a routine of regular long walks, to help him work off some of his pent-up frustrations. Cesar demonstrates the proper way to walk, by keeping the leash high up on the neck for maximum control and giving quick corrections by pulling sideways on the leash to snap Coach out of any unwanted behavior. "That little tug is for Coach to understand that I am now in control of his reactions."

On a return visit, Cesar brings a backpack to put on Coach during their walks. The backpack represents the concept of giving Coach a job while walking. "Since you guys are doing really good walking with your dog and involving him more in your daily life, a backpack is going to help you to intensify the challenge on the walk."

Cesar is delighted to have saved Coach from an unnecessary fate. "I think Coach is very happy to be alive, to tell you the truth. I am not a psychic, but I can definitely feel that he trusted me in the matter of an hour. Is he grateful? Absolutely! That's just the beauty of dogs. They're grateful when they're next to a person who truly understands what is best for them."

Mixed-Up Chow

Name: Stewart

Breed: chow–golden retriever mix

Catherine, Calvin, Andre, Cesar, and Deborah walk with Stewart.

Damon and Deborah Carr got Stewart from the pound, as a birthday gift for their daughter, Catherine. She was also the only dog who wasn't barking. Deborah recalls. "We thought, 'Oh good, the quiet one.'"

But at home, this chow–golden retriever mix was no longer silent. "She really hasn't shut up since," Deborah says with a laugh. In addition to her constant barking, Stewart seems to have multiple personalities—sweet at home, a terror outside, friendly to some people, aggressive toward others. Damon and Deborah are most concerned about how Stewart relates to children. She seems to be afraid of children and barks at them constantly.

Cesar has worked with nervous, aggressive chows before, but he never blames a dog's problems entirely on its breed. "Just because she's a chow, that doesn't mean she's going to be nervous or aggressive. This comes from the dog in her, not the breed," says Cesar.

Since one of Stewart's scariest behaviors is her fearful aggression toward children, Cesar calls on his own sons, nine-year-old Andre and five-year-old Calvin, to assist in Stewart's treatment. They stay safely on one side of Cesar as he walks Stewart on the other. "This is the best way you can rehabilitate dogs if they are afraid of children. She can begin by walking next to children." Cesar explains that kids move, sound, and smell very different from other humans, and that can make a nervous dog even more anxious. Cesar recommends that the Carrs not let people just come up and pet Stewart during her rehabilitation. They should politely tell people that Stewart is "in training."

Deborah and her family are thrilled by their experience with Cesar. "I think it's fantastic! This will make such a difference to our lives! Oh, my goodness."

What's It All About, Alfie?

Name: Alfie

Breed: bulldog

(episode 126)

Alfie is a three-and-a-half-year-old English bulldog who has been pampered by actress and television host Daisy Fuentes. After about two years, Daisy and her fiancé, Matt, noticed that Alfie was becoming defensive and aggressive, especially to people coming to their front gate and into their house.

Daisy with Alfie and Cesar.

Alfie's hostility seemed to escalate when Rita, a two-year-old wheaten terrier, joined the family. According to Daisy, "Rita jumps all over everybody—it's very annoying. Alfie just looks like a tank coming at you. He has snapped at a couple of people, he's broken the skin. I'm just very worried that he's going to hurt someone bad one time and that he'll be taken away from me."

Once Cesar talks to Daisy, he gets a better handle on the situation. "Alfie suffers from aggression; Rita suffers from a hyperactive state of mind. They both are side effects caused by lack of exercise and lack of discipline."

Cesar asks Daisy how she corrects Alfie when he misbehaves. She says she yells at him, then puts him behind a gate, but he refuses to settle down after that. Cesar counters, "So he didn't get the message of the discipline when you did that. If we don't stop him, he will keep biting people. This is not going to stop until somebody sets up new rules."

According to Cesar, when humans shower a dog with affection and nothing else, it's really more for the owner's satisfaction than the dog's. "The human is not really fulfilling the animal. So we begin backward . . . every single day. When a dog feels that the human does not represent a one-hundred-percent authority figure, it's just not going to listen to the human."

Cesar begins today's rehabilitation at Daisy's front door, where any visitor tends to trigger Alfie's aggression. Cesar watches while a *Dog Whisperer* crew member comes to the door and Daisy fruitlessly tries to get Alfie to get back from the door and sit on his pillow. Cesar observes, "Your style is just to move the dog away from the front door without really making the dog submit to the situation. You make him go away when his mind is still unstable. What I would do is, I would come and bump against him." Alfie looks up at Cesar when he is touched. "Once he looks at me, then I move forward."

When someone steps on a cheeseburger squeaky toy, Daisy is reminded of one of Alfie's other issues. It is impossible to take any toy away from Alfie once he starts chewing on it. Cesar demonstrates how a pack leader handles that situation. He takes the toy and puts it down hear Alfie. "Before I give him the toy, he can't touch the toy. He's not going to get it if he does any excited behavior. He will get the toy if he does patient behavior."

When Alfie eventually backs away from the toy and rolls onto his back, Cesar gives the bulldog a friendly belly rub. "I reward this. This is the highest level of submission."

When Daisy tries to get Alfie to drop his toy, she is not as successful. "When I did it, it didn't work so well. But we both need to practice a little bit. This is new to both of us. After Cesar showed him who was the dominant male, Alfie came around and just wanted to lie down by him instead of me!"

Daisy admits, "I will probably still treat them as children or refer to them as my kids, which I know is wrong but I'm just being honest. But I will keep in mind and realize that they are animals."

Showdown with Shep

Name: Shep

Breed: German shepherd

Cynthia Holvenstot has overcome many obstacles since that fateful day when gang members opened fire at a party, and a stray bullet traveled four blocks, piercing her spine. But for the wheelchair-bound Cynthia, there's still one obstacle that she just can't seem to beat: Shep, her fearsome white German shepherd.

Cynthia's son Joseph found Shep abandoned behind a convenience store and lured him home with food. Although Shep is friendly and playful with Joseph, Cynthia, and her other son, Ricky, the dog bites anyone he does not know, often without warning. In addition to wanting to cure Shep's aggression, Cynthia holds on to one other hope. "I would love to be able to walk him, but that's a dream. He's too strong. Being in a wheelchair, I'm afraid that if I did try to walk him, I'd go off like a roller coaster."

Cesar shows Cynthia how to walk Shep.

When Cesar arrives, he assures Cynthia that her dream of walking Shep can come true, but first he's curious to know how much exercise the energetic Shep gets every day. Cynthia tells him that her two boys play with Shep for fifteen minutes in the backyard every day as one of their chores. Cesar counters, "That's just excitement. That's like taking kids to Chuck E. Cheese versus taking kids to piano lessons. Piano lessons will make calm and submissive kids, put them into a different state of mind, but Chuck E. Cheese gets 'em hyper."

To help Cynthia achieve her dream, Cesar has to confront Shep and let him know there's a new sheriff in town. Cesar's mission is a risky one: a showdown with an attack dog on its own turf, and Cynthia is terrified that Cesar will be hurt. When Cesar, armed with only a 35-cent leash, arrives at the gate to the backyard, Shep immediately starts barking ferociously. Cesar calmly and assertively steps inside. Shep runs wildly around the yard, barking the entire time. Cesar sees a plastic garbage can nearby and picks it up, preparing to use it to block any attacks from Shep.

Cynthia ultimately was not able to handle Shep, but she does have one of Shep's puppies, named Dora, which she has trained from birth how to help her using Cesar's techniques. Her sons helped Cynthia train Dora to pull the wheelchair if she needs it. Dora goes with Cynthia every weekend to the Santa Monica pier. Dora walks right beside Cynthia without a leash.

Cesar approaches Shep, who has his back against the wall and is still barking. Using energy and body language as his only "weapons," Cesar gives his signature "*tsst*" sound and says firmly to Shep, "Relax." The dog stops barking. Cesar holds out the leash, which has a loop at the end. Cesar slowly, gently places the loop over Shep's head and around his neck, then leads the now submissive dog back out to the front of the house. Cynthia is blown away. "I got a chill through my whole body."

Cesar and Shep join Cynthia in her wheelchair for a stroll down the street. Cesar keeps Shep right at his side during the walk, and Shep gives him no resistance at all. Cynthia's hopes are rekindled. "I'd love for Shep to be a service dog. I thought it was out of reach, but now it seems that he might actually be able to do that one day."

When Cesar hands Shep's leash over to Cynthia, she is surprised at how gentle he is. "He's not yanking or pulling, it's actually cruise control. I walk my dog, he walks me, we walk each other, and we're cool."

But all is not cool. Cesar returns to Cynthia's house three weeks later after learning that Shep has bitten a neighbor. Cesar decides to show sons Ricky and Joseph how to control Shep on a walk and then the way to handle the dog when he turns aggressive. First, Cesar shows the boys where to put Shep's collar. "Remember, it requires less pull when the leash is all the way on the top, because that's the most sensitive part of the neck. When you guys used to walk him, he would pull you. You were following him. Now he's following us."

Cynthia and her boys have their work cut out for them, but Cynthia has hope. "This was a dream come true. I hugged Cesar for it. At first I was scared for him, and then I was amazed by him, and now I'm blessed by him."

Postal Dog

Name: J

Breed: beagle

Years ago, Janet Cantebury and her kids brought home a darling dog named J from the pound. Or so they thought. Janet recalls. "When we took her home, she became this sort of flaming, unmanageable monster." Janet always warns people about J and makes sure they approach with caution, because she worries that J will bite for no reason.

Janet's problems turned into a living nightmare when J had a close encounter with one of man's best friend's biggest adversaries—the letter carrier. "J nipped her pants leg and actually broke her skin. A few minutes later, a person came running up on the lawn and took a bunch of pictures, then drove away. That turns out to have been the letter carrier's supervisor."

A U.S. Postal Service supervisor advises dog owners about the dangerous problems postal employees confront every day. "It is a very serious matter. If dogs can't control themselves, then their owners have to control them. And it's the owners who ultimately are held responsible if something happens to our letter carriers." In Janet's case, the Postal Service refuses to continue delivering mail to her door.

"Then the Department of Animal Control showed up. They said they may come and quarantine the dog. Then I got a letter from my insurance company, saying that they were going to cancel my insurance. Finally, there was a letter from a lawyer saying that I was being sued by my postal carrier."

In desperation, Janet turns to Cesar for help. From the moment Janet opens her door, Cesar gets an eyeful. "J exhibited panic right away. After that he showed tension, after that he showed nervousness, and then he showed fear. This dog is carrying all the bad energy that's possible."

Cesar notices that Janet's own nervous energy is contributing to J's issues. Cesar believes that J needs a pack leader who is calm and in control. "I'm not saying don't give affection to a dog. It's just not good to give affection when the mind is anxious."

Cesar allows J to "check him out," by ignoring the dog while she sniffs and explores. When J finally relaxes and lies down, Cesar pets the dog like he's giving a gentle rubdown, using the tips of his fingers on J's body. "I massage dogs in a way that they do with each other. Dogs bite each other to stimulate each other's muscles.

When the postal service told Janet that it would never deliver mail to her home as long as J was there, she decided to adopt him out to a family that runs a beagle rescue. He's much happier there and is doing great.

Behind the scenes

MPH Entertainment rented Cesar a generic mail carrier uniform from a costume company. If you look closely when you watch the episode, you'll see it's not the official uniform of the United States Postal Service.

Key Cesar Tip

The U.S. Postal Service takes the physical safety of its letter carriers very seriously. It's up to dog owners to be responsible, or else they may find themselves in Janet's situation.

I send them to a higher level of relaxation by giving a good deep massage."

Before Cesar's visit is complete, he's got one more trick up his sleeve. He dresses up in a mailman's outfit and goes for a walk with Janet and J. "This is very unusual, that a mailman would actually take a dog for a walk, especially a dog that went after one of them. This way he develops a connection with the mailman."

Cesar wants Janet to practice calm-assertive behavior around J to establish herself as his boss, not his employee. "By doing the things that I do, I have actually been encouraging the behaviors that I hate. In healing myself, by getting control of the situation, I'll heal J."

Battle of the Boyfriends

Name: Boyfriend

Breed: herding mix

(episode 126)

Anita Eble's home used to be a happy menagerie of people and animals. But this idyllic life was turned upside down when Anita found herself with two boyfriends. Boyfriend, a four-year-old herding mix, just doesn't get along with Anita's other boyfriend, David Kovach—in fact, he's bitten David four times. David is convinced that Anita's house just isn't big enough for two boyfriends. He says, "Being bit four times is definitely my limit. If it was up to me I would have put the dog down quite a long time ago."

Cesar with the four-legged boyfriend.

Since then, Anita has kept the canine Boyfriend confined in a large backyard pen. "I have called dog trainers and no one, for no amount of money, would come out and even try. Everybody told me to put him down."

Once Cesar hears more about Boyfriend's story, the picture begins to become clear. "Boyfriend was *afraid* in the beginning. So when we don't understand the fear, then it becomes something that we actually nurture. We can create a fearful, aggressive dog."

Cesar learns that Anita's way of punishing any dog's bad behavior is to put it in a cage. When Cesar asks, "So you put him away, like a time-out?" When Anita nods in agreement, Cesar tells her, "In the animal world, time-outs don't exist."

Anita tells Cesar that she is afraid Boyfriend might bite her and that when he acts up, she yells at the dog. Boyfriend David adds, "I'm concerned whether or not Anita is gonna be able to do it. I'm concerned that after everything, I'm gonna get bit again." Cesar is more concerned about David's attitude. "He's not giving him a chance anymore. In his mind—it's done. He's blaming the dog. And this is not about blaming the animal; it's about really taking full responsibility. It's not the dog's fault."

Although Anita is nervous, Cesar lets himself into Boyfriend's large pen and sits

Follow-up ❀ ❀ ❀

Anita is very happy with Boyfriend's changed behavior. He is able to get along easily with the other dogs in the backyard and loves going on long walks with Anita. Though her human boyfriend, David, moved out, Anita says they are still together as a couple.

down with his back to the dog. "When I walk in there, I have to be calm and assertive, but he was letting me know that he was close to striking me. I turned my back to him and waited." Common sense might dictate that this would make Cesar a target, but he knows what he is doing, "This is just allowing him to calm down next to me." In fewer than five minutes, Boyfriend lies down calmly next to Cesar.

Cesar attempts to show Anita the basics of how to walk Boyfriend. "We can't challenge him too much during the walk because he's way too sensitive, he's right at the edge of coming after us and releasing his frustration. So we really have to get into the role of being the dominant one." Cesar demonstrates that Boyfriend has to be calm and submissive before they can lead him out of the pen on a leash. But he has doubts about Anita. "Right now Anita's at level zero of leadership. So the owners have to do their homework and at least get themselves on level three, and then I can take it from there. Without their commitment, we're not going anywhere, and the dog will go right back to the negative behavior."

Next, Cesar brings the two boyfriends together. Anita remarks, "David's never ever been this close to this dog without being bit." Cesar tells them, "David has to become part of the strategy here because they have some friction going on with each other. David is part of the family, but in Boyfriend's eyes, he is not part of the family."

Even David is willing to give his rival another chance. "I think if I can be a little bit more peaceful, it'll help out immeasurably."

Chapter 2

Aggression Toward Dogs and Other Animals

Stephanie and Amir with Churchill.

Raging Rottie!

Name: Churchill

Breed: rottweiler

(episode 109)

For Stephanie Kaspian, it all began with a dream about dogs. The next morning, Stephanie told her husband, Amir, a Los Angeles firefighter and paramedic, that they had to go to the pound, just to *look* at some puppies. But Amir knew the real story. "If I didn't pick out a dog, I'*d* be in the doghouse."

They settled on an adorable rottweiler puppy named Churchill and brought him home. Inside their apartment, Churchill is as sweet as can be. Outside, it's a different story. Amir says, "Every time I would take Churchill on a walk, he would go berserk."

"When he sees a dog, he'll jump up and down and his hair stands on end. He growls and barks, and it doesn't matter what size the dog is. It could be a Saint Bernard or a little toy poodle," Stephanie adds.

Although Churchill seemed to be aggressive only toward other dogs, the gravity of the situation increased when the dog bit a neighbor who was petting him. For Amir, that was the last straw. "As soon as that happened, I told my wife, Churchill's gone." In Los Angeles County, if a dog bite breaks the skin, the offending canine must be quarantined for ten days. Stephanie and the neighbor bitten by Churchill both convinced Amir to give the rottweiler one more chance. Then they contacted Cesar.

When Cesar meets with the Kaspians, Amir tells Cesar that he believes Churchill is a "done deal, meaning, I've talked to people who train dogs and rescue dogs, and everything I've read about him being a male rottweiler says that, at his age, being two and a half years old, it's too late. He'll never socialize with dogs. Only a miracle could make that happen."

When Cesar asks Amir, "Would you consider it a miracle if you could walk Churchill with another dog next to you today?" Amir nods and replies, "Everything I've read about you, Cesar, seemed awesome. But I gotta see it with my own eyes."

Cesar is ready to take on the challenge of Churchill, but first he needs to walk with him alone, without the negative energy of Amir and Stephanie, who are already anticipating defeat. Leaving the Kaspians behind, he takes Churchill down the street and around the corner.

Sometimes Cesar needs an assistant to help in a dog's rehabilitation. For this case, Ilusion arrives with reinforcements, including a retriever named Benjamin. As soon as Churchill sees Benjamin, he begins to jump and react. Cesar starts to walk, with Churchill on one side of him and Benjamin on the other. Whenever Churchill tries to fight or attack, Cesar gives correction with quick tugs of the leash. In less than two minutes Cesar's calm-assertive energy has eliminated Churchill's aggression. "I didn't allow him to escalate too much. The moment I grab the leash, I'm already in control."

Minutes later, when Cesar comes back around the corner walking two calm dogs on either side, Amir is stunned: "You gotta be kidding me!" Cesar tells the couple, "This is just step number one: to actually convince him that he can't do that behavior anymore, because it's a vicious cycle that he has lived with for months."

When Cesar hands Churchill's leash to Amir, the firefighter immediately gets tense. As the two men walk next to each other, Cesar makes the process relatable to Amir's profession. "It's like being a paramedic. When somebody panics, you have to be the calm, assertive one, because you know best."

Cesar tells Amir and Stephanie that whenever they take Churchill for a walk, the dog's focus needs to be entirely on them. Whenever Churchill gets distracted, they need to correct him with a little tug on his leash and get Churchill immediately to refocus on them.

Cesar says, "I'm very proud of Amir because he was a very skeptical guy, then here he is participating. And in this case he wants to be the best dog owner that Churchill can have." Amir also has praise for Cesar. "This was a miracle, man. Cesar saved Churchill's life. I was ready to get rid of him, but now . . . I see that there's light at the end of the tunnel."

Follow-up ❀ ❀ ❀

Amir and Stephanie have become Churchill's pack leaders and no longer have any trouble with him. They even have a new member of their pack, a two-year-old son named Dominic, who also gets along great with Churchill. They are both overjoyed that Churchill has been able to remain a loving, active part of their growing family. After adopting another dog from Cesar, the formerly skeptical Amir has become a true "Cesar believer."

There's Something about Emily . . .

Name: Emily

Breed: pit bull

Emily.

For Jessika Palmer, it was love at first sight when she saw Emily, especially since she had a heart-shaped brown spot on her side. Jessika's dad, Dave, didn't really want Jessika to get another dog, but he fell in love with Emily as well, so the deal was sealed.

Unfortunately, this seemingly sweet pit bull has spent most of her six years confined to the Palmers' backyard. When Dave or Jessika takes Emily out into the world, she shows another side of her personality—a dangerous aggression toward other dogs. Emily is so dog aggressive that Jessika can't walk her, so Emily lives in confinement, totally secluded from any possible dog encounters.

Even though pit bulls have a bad public reputation, Cesar has great affection for this powerful and often misunderstood breed. During their initial consultation, Cesar learns that the Palmers pretty much let Emily get her own way around the house. Cesar wonders whether there's a parallel between the way Emily runs the household and the way Dave raised Jessika. "I got away with everything!" declares Jessika. Cesar notes, "Emily controls the household, controls the dad, controls the daughter—and that just gives her too much power. To really fulfill her life, she needs to have three things: physical activity, which is the walk; psychological activities—rules, boundaries, limitations—and then the affection."

It is late in the afternoon when Cesar begins working with Emily in the Palmers' front yard. Cesar asks Ilusion to walk past Emily with Daddy, one of the balanced pit bulls from their pack. Cesar quickly determines that Emily's level of violent behavior has reached what he calls the "red zone." When Emily starts lunging at Daddy, Cesar makes Emily lie on the ground by keeping his hand on her neck. "This is a very powerful breed. And without us releasing the power, this power becomes frustration. This is a breed that was meant to be a gladiator. Gladiators will choose to fight as an option to release frustration."

Cesar takes Emily for a walk around the block several times to try and drain her energy. Even though Cesar is eventually able to walk Emily and Daddy together, he recommends that Emily spend six weeks in his Dog Psychology Center to be resocialized by living with a real dog pack. Cesar declares, "This is as bad as it gets. There's a lot of bad energy inside her."

Back in her own neighborhood, Emily was a terror. Now she's about to be scared straight. When they arrive at Cesar's center, Emily is met at the long fence by fifty imposing dogs, including pit bulls, rottweilers, and German shepherds. Virtually all these dogs had serious issues that Cesar fixed by utilizing his "power of the pack" method. "A dog is a pack-oriented species. And humans are a pack-oriented species; we need a group of people to be with. We call that family. So a pack of dogs for a dog is nature. It is part of who he is," says Cesar.

Emily resists when she first sees all the dogs, but Cesar corrects her with a pull of the leash and then brings her inside the gate to meet the pack. She is instantly surrounded by dogs of all breeds and sizes trying to sniff her. "It's like swimming with sharks without being bitten," says Cesar. Whenever Emily starts to charge or make an aggressive move on a pack member, Cesar corrects her by touching her neck firmly with his hand. "Every touch that I do is because she gets fixated on something, she gets too tense, and I have to direct her to another state of mind by touching her."

During her stay at Cesar's boot camp, Emily gets exercise on a treadmill and by Rollerblading with the pack. Two weeks into her treatment Emily is improving, but she's still not entirely comfortable within the pack. When Dave and Jessika arrive at the center to visit Emily, Cesar warns them, "Now, one thing that can happen is there's a possibility that she will attack a dog, because this is what she used to do around you." Sure enough, When Dave walks with Emily through the pack, Emily tries to attack another dog. Cesar immediately puts her on the ground, into a submissive position. "Every once in a while, we're going to see a fight or a bite—which is part of the program, unfortunately," says Cesar.

After forty-three days of boot camp, Cesar is finally able to have Emily be in the pack without her trying to attack anyone. When he brings the pit bull back home, Cesar instructs Dave and Jessika how to walk with Emily and how to give her corrections

Although Emily loves the treadmill and is in great shape, she still doesn't get along with other dogs. Emily now lives with Jessika in Nevada.

with a quick snap of the leash whenever she starts to become aggressive toward another dog. "Their assignment is to walk around their neighborhood, to walk around dogs. They have to learn to pass by dogs. If they achieve that, I think that is a good step for them. But it's not going to be an easy street."

Jessika, dabbing tears from her eyes, says, "I'm really, really grateful for this experience. I think that Emily totally deserves a good life, because she means a lot to me."

Aggressive Alice

Name: Alice

Breed: mixed

"I've rescued like a thousand dogs. Once you pick up a puppy, you can't just walk away, you've got to bring it back," says Karen Erbach. When Karen found eight-week-old Alice on the street, she turned out not to be a sweet little puppy. Instead, Alice is not only aggressive toward dogs on the street; at home, Alice has become the nasty little sister to Katie, an Akita, and Stanley, an Akita-husky mix.

Karen relates how an Alice surprise attack begins. "They'll just be sitting here; maybe one will walk by the other. They look at each other, there's all this secret silent information being exchanged. I can see it. And then suddenly, Alice has taken out a piece of Katie's ear." Patrick Lawlor, Karen's husband, adds, "We're always at kind of a yellow or orange alert. We're never really able to just completely relax."

When Cesar arrives, he asks whether Patrick and Karen can think of anything—like food or toys—that might trigger an attack. Karen replies, "It's usually about a look. Or they'll brush against one another, or it's a perceived injustice." Cesar also learns that the couple believes that their Akita, Katie, is the dominant member of their pack.

Cesar is surprised to learn that the couple looks at Katie as "kind of their baby," allowing the Akita to sleep on the bed with them, while the other two dogs remain on the floor. Karen asks Cesar whether he has a dog who's a favorite. "Imagine if you send a dog to me and I have a special dog, then it's not fair," replies Cesar. "I love 'em all the same. If I get a rescue dog from the street, he will get the same treatment as when some celebrity sends me his or her dog. No difference. They're all number two to me."

"And who's number one?" asks Karen. "I am," says Cesar in no uncertain terms.

Cesar begins Alice's rehabilitation by working with her away from her own pack. Cesar holds Alice by her leash while Ilusion assists by using two dogs from their pack as temptation. At first, Alice appears tense but doesn't lash out at the strange dogs. When Alice growls, Cesar snaps his fingers loudly and she stops. Patrick notes, "So she was given a warning that time." Cesar answers, "And I let her know that that behavior is unwanted by me."

Next, Cesar walks Katie with Alice to see how the favored dog acts on the leash.

When Katie sees a neighbor walking a German shepherd, she starts to get agitated. Cesar says, "I asked Katie not to react, but the spoiled little girl that she is, she says, 'I'm gonna get my way.'" When Katie and Alice get into a fight, Cesar stops it immediately by pulling the two dogs apart and then keeps walking with them down the street while he talks to Karen and Patrick. "So who triggered the fight? Is it the aggressive dog, or is it dog who is spoiled? The whole fight was initiated by Katie."

Once Alice and Katie are calm, Cesar decides to bring Stanley to join the pack. All three dogs walk calmly with Cesar. "The more they do this kind of behavior together, the more they learn to tolerate each other. You all have to learn to be relaxed—together."

Both Karen and Patrick say they are ready to make changes. "Every morning we're going to get up and take the dogs out for a walk. And we are going to stop showing favoritism to one over the others," claims Patrick. Karen adds, "I think Cesar's lessons are bigger than just taking care of dogs. They're really life lessons."

A Prayer for Nicky

Name: Nicky

Breed: rottweiler

Kathleen Daniels and her son, Donald, are providing a loving home for their three-year-old rottweiler, Nicky, that once lived in a homeless camp. When Kathleen adopted Nicky, she was stunned to find out that he had been called Cesar when he lived in the camp, the same name as her own rottweiler that had recently died of cancer. According to Kathleen, "In a spiritual way, I felt like this was all meant to be."

But whenever other dogs come around, Nicky reveals a dark side. "He gets to a level of aggression that's just so bad it's horrifying to be around him," says Donald. Kathleen believes Nicky's hostility was related to his former life, when he was

Kathleen and Nicky outside the Dog Psychology Center.

tied up to a wire much of the time. After Nicky was rescued by an animal rights advocate, a veterinarian removed the wire, which had grown into the dog's neck, leaving him with thick scar tissue and an almost total loss of feeling there.

Kathleen renamed Cesar and began calling him Nicky when she brought him home. Kathleen says, "I knew from that day forward my son could walk him because he's strong, but I couldn't because I have osteoporosis, and I couldn't really risk having a broken bone." However, Donald's walks with Nicky are filled with tension and dread as Nicky leaps at almost any dog that comes their way. Kathleen prayed to find a solution to her problems. Then she heard about the *Dog Whisperer* series and contacted the producers.

Because of the severity of Nicky's aggression, especially while being walked, Kathleen purchased a prong collar to help keep the ninety-two-pound dog from attacking other animals. "I'm an animal activist and I love animals. I don't really like pinch collars, but I think you have to be responsible with these dogs and not let them hurt another dog. So I tested it, and it felt like it put pressure on his neck but didn't pinch it," Kathleen tells Cesar.

"Whatever tool works for the person, works for me," Cesar says.

Cesar wants to make sure Kathleen and Donald know how to use the collar correctly and responsibly. "The purpose of this collar is to mimic the bite of dogs. When you pull, the dog gets the sensation of being bitten, but you have to learn how to pull properly, and you have to learn when to pull. If you use too much pressure or too much tension or a lot of strength, you can dig holes into the dog's neck, which becomes detrimental to its psychological being and, of course, the body."

To evaluate Nicky further, Cesar invites Kathleen and Donald to his Dog Psychology Center. Here they'll observe how he interacts with the forty rehabilitated dogs in Cesar's pack. At first, Nicky seems to handle being surrounded by the pack, but when he lunges at a white German shepherd, Cesar takes the leash from Kathleen to give Nicky a correction. Then Cesar asks Kathleen and Donald to wait outside the fence while Cesar brings Nicky in to meet the pack a second time. When Nicky gets near a pit bull named Buddy, he jumps and the two dogs try to go after each other, even though at that moment they are on opposite sides of the fence. Cesar takes both dogs and makes them lie down on their sides. Buddy immediately rolls on his back with his legs in the air while Nicky lies on his side. "Buddy was not trying to be enemies with him, he was trying to actually smell him, create a friendship with him. And Nicky did not know how to be a friend. That was fence fighting and we don't allow fence fighting. They're both getting a correction because they both did the same thing."

Kathleen agrees to leave Nicky for a fourteen-day stay at the center. Cesar believes there is one key obstacle to Nicky's rehabilitation: he's overweight and can't keep up with the pack during group walks. Fortunately, the center doubles as a health spa where Cesar puts Nicky on a regular treadmill routine. Cesar also brings a white German shepherd named Lobo in to walk around the treadmill area while Nicky works out. "When Nicky first came here, he got into a fight with a white German shepherd. So now he has to learn to exercise next to white German shepherds."

Over the next several days, the calories burn away and so does Nicky's aggression. "Nicky not only became okay with other dogs, he actually made a best friend, when before he never had a friend," says Cesar.

When Cesar brings Nicky back to Kathleen's home, he has a surprise for her—several dogs from the pack have come along for Nicky's homecoming! Kathleen starts to cry as she watches her once fearsome dog interact happily with the other members of Cesar's pack. Kathleen exclaims, "I am blown away! He had all these dogs with him, but they are in his environment and he is allowing them to be here. I'm witnessing a miracle!"

For a case as serious as Nicky's, the Danielses will need to work with him daily to continue his rehabilitation. Cesar will make follow-up visits. "We never finish with the rehabilitation in only fourteen days, but they can see that this social way of being is possible. Nicky let go of the past and now Nicky is living in the present."

Her prayer answered, Kathleen is filled with hope. "It was like an epiphany, just to see that he was able to change so dramatically in two weeks. By going through this type of experience, I can encourage a lot of people in the community to take these animals. We don't have to euthanize them. On the other hand, I look at my own abilities as his pack leader and what it is I have to work on. So it's been a journey for me too."

Follow-up ❈ ❈ ❈

Kathleen and Nicky are doing great, and Cesar considers them to be two of his proudest success stories. Kathleen now does accounting work for Cesar's Dog Psychology Center and the now popular Nicky is able to visit his pals frequently.

Serving Justice

Name: Justice

Breed: pit bull

(episode 122)

Fourteen-month-old Justice was a gift to Robert Bias from his godmother. Before Justice arrived, the top dog in the Biases' yard was Smokey, a nine-year-old retriever-Lab mix. Smokey has always been easygoing and laid back, but he's increasingly being harassed by the new dog in the family. Smokey has to defend himself against Justice's relentless aggression, which Robert fears is becoming more and more serious.

Justice has a lot of energy to burn, but she seems afraid to go for a walk. Ever since Justice escaped from the backyard and was hit by a car, she refuses to leave the yard. There, she aggressively barks at other dogs and takes out her frustrations on either Smokey or the trash cans. Justice can usually be found with something from the trash in her mouth. Robert says, "I had a muzzle to keep her out of the trash and keep her from biting my Smokey, but she ate the muzzle up too."

When Cesar arrives, he learns about one more problem: Justice apparently wants to kill the family birds. Cesar has a plan for that kind of behavior. Cesar holds Justice by her leash, brings her to the cage, and desensitizes her to the birds by making her wait, without letting her make any kind of move to attack them. He "bites" Justice on the neck with his cupped hand when she fixates on the birds too much. "If you take the bird away from her, you make her reaction more intense, so then she goes after the bird. Right now she comes to where the bird is, and I am making her submit to the bird."

When it's time to go outside, Cesar decides to use a lure to get Justice to walk. He waves some food near her nose to encourage her to walk toward him. "My goal is always to motivate the nose, so that the nose moves the brain, and without us giving her the food. We're just offering the scent. So we're motivating the mind."

But Robert can't seem to get Justice to respond the way she did with Cesar. When Robert uses the food, he tenses up without realizing it. Cesar tells him, "Once you offer food, you can't use tension. Because then food means tension. You can't really invite a dog to follow you with tension when she's already tense. The energy that we need to share is like a little tug on the leash and then relaxation." Gradually, Robert gets the hang of it.

His mother, Elaine, is very hopeful. "She will be a good part of the family now." Robert adds, "Justice can be served."

Follow-up 🐾 🐾 🐾

Robert had a busy schedule with school so he was unable to give Justice the amount of walking she needed.

A Puzzle Named Pepsi

Name: Pepsi

Breed: German shepherd

(episode 120)

Pepsi was a tiny German shepherd puppy when Marcela Gonzales brought him home to her husband, Bartolo. Now that Pepsi is three and a half years old, he's very protective of Marcela, the only one who walks him. Not only does Pepsi go after strangers and smaller dogs in the neighborhood, he is also very aggressive with the Gonzaleses' cat, Kitty Love. According to Marcela, "I'm afraid that he's gonna kill her."

For Cesar, every case becomes a detective story. Usually he gets his best evidence from the owners. In Marcela's case, Cesar learns that she is the only one of eight brothers and sisters who has no children. "That space has to be filled with something. In America we fill that space with dogs, cats, and other animals. So Pepsi and Kitty Love are your kids."

When Cesar asks Bartolo whether he gives corrections to Pepsi, he tells Cesar that he doesn't spend much time with Pepsi, that it's his wife's dog.

Cesar gets another important clue to Pepsi's problem when a member of the camera crew gets too close to Marcela, and Pepsi begins barking angrily. "What was happening here, it was a case of overprotection. Marcela was overprotecting Pepsi, and Pepsi was generating the same behavior toward her. He could really hurt somebody."

To solve this case, Cesar decides he needs to take Pepsi out alone. Whenever they walk near another dog in the neighborhood, Cesar doesn't want Pepsi even to look at it. "Tsst! We want Pepsi to learn to ignore the dog. We want to see ears back, we want to see a dog that is docile, we want to feel that submissive energy before we put him around a cat. My biggest challenge is going to be when Marcela comes into the picture because if he sees Marcela a block away, he is going to try to control the situation."

When Cesar walks back to the family's front porch, Marcela is holding Kitty Love on her lap. "When Pepsi focuses on the cat, when he gets fixated, he needs to get a correction. This is a correction." Cesar gives a quick tug on the leash to redirect Pepsi's attention from the cat to him. "As you see, I'm not using force. I'm just getting my point across."

Next, Cesar begins to work with his main suspect in the case: Marcela. Before she can improve her relationship with Pepsi, Marcela needs to come clean about her own issues. "She has to let go. She has to let go of the fact that Pepsi is not a human, and that Bartolo can participate in the relationship with Pepsi, and that is only going to make their world better." As they walk together, Marcela confesses, "I'm the one who was keeping him away from everybody. I'm the one who was not being trained."

Cesar's homework for the Gonzales family is two-fold: long daily power walks with Pepsi, which include both husband and wife, and immediate, consistent corrections before Pepsi's possessive behavior can escalate. Rehabilitating an aggressive dog like Pepsi will take leadership and consistency. But in just one afternoon, Cesar has helped bring all the members of the Gonzales family a little closer together. Bartolo says, "Now I feel like I'm getting closer to him, because she's letting me."

Follow-up ✤ ✤ ✤

Pepsi is doing beautifully on his walks now, but never did make friends with the cat.

Jake

Name: Jake

Breed: shepherd–Labrador retriever mix

In June 2002, Curb Your Enthusiasm director and producer, Bob Weide, was surprised to discover a fresh new face. On a trip to the SPCA, Bob was intending simply to drop off some cat toys, when a dog named Jake gazed at him with what Bob describes as "Rudolph Valentino" eyes. Bob immediately called his wife, Linda, who came over and began to cry as soon as she saw the dog.

The shepherd-Lab mix quickly became a superstar in the Weide household. Unfortunately, just like a pampered celebrity, Jake started to spin out of control. Walks with Jake became like a suspense thriller, with Jake's hackles going up and charging whenever he saw another dog. This battle of the leash has bruised Linda's hands and possibly given her tendinitis. Linda recalls, "One of my fingers was almost broken. I'm really starting to think that this is not behavior; this is who he is, and I'm not convinced that anything can be done. There's no hope."

Cesar hopes to play a key role in this production and to see if he can help create a happy ending. Cesar's first task is to understand everyone's role in this scenario. After hearing the backstory from Bob and Linda, Cesar picks up a hint when the Weides tell him that Jake has no problem playing off leash with other dogs at the dog park. He believes that Jake is frustrated by the leash and has come to view walking as a negative experience. "When the leash is an uncomfortable experience, then everything around it is suspect."

When Cesar asks Bob and Linda to show him how they get Jake ready for a walk, he notices several basic mistakes. He notes that Jake gets too excited in the kitchen when they put his leash on and then pulls toward the picture window without getting a correction. When Linda cries out "wait, wait, wait" several times, that seems only to intensify Jake's excitement. Finally, Jake leads the way out the door in a very excited state of mind.

Cesar decides to produce a "remake" of getting ready for the walk. He waits until Jake is calm before putting the leash on him. Then Jake has to sit before Cesar opens the front door. Cesar goes out the door first, motions for Jake to follow him, and then has Jake sit again while Cesar closes the door. "From this point on I make the decisions which way we should go. So at the moment, he is in a good state of mind. And for right now there is no tension on the leash."

When Jake spots a dog and starts to react, Cesar gives the dog a correction with a short quick jerk of the leash, redirecting Jake's attention back to him.

The Weides then show Cesar the house where Jake's reactions are the worst, even when the neighbor's dog isn't in the front yard. Cesar heads right for the front door of the house. "Instead of going away from the situation, I move into the situation. Rehabilitate the problem by fighting the situation." When Cesar walks to the house, he gives Jake several quick corrections with the leash until the dog finally settles down. Then it's Linda's turn. Cesar notices that when Linda gets nervous, her arms tense up and make the leash too taut. "Her body language was speaking for her; she didn't realize that she was holding the leash with tension."

Linda's subsequent attempts to approach the house get better and better with every "take," and ultimately she is thrilled with the afternoon's performance. "Honestly, I did not think that anyone would be able to change Jake's behavior. I thought that this was just who he is. Cesar has changed my life. I can't wait to walk with Jake at any time now. I can't wait to implement what he's taught me and it's a whole new day."

Follow-up ❀ ❀ ❀

Jake is now the perfect dog with Bob, but Linda is not having the same results. She struggles to get Jake to mind her and is still working to implement Cesar's advice.

Chapter 3

Fears and Phobias

Kane awaits his rendezvous with the dreaded linoleum.

The Shiny

Name: Kane

Breed: Great Dane

(episode 101)

Kane is a lumbering, lanky mass of Great Dane, a dog more likely to drool on you than to growl at you. If Kane decides he does not want to go somewhere, then, Kane is simply not going and no one is going to change that. And much to his owner's chagrin, Kane will not go anywhere where there happens to be shiny floors.

Gentle giant Kane is terrified of all shiny surfaces. His phobia began one year earlier, in the elementary school where his owner, Marina Dahlem, teaches. Kane was running down the corridor of the school when he slipped and slid on the linoleum floor, smashing hard into a glass wall. Marina recalls,

"He's been traumatized ever since then." Marina, who likes to bring Kane to school for events with the children, now has to haul along a kind of "security blanket" wherever she goes. "I have a special carpet that I have to roll out for him. So he goes into the entrance because he's familiar with that carpet from home." Unfortunately, Kane's veterinarian's office also has linoleum floors, so Marina has to go through the carpet ritual whenever Kane needs medical care.

When Cesar sits down to discuss Kane's situation with Marina and her son, Emmett, he is able to size up the situation pretty quickly. Marina admits she overreacted when Kane hit the glass and ran to comfort him. According to Cesar, "By giving an animal affection when the mind is under stress, she is nurturing the behavior. She was seeing Kane as a human being."

Cesar decides that now is the time to get Kane over his phobia of shiny floors. First, he takes Kane on a long walk with the dog right by his side, in order to create a bond between them. "I needed him to trust me as soon as possible. And the walk is one of the most primal activities for a dog, to create both trust and respect." In fact, at 160 pounds, Kane actually weighs five pounds more than Cesar, so respect is going to be a vital part of this equation.

As Cesar walks closer to the school's front door, he increases his pace with Kane until they are almost trotting. They bound up the school steps together, and Kane finds himself inside the school and standing on the dreaded linoleum floor before he even realizes what happened.

Kane freezes, then starts panting heavily, but Cesar stands firm . . . and calm. "We just stayed by the door for three to five seconds. Those were the hardest seconds of his life. He knew I wasn't going to give up. I knew if I stayed there with him and didn't allow him to back away, that he was eventually going to move forward." After waiting just a few more seconds, Cesar takes one step farther into the school's corridor. Kane tentatively follows him. Cesar takes another step. So does Kane. Cesar pulls up a chair and sits down. Within thirty seconds, Kane starts taking a couple of tentative steps on his own. "He's doing it!" Cesar says quietly.

After only a few minutes, Cesar has Kane walking up and down the hall, then in and out of the school doors and back down the hall again. Next, Cesar asks Marina and Emmett to join him. In minutes, Cesar has Marina and Kane entering and exiting the building with Kane. "It's a miracle! I was just overjoyed! It

Follow-up 🐾 🐾 🐾

Marina happily reports that since that day at the school, Kane has never again had a problem with shiny floors.

really was like a milestone, a complete milestone for him," exclaims Marina. From the moment Cesar first brought Kane in the door until he was walking calmly through the building with Marina, fewer than eleven minutes had elapsed.

Kane passes this test, but his final exam will come in just four days. Marina wants to bring Kane into the school to celebrate his second birthday with her class. Using the calm-assertive energy she learned from Cesar, Marina confidently gets Kane out of the car, up the steps, and down the hall of the school without even a moment's hesitation by Kane . . . or Marina.

Cesar joins all the kids at school in celebrating Kane's birthday . . . and celebrating Marina's new-found confidence. "Actually, it's a very beautiful lesson—that you don't have to suffer instability for your whole life," Cesar says. "You can move forward and let go of any kind of issue you might have."

Key Cesar Tip

Giving comfort and affection to a dog when it displays nervousness, fear, or aggression will nurture the unwanted behavior.

Scared Family Dog

Name: Ruby

Breed: vizsla

(episode 103)

Vizslas have a reputation for being faithful and obedient. This intriguing rare breed was rescued from possible extinction by Hungarian expatriates during World War II. But Ann and Larry Klein's vizsla, Ruby, has a dark side. "From the minute we brought Ruby home, it was instant terror. She was constantly biting us, biting our clothes, tearing our clothes," recalls Ann.

Ruby seems to be scared of almost everything, even inanimate objects, and is also afraid of the water—odd for a breed that usually loves swimming. However, the Kleins' biggest concern about Ruby is that she can become extremely possessive and aggressive. According to Ann, "When she grabs a sock, or there's food she shouldn't have, or even if she has a bone that she's chewing, you can't get near her. Sometimes I'll have to push a chair at her to get her to back away."

The Kleins are desperate, feeling that they have to find a way to stop Ruby's aggression, or they will have to give her up for adoption. With ten-year-old twins and lots of youngsters coming over to the house, the Kleins are unwilling to take that kind of risk. "We've tried to desensitize her by sitting here and petting her [while Ruby growls], saying, 'It's okay.' But it never stops. She never relaxes." Larry sighs.

The Kleins relate how they try to sooth Ruby when she's being possessive or fearful. Cesar tells them they are nurturing the unwanted behavior by giving affection to a dog when its mind is under stress. In fact, Ann is constantly petting the nervous Ruby during Cesar's initial consultation. "You're giving affection when the mind is unsure. So right now, her tail is between her legs and she's facing the other way. She wants nothing to do with us, but she receives affection in the meantime. You are loving her unstable state of mind."

After the consultation, Cesar puts a leash on Ruby in order to give her corrections whenever she exhibits aggressive or possessive behavior. He decides to challenge Ruby's possessiveness while she has one of her precious bones on her bed. Referring to the leash, Cesar says, "No tension on it until she shows aggression." When Cesar moves to take the bone off the ground, Ruby instantly snaps and bites him. But Cesar doesn't back off. "There is no backing away." After Cesar pulls Ruby slowly off her pillow, the dog begins to relax. Then Cesar instructs Ann to give the bone to Ruby, and then take it back in a calm-assertive manner. When Ruby starts to growl, Ann responds with a firm "No!" and Ruby lets her take the bone away without further incident.

There are still more phobias Ruby needs to face. Cesar dons a wet suit and, with Ruby still on the leash, walks firmly out to the backyard and down the pool steps into the water. Ruby hesitates a bit, but Cesar pulls her in behind him. "I was expecting a little challenge in the pool, but it didn't take much for her to get in the pool. It was almost immediate." Cesar tells the Kleins as they watch in astonishment while he continues to swim with Ruby, "From this point on, you just have to lead her to the water."

After seeing the changes in Ruby in just a few hours, the Kleins are optimistic that they can become Ruby's pack leaders. According to Cesar, "This is just the beginning of Ruby's rehabilitation in order for Ruby to get back to normal."

Follow-up ❧ ❧ ❧

Despite many valiant efforts, the Kleins were never able to get Ruby to a point where they felt comfortable with her. They were advised to put her to sleep, but Cesar offered to take Ruby in and make her part of his pack at the Dog Psychology Center. After spending several months at the center, Ruby slowly came out of her shell. She is no longer territorial or possessive and has shaken off most of her fears, although she can be shy around strangers. But she loves to swim and go Rollerblading with Cesar and her beloved pals in the pack.

Behind the scenes

Although Cesar was able to control Ruby, *Dog Whisperer* crew members had to remain cautious and as far away as possible from her during the filming, since her aggression was so unpredictable. Bryan Duggan, one of the cameramen, actually was bitten. Now the same crew can be around her frequently at the Dog Psychology Center without incident.

Make Room for Rana

Name: Rana

Breed: Sheltie

(episode 103)

Rana the toaster dog.

Even though Rana graduated as the valedictorian of his obedience class, Karen Adams and her daughter, Alanna, are perplexed by his increasingly strange behavior. In fact, Rana's crazy conduct has turned Karen and Alanna's peaceful domestic life into toast. Every time the toaster pops, Rana goes into a frenzy, barking and twirling relentlessly. According to Karen, "We avoid making toast. We've even been known to take him and put him on the patio while we make toast."

Karen has even been bitten by the agitated animal during a breakfast melee. Karen and Alanna now find their first meal of the day a real challenge. In addition to the toaster, the microwave sets Rana off, as does the ringing telephone. Despite their love for the dog, Karen and Alanna are tired of altering their lives for Rana.

Cesar agrees to try to help Karen and Alanna find a way out of their toastless hell. He quickly determines that the two women have been treating their Sheltie like a human. "He's your baby. A lot of people think that their dogs are their babies. It's good therapy for the human, but it's not so good for the dog. So what we have is a dog that's in control of the household."

Cesar delivers some surprising news. "It takes ten seconds for a dog to know what position you have in its life. Ten seconds. If you share affection in the very beginning, you become a follower. But it's never too late to turn things around, that's the good news. But you've got some work to do."

When Karen brings out the dreaded toaster, Rana runs into the other room. Cesar says, "We have to stop that running away behavior because every time he runs, he wins."

Cesar brings Rana into the dining room and gently but firmly holds the dog while he pops the toaster repeatedly next to him. "We are not going to hurt him, we are just going teach him a lesson that this toaster shouldn't make him nervous, afraid, or anxious." Cesar continues to hold Rana as he continues to pop the toaster. "This is about making the mind calm-submissive. This is not dog training, this is dog psychology."

With Cesar's guidance, Karen uses a leash to try to manage Rana's kitchen etiquette. "The good thing is, this leash helps make him submissive, so anything that happens around that is not going to affect his state of mind." Cesar also recommends that they correct Rana the moment he begins to bark and not wait until he is in a full frenzy.

Just before Cesar leaves, he offers a final tip. "Remember, this is your home, not his home."

Follow-up ❁ ❁ ❁

Karen is not able to stop Rana's toaster attacks, but she has decided to live with his quirks because she loves her dog so much.

Hell on Wheels (episode 105)

Name: Harry

Breed: shepherd mix

Cesar with Janet while Harry looks out for wheeled objects.

Harry creates a heap of trouble for retired schoolteachers Janet Parker and Beverly Keeley. "He's a good dog, a good protector, but he has a couple of faults that drive us crazy," claims Janet. "He'll take after anything on two wheels," Beverly adds. "Any time a bike, a skateboard, or anything like that goes by, he goes crazy." Yes, life has gotten a little hairy with Harry, their seven-year-old German shepherd mix. But the two women are determined to find a solution.

Cesar is ready to ride to the rescue, but for this case, he brings along a posse. Ilusion, Andre, and Calvin, plus their collection of bikes, skateboards, and Rollerblades, are ready to put Harry to the test during Cesar's rehabilitation process.

After Cesar hears the basic story from the two women, he says, "Harry has anxiety and fear that have turned into aggression. He releases aggression toward things that make him afraid, or anything on wheels that gets him excited, gets him nervous. So Harry tries to gain dominance over them. That makes him an anxious, fearful, dominant dog."

First, Cesar takes Harry on a five-minute walk to begin the bonding process. Then Cesar asks Calvin, Andre, and Ilusion to ride bikes past Harry so Cesar can give corrections by pulling quickly on the leash every time Harry makes a move on a wheeled object. "I'm always very happy when my whole family is involved in the rehabilitation of dogs. It's a win-win situation because I get to help the dog and my kids get to learn about rehabilitating dogs. One thing I know is that I will never put my kids or my wife in danger."

Once Harry seems calmer around the bikes, Cesar gets on a skateboard himself and leads Harry on the leash while rolling down the sidewalk, giving Janet and Beverly a thumbs-up as they pass. "It's making me cry just to see it," says an amazed Janet. Next, Andre joins him on the skateboard and takes over Harry's leash. "I wanted Janet and Beverly to see that my son can also do what I was doing. So it's not just me. It's anybody who is sharing calm-assertive energy during the rehabilitation."

Even though Harry now seems more at ease, his rehabilitation is far from over. Cesar takes Harry onto the grass near the sidewalk and has the dog sit next to him. Then Cesar signals for Calvin and Andre to ride their skateboards just a few feet away from Harry. When Harry fixates on a skateboard or tries to attack it, Cesar gives him a light tap with his foot on the hindquarters to get Harry's attention. Now Cesar has Janet and Beverly take turns giving Harry corrections as needed when Cesar's skateboarding sons roll by.

But the road to Harry's rehabilitation isn't going to be a smooth one. Cesar recommends they work with Harry every day to make sure that *they* are now in charge. According to Janet, "When I saw that the kids could do it, I knew that we could do it." Beverly adds, "It's just going to take practice and a lot of work."

Stubborn Shih Tzu

Name: Seuki

Breed: shih tzu

Even though she's retired, Eula Manocchi still thinks of herself as a mother—both to her forty-three-year-old son, Anthon, and to her "daughter," a five-year-old shih tzu named Seuki. But sweet Seuki has a stubborn streak. Whenever Seuki is without a leash, she runs after strangers. "Every time she hears a voice, she runs to that person who's speaking, like, 'Hello, my name is Seuki. Who are you?'"

Seuki's more serious issue is about walking . . . or rather, *not* walking. For four years, Seuki has simply refused to walk on a leash, or even stay on one. Seuki's no-walk policy is particularly frustrating for bachelor Anthon. "Because there's nothing better I'd like to do than to take her for a walk. That's one way to meet girls, too, 'cause they love dogs."

One of Cesar's rehabilitation techniques is to get a sense of a dog away from its owners and home environment. So Cesar carries Seuki about a block away as he formulates his approach. He also brings along a very basic leash to use in Seuki's rehabilitation. "What I'm creating is that the leash is going to bring her home. So there's going to be a positive association between this leash and her."

After Cesar puts the leash on Seuki, she begins walking almost immediately. At the first sign of hesitation, Cesar gently taps Seuki on her rear end. "See, just me touching the back part of her, it helps her to move forward. It's not always the leash; you have to find parts of the body that can trigger the reaction you're looking for."

Cesar then shows Eula and Anthon where to tap Seuki to get her moving. He even suggests that it's okay to lure her to walk by using a food reward. After four years of not being able to walk her dog, Eula is ecstatic. "I want to show her off and show my friends what she can do."

Follow-up ❖ ❖ ❖

Seuki will walk on the driveway, but Eula still has to carry the dog away from the house in order to get her to walk home.

Hose Dog

Name: Buddy

Breed: beagle

One day John Johnson asked his nine-year-old daughter, Alexandra, to come out into the backyard. When she came outside, he surprised her by saying, "You've got a puppy!" Johnny had picked out Buddy, a beagle–American coonhound mix, from the pound. Alexandra says of Buddy's beguiling brown eyes, "He's got a bunny rabbit's eyes and a puppy's body."

Buddy has an overwhelming fear . . . of water. According to Johnny's wife, Christine, "It started out just when you put the hose on and he would run and hide and get in the house and get under a bed." John adds, "It's not just turning on the hose, it's pretty much just water altogether. It's almost inhumane at times to watch him go through this fear of what's happening to him."

After speaking with the Johnsons, Cesar is really concerned for Buddy. "Living in fear for eighteen months is horrible! The dog is living in an environment where he is not thoroughly comfortable. Here is a case of a hyperactive dog with a very laid-back family and a very easygoing family with regard to discipline. The family is not practicing the leadership role with the dog."

Due to Buddy's extremely high energy, the Johnsons also can't control him on walks. When Cesar puts a leash on Buddy and takes him outside for a walk, Buddy flails and pulls, so Cesar starts running. "It's easier to drain his energy or to accomplish taming the animal if you accelerate the speed. When a dog is bucking like a wild horse, it's really hard for someone who has no experience to control this dog."

Having drained Buddy's energy, Cesar brings the dog to the Johnsons' backyard to make him confront the dreaded water hose. At first, when Buddy resists, Cesar keeps him close to the hose with the leash. "At this moment you don't talk to the dog, you don't say, 'It's okay.' Since he is not completely calm-submissive, whatever you say is not going to benefit his state of mind. At this point please do not feel sorry for him, because that is not going to help him, either." True to Cesar's prediction, Buddy panics for a few seconds—then relaxes.

Cesar then has members of the family hold Buddy's leash while keeping him close

Buddy is still afraid of water. The family says they followed Cesar's instructions, but nothing seemed to change. Now Buddy stays in the backyard with another dog to play with.

to the water hose. After just a few minutes, John is able to turn the water hose on without Buddy panicking. "I tell you what, this is amazing, I've never been able to do this," says an incredulous John.

"This is a very simple case to me. The whole family has to follow up with the program, so this way Buddy sees everybody as the pack leader. If this family stays consistent for the rest of Buddy's life, Buddy will be the perfect dog!"

Petrified Pit Bull

Name: Julius

Breed: pit bull–Dalmatian mix

(episode 117)

"Julius is afraid of everything. He's extremely nervous. Spooked all the time. If I put down a coffee cup too hard, he bolts. If there are leaves and they rustle, he bolts. When the gardeners come to cut the grass on Mondays, he panics and he pees and he vomits," Sharon Noble says with a sigh.

Sharon and her husband, Brendan, rescued Julius, a pit bull–Dalmatian mix, after learning the dog had been abandoned in a field when he was only five weeks old. When the couple brought Julius home, he was constantly having accidents in the house and vomiting an average of ten times a day for the first three weeks. Julius refuses to leave the house for anything, sometimes not even budging from a particular spot.

When Cesar arrives for the consultation, Brendan tells him, "The only place where he's calm is here inside the house. This is his sanctuary." Brendan is concerned that the Dalmatian breed tends toward nervousness, and this is one of Julius's key issues. But Cesar doesn't see it that way. "It's not the breed that has created this problem; it's whatever happened to him in the beginning. The dog is traumatized."

Cesar is familiar with what can happen when people rescue a dog that was abandoned or abused. "They have huge hearts, but they give affection when Julius is having fear. Love is not going to rehabilitate a psychological problem. Dogs don't follow lovable leaders and they don't follow emotional leaders. They follow calm-assertive leaders."

Cesar begins by confronting Julius's greatest fear—going outside. Sharon and Brendan have been using a haltie, a collar designed to fit over Julius's face that gives them more control on the walk. But Cesar feels that Julius has a negative association with the haltie, so he decides to use a choke chain for the walk instead. When Cesar exits the house with Julius on the choke chain, the dog is clearly more comfortable.

Until Julius's owners prove to him that they're strong leaders, he will never trust them enough to let go of his fears. To help Sharon become a leader, Cesar asks her to draw on the skills from her career as an actress. Taking on the role of director, Cesar

Sharon and Brendan report that Julius is a much more relaxed, obedient dog. He is still sometimes nervous on walks, but Sharon and Brendan admit they've been too busy lately to work with him as they should. But whenever Brendan corrects him using Cesar's techniques, Julius complies. When they have guests at their house, Julius is even able to relax and be affectionate around them. Brendan says there's no question that Cesar's techniques work.

Key Cesar Tip

Use the power of your mind and imagination to increase your leadership skills. If you are unsure of yourself when walking your dog, imagine yourself to be a person or character who represents strength to you. It worked for Sharon!

tells his actress to become like the ancient Egyptian queen Cleopatra. "Cleopatra was a dominant woman. Beautiful and dominant. Let's go, Cleopatra. Shoulders up. Remember, you are Cleopatra."

Sharon takes Cesar's direction well and becomes regal in her bearing and her walk. Julius picks right up on her new energy and relaxes. When it's Brendan's turn to walk Julius, the dog begins to act frightened again. Cesar tells him, "You didn't set yourself to win, sir. When you grabbed the leash, you didn't set yourself to be in a comfortable position. Get comfortable. Feel proud!"

Sharon and Brendan will need to grow into their new roles before Julius can release all his fears. Brendan admits, "I didn't recognize that giving Julius affection when he's apprehensive reinforces the apprehensive behavior." But today they've taken an important first step toward becoming true pack leaders.

Pampered Puli

Name: Slick

Breed: puli

Slick seems to have it all. He has a luxurious home in Beverly Hills and two super-successful owners, Academy Award telecast producer Michael Seligman and his wife, event planner Teresa Cusik. Slick is a puli, a rare breed of sheepdog that originated in Hungary and even came close to extinction. Today the breed is best known for its skill in obedience and performance in the show ring.

You'd think this pampered puli would be the happiest dog in Los Angeles. But Slick is too terrified to appreciate his Hollywood home. Eighteen months earlier, Michael rescued Slick from a tragic existence of living in a crate for up to fifteen hours a day. According to Michael, Slick has been so traumatized by his past that he isn't able to enjoy his wonderful new home and luxurious lifestyle. Slick is constantly hiding behind Michael's legs, riddled with fear.

Slick's problem gets worse when he goes to the dog park. He's so insecure around other dogs that he acts out, often aggressively.

Cesar learns that Michael and Teresa react to Slick's panic attacks by giving him affection and speaking to him in high, reassuring voices. Cesar explains, "You are sharing affection at the wrong time. When the mind is fearful, if you come and say, 'It's okay,' you are really saying that it's okay to be fearful. That's why Slick hasn't overcome his fearful side."

After the initial consultation, Cesar decides what Slick needs. "In order for us to bring back balance to an animal that is pack oriented, we have to put him around a population of dogs." So off they all head to Cesar's Dog Psychology Center to help give Slick some better social skills. According to Cesar, "I knew that once Slick was there, among those dogs, that my pack was going to influence him to become more of a regular dog."

First, Cesar has Michael and Teresa walk into the center where Cesar's thirty-seven dogs can sniff and check them out. Teresa found the initial experience unsettling. "It's a little overwhelming at first. When you come in and you have all these dogs that could probably kill you, and you're walking in and they're very mellow. You have to realize that it's you, you're in charge."

Michael Seligman called the *Dog Whisperer* producers shortly after filming to tell them that Slick had reverted back to his old self and that Cesar's rehab session didn't "stick." Cesar's response was that he's not an appliance repairman who comes in and with one session fixes the problem forever. It's up to Michael and Teresa to change their own behavior in order to get the behavior they want to see in Slick.

One of Cesar's first recommendations is that they trim the hair that hangs over Slick's eyes so he can see better. "Dogs use nose, eyes, ears in that order. So in his case, he has no eyes, so my pack is going to view him as a weird dog."

Once Cesar puts Slick's hair in a ponytail and out of his face, he brings the puli in to meet the pack. Slick immediately has a couple of bad reactions and starts barking. Cesar corrects Slick by pulling on the leash and using his familiar "*tsst*" sound to get Slick's attention. Then Slick moves toward Teresa. "He's gravitating to you because with you he becomes dominant. And every time he behaves this way, you have to turn around and remind him that this bad behavior is unwanted by you from this point on."

With just a few corrections, Slick is walking around through the pack, sniffing and investigating like a normal dog. Once Michael and Teresa see that Slick can have normal interactions with other dogs, they have cause for hope. "This consultation has definitely changed our life. But now we've got to do the work and have the follow-through. It's actually hard 'cause I want to tell him he's being a good boy and run up and give him a big hug. But I can't do that. Not yet. So now we have to learn how to think like a dog."

Dependent Dobie

Name: Sunshine

Breed: Doberman pinscher

(episode 119)

"*The thing that* happened with Sunshine, I know she was a God pick. I know she was supposed to be with me," says Michelle Bird. It wasn't long before Sunshine's extraordinary beauty became apparent, so Michelle decided to enter Sunshine in dog shows. Sunshine shined brightly in the show ring and won several ribbons.

Despite this success, Sunshine has issues. Ever since Michelle and her husband divorced, and Sunshine's closest Doberman companion died, the dog has become overly attached to Michelle, whining incessantly whenever she's left alone. It's come to the point where Michelle can't leave her apartment without Sunshine—even to go out on a date. "My life is at a standstill right now because of Sunshine's separation anxiety. She won't stop crying. So I take her with me everywhere I go." Michelle sighs.

During their initial meeting, Michelle admits to Cesar, "At this point, Sunshine is my life." She starts to cry as she tells Cesar how Sunshine's behavior changed after her other Doberman, Zed, passed away. Cesar gently offers his opinion. "Fear is not something they're born with. It's something that they learn after they're born. Sunshine now represents so much to you that Sunshine sometimes is not even a dog. You're not balanced, so she's not balanced." When Michelle immediately promises Cesar that she is ready to change and start treating Sunshine like a dog, he is taken aback. "That's awesome! I was not expecting that one! Now you're going to make me cry."

Cesar's first order of business is to correct the way Michelle walks Sunshine, or rather, the way Sunshine walks Michelle. He shows her how her long Flexi lead allows Sunshine to be out front and in control every time they go for a walk. "Once we are leading the dog, she can't get distracted by anything. That's just part of the psychological challenge. You want her to be totally focused on you." Cesar also tells Michelle that she has a head start because Sunshine already knows how to walk next to her with the collar high on the neck when Sunshine is with her in the show ring.

Michelle is thrilled when Sunshine seems to get it right away, walking next to her without any problem whatsoever. "What Cesar's telling me to do is to make it very clear in her mind who the pack leader is. And once she establishes that, I have a feel-

Follow-up · · ·

Sunshine improved greatly when Michelle followed Cesar's suggestions while on the walk, and she could even be left alone in the house without having separation anxiety. But an even greater change took place within Michelle. She says she had "an epiphany" because of Cesar, changed her job and her life, and is now a "dog whisperer" in Utah. Sunshine passed away of natural causes in February 2007.

ing that all the other issues like the abandonment stuff and the separation anxiety will go away."

Michelle adds, "You know, you can't see it until you're willing to literally listen and accept that something you're doing is influencing the whole thing. When Sunshine fell in beside me and walked like a regular dog—like the dogs I've had in the past—I felt the most incredible sense of elation. What I really felt was just absolutely a total sense of freedom."

Chapter 4

Obsessions

Brooks.

Big Lights—Big Problem

Name: Brooks

Breed: Entlebucher

(episode 105)

Actions have consequences. Perhaps Lorain Nicholson's brother-in-law wasn't thinking about that fact when he first used a laser light pen to entertain Brooks, the Entlebucher mountain dog belonging to Lorain and her husband, Chuck. According to Chuck, they were using the laser pen "to play a game, Chase the Dot." Lorain adds, "It was such a fun game that ever since then Brooks has been looking for the elusive light. He's never stopped looking for it and he's five now."

The moment Cesar enters their house, he witnesses Brooks's relentless light obsession. Cesar declares, "We have to go all the way back to the source.

This kind of behavior doesn't just happen." During their consultation, Lorain tells Cesar about Brooks's early days, when they introduced Brooks too quickly to another puppy and scared him. "Another time we took him for a walk around the block and a car backing out scared him to death. I think that it made him a little uptight. Just too much, too fast."

Cesar responds, "And that becomes like a nervous breakdown. The light obsession was the end of his nervous breakdown. That's what happens to dogs when they develop this behavior of being obsessive over something, because they know they can take over. With other situations or other dogs, they know that they can't control that. But with the light, he became the dominant one. But he became the dominant one in a very obsessive way."

Since Brooks is usually an obedient dog, Lorain and Chuck have stopped using a leash when they walk. But Cesar wants the Nicholsons to start using a leash again. With this tool they can begin to correct Brooks's obsession and reassert their leadership role. Cesar suggests they also keep Brooks's head up with the leash while they walk on the trails near their house. "We have to stop his behavior of looking at the ground. We're not going to give him the option to look down."

When they are back in the house, Cesar tells them, "Knowing that we have a dog that has less energy now from the walk, it will be easier for us to start working on his fixation in the house." Cesar keeps the collar and leash on for this part of the exercise. Every time Brooks makes a move on any kind of light, Cesar gives the dog a quick correction by pulling on the leash. It isn't long before Brooks is looking up to Cesar, waiting to see what he should do next. "His concentration is going to move from the floor or the light to somebody else, which is me."

This is an exercise Cesar wants the Nicholsons to practice all over the house until Brooks no longer fixates on a light anywhere in the house. Lorain was surprised to see how quickly Cesar worked his magic. "It was instantaneous. It was unbelievable. I mean, it was just like the dog is waiting for direction."

Follow-up 🐾 🐾 🐾

Brooks is now completely cured of his light obsession.

Chuck says, "It's just going to be a lot of work to keep him focused, to keep him learning not to look at the lights." But Lorain is determined. "We can help our dog to live a better life, to be a happier dog, and we owe it to him to do this and stick with it."

Manic Miniature Pinscher

Name: Caper

Breed: miniature pinscher

(episode 117)

Daniela Schnebly wanted a little dog she could take everywhere. It was love at first sight when she saw Caper at a local rescue organization. She quickly realized that Caper only did things her way. But Daniela's main concern about Caper has to do with her one big fixation. "Basically, it's a ball obsession. Once she sees a ball, she wants to control the ball and possess the ball. It doesn't matter what's going on around her. You could give her a steak, but nothing else matters to her except that ball and where it's going. It's her religion, her drug of choice." Daniela's boyfriend, Chad, sighs. "We just want the dog to be more . . . doglike. Just be around us without being so obsessive."

Chad and Caper play ball.

Cesar watches Caper play ball for only a minute or so before he gets the picture. "The way Caper is practicing this exercise is like she's *reeeally* obsessed. Caper's problems come down to three different things: hyperactivity, a dominant state of mind, and obsession. When these three things combine, you have a bomb."

Cesar tells the couple that they need to strictly enforce new rules for Caper. But Chad and Daniela aren't comfortable taking on the role of Caper's boss. According to Chad, "We don't really discipline the dog per se." Daniela adds, "I don't like it. It just makes me unhappy."

"So you want freedom without working for it?" asks Cesar. "Probably," Daniela admits. Once Daniela and Chad commit to buckling down and working with Cesar, they all head outside to deal with Caper's ball mania. Cesar puts a tennis ball on the grass and waits for Caper to run up and claim it. When the dog does, Cesar reacts immediately by touching Caper's neck to make her back away. "Instead of using choke chains and leashes and all that stuff, I'm using my hand. It's like I'm biting. So I'm claiming the ball. She can look at the ball but she can't touch the ball."

Follow-up ❀ ❀ ❀

Daniela says Caper is now a wonderful companion. She comes when called and is no longer running off. Caper walks very well on the leash and is much better when playing ball—though she still can't get enough of it.

Cesar slowly moves the ball away with his foot. When Caper starts to move at the ball, Cesar no longer feels the need to give Caper a physical correction; instead he gives a firm vocal "*tsst.*" Caper backs away and looks up at Cesar instead of at the ball. "She redirected her attention from the ball to us now. Once she achieves calm-submission, then I'm going throw the ball."

When Caper is calm, Cesar kneels down and holds her by the collar. Then he throws the ball, but he doesn't allow Caper to run after it until she is calm again. "I didn't send her when she was very anxious. I sent her when she went into a relaxed mode. So she's getting the picture now that the only way she's going to go get the ball is when she practices calm-submission."

Cesar has Daniela and Chad practice the same thing. Caper can go after the ball only when they let her. Both of them are surprised by the rapid change in Caper's behavior. Daniela says, "It's taught us that we're as much a part of this dog's behavior as the dog. I feel like she's a different dog. Chad adds, "It's not the leash, it's not the collar, or the weather. The way that you act is all that it is."

Twirling Dog

Name: Ava

Breed: pug-Pekingese mix

(episode 108)

Ava means the world to her owner, Nadia Crimm. Nadia decided to get Ava after her beloved English bulldog Barclay died of cancer. Nadia found Ava at a local shelter and immediately fell in love. But as soon as Ava arrived at Nadia's home, the problems started almost immediately. "She loved people, but she would cling to you. And then I noticed her little twirling issues too."

Ava twirls . . . and twirls . . . and twirls. And when she's finished twirling, she twirls some more. According to Nadia, "Her twirling basically expresses any emotion—happy, sad, nervous, scared, anxious, or excited. It's become a problem because she does get underfoot when she twirls. It makes me dizzy sometimes. It's always counter-clockwise. I have no clue why that is."

Before he arrives, Cesar wonders whether Ava could have a medical condition that's beyond his expertise. "Sometimes there is a neurological problem that needs medication, and I'm not a vet." But once Cesar sees Ava in full twirling mode, he says, "When a dog or animal lives behind walls for too long, that gets it crazy—very, very crazy. This is not neurological, this is psychological. This is a dog that is desperate for help. Spinning around has become a way of her fixing herself, until she gets really tired and lies down. And then she goes and spins again."

Cesar's prescription: "Three things we need to be balanced: exercise, mental stim-ulation, and affection. By really being committed to exercise, discipline, affection, you will slowly see that the spinning around will go away."

Cesar begins the walking exercise by moving Ava's leash higher up on her neck. He always recommends this position, especially for hard-to-handle dogs. "When the collar slips to the bottom of the neck, the nose goes to the ground and the dog can go anywhere it wants, and in her case spin around. But when the collar is all the way on the top, the dog can't do it."

Nadia is amazed at the rapid transformation. "It was really easy once he put that on her; she changed instantly. So I guess that it's mind over matter—she's gonna learn how to not spin." Cesar replies, "Because you're blocking the behavior that you don't want her to do." Cesar also recommends using the leash to stop the spinning inside the house as well. "We're not using the leash to make her sit down; we're using the leash just to stop the spinning."

With Cesar's guidance, Nadia comes to a new understanding. "I thought that the twirling at first was kind of cute, but after talking to Cesar, I see now that's it's because of problems. It's like children—they need rules and boundaries, and they like routines. And I think that if I give that to her, she'll be a happier dog."

Running Beagle

Name: Lizzie

Breed: beagle

(episode 124)

Lizzie is a three-year-old red tick Elizabethan beagle that runs and runs and runs until she drops. When Michael and Claudia Ortopan first adopted Lizzie, Claudia recalls, "We brought her home because she was so sweet. And then she just started this pacing thing. Pacing from the bedroom, down the hall, into the kitchen, and then turns around and goes back again." Lizzie makes laps in the backyard so continuously that she's worn the grass down into a dirt track.

Cesar tells the couple how an obsession like Lizzie's can get started. "You adopted her even though she was shy, timid, insecure. And when you brought her home you gave her the whole house. She wasn't ready for that. So she got nervous and started pacing back and forth. You didn't give the dog a positive activity right away. Every time we rescue a dog from a shelter, the best thing we can do is take it for a good long walk. I'm talking about a one-hour walk at the minimum. So it gets to know you as the new owner, as the new pack leader."

Cesar decides Lizzie needs both mental and physical stimulation to counteract her anxious obsessions—which is what she'll get on a treadmill. Cesar tells them, "Every time we have a psychological problem—in this case, obsession—a treadmill can help you to achieve calm-submission because it becomes a challenge to the mind. It becomes a challenge to the body. It becomes like this healthy medication for the obsessive behavior."

Cesar puts a leash on Lizzie so he can control her during this new exercise. To help get Lizzie used to the machine, Cesar has her walk on and off the treadmill when it's not running. "Once she's on it, and she feels comfortable on it, then we can turn it on." When Cesar turns the treadmill on, Lizzie starts walking hesitantly. Cesar holds her leash at the front of the treadmill so Lizzie is walking toward him. The ultimate goal is for Lizzie to be able to enjoy the treadmill without a leash but always with supervision. By burning off some of her excess energy here in a focused way, she'll have less need for obsessive outlets like her endless backyard racing.

Follow-up ❁ ❁ ❁

When Claudia got a job that resulted in Lizzie being alone all day, the family gave her to a beagle rescue and Lizzie has since been adopted by another family.

Claudia is surprised to see how quickly Lizzie takes to the treadmill. "I could see her focusing in on the treadmill, which I thought was kind of amazing. So that makes me feel a lot better about the whole process. I think the treadmill will be a good thing, and I think it'll work."

Catch It If You Can

Name: Garrett

Breed: German shepherd

Sheila and Joel Malavasi bought Garrett, a German shepherd, from a breeder to be a companion to their other dog, Keela. The breeder did tell Sheila and John about Garrett's tendency toward tail chasing, but other than that, Garrett was a normal, healthy puppy. They brought Garrett home, and at 5:00 a.m. the next morning, they were awakened by sounds of Garrett chasing his tail and barking. Garrett's tail obsession is so relentless that Sheila has stopped taking him on walks.

The constant spinning at home has been going on for seven years. One time Garrett actually caught his tail while he was spinning, and he kept spinning until there was blood all over the kitchen and entryway. They took the dog to a special veterinarian in Orange County who thought Garrett had a pinched nerve and was twirling to relieve the pain. Five thousand dollars in vet bills later and the dog is still spinning. They tried doggie Prozac, but that seemed to make Garrett aggressive . . . plus it had no effect on his spinning. At this point, Sheila and Joel don't think Garrett will ever stop spinning.

Cesar explains what he believes is the cause of Garrett's behavior. "When a working type of dog has nothing else to do, that's what they do. Some start pacing back and forth. Some go around in circles, because they're anxious. They're ready to work and they have no job. The walk has a lot of power. The walk is much stronger than Prozac."

Cesar demonstrates how to take control of the walk. "Now, the human always goes first and the dog follows. At the moment he starts pulling to go in front, you pull up on the leash. At the moment you pull up, the brain stops." Within a minute or two, Garrett is walking calmly at Cesar's side. Next, Cesar brings out another part of his recommended remedy—the backpack. "I knew that he wasn't being challenged. The backpack is going to intensify whatever he is doing. He is now carrying something for you. You give this guy a job, and that spinning thing will go away. Now he looks like a German shepherd with a purpose."

Sheila observes, "When Cesar put that backpack on, there was definitely a difference in Garrett's whole manner." Joel adds, "Almost looks like when he put that on he had something to do that controlled him and his mind."

Follow-up * * *

Sheila and Joel walked Garrett using the backpack, and his tail-chasing behavior gradually diminished. After he was diagnosed with a degenerative disease, Sheila made the difficult decision to put him to sleep. She has since brought home a new young shepherd and now uses what she learned from Cesar to be her new dog's pack leader.

Cesar recommends that the dog still wear the backpack for a while, even inside the house. "The reality is that we can't supervise our dogs twenty-four hours a day. So I suggest they put the backpack on Garrett from two o'clock to four o'clock every day."

Cesar's message sinks in with Sheila. "You have to continue doing it; you can't just do it for a week or a month. It's like anything; it has to be a way of life."

Chapter 5

Territorial/Possessive

Percy's posterior poses no problems for Diane.

Percy's Peculiarities

Name: Percy

Breed: West Highland white terrier

(episode 122)

Percy is a playful little pup with a cheerful disposition. Just don't go near his butt.

"When I touch Percy, he's all right at the top and in the middle, but when I get down to the end, he will turn and snap right at my hand. And if he could get my hand, he probably would," says Diane Engstrom. According to Diane, "I had X-rays done on his back and hips and it looks fine. He's a good dog, I think, it's just these peculiarities."

Cesar often deals with rescue dogs that have psychological issues. But unlike human psychologists, he's less interested in what caused the problem in the past than on how to correct it in the present. First, Cesar wants to know how Percy behaves on a walk. "He just sniffs a lot. He doesn't lead the way. It's more me pulling. And he'll stop at everything. He's not an easy one to take for a walk because I tend to get a bit impatient with that. I'd rather him walk ahead."

Cesar goes right to the shank of Diane's issue. "This is the story behind your life—that you get impatient very quickly, right? You try something and when it doesn't fit your expectation, then boom, you give up. You find a wall, and that's it. You stop."

When Diane admits that she doesn't follow through with Percy, Cesar asks why and she replies with one word: "laziness." Cesar replies, "I love that you admit it, because all the problems that you have with Percy have to do with discipline."

Diane is curious to know where Percy's don't-go-near-my-rear issue comes from. Cesar explains, "It could have come from a vaccination, from a shot, from anybody checking out his rear end when he wasn't ready to be checked out back there, and then he solved the problem by snapping, and from that point on nobody can touch that part of him."

Cesar begins the rehabilitation process by addressing Percy's most pressing problem—his delicate derriere. He loops a leash around Percy's neck and immediately starts rubbing Percy's behind. "What I did right away was catch him by surprise. Also, I am putting the leash all the way on the top of the neck. When the leash is up high, he can't turn his head to bite me. I'm just keeping his head forward."

Diane is amazed that Percy is letting Cesar rub his hindquarters. Cesar continues, "Percy got the point that I wasn't going to allow him to manipulate me the way he manipulates others." Whenever Percy starts to react to Cesar's touch, he gives a correction by pulling up on the leash, accompanied by a loud "*tsst.*" "And right after he throws a tantrum, we go and touch him again just to let him know that his behavior is not going to make us back away."

When it's Diane's turn, she has no problem as she pets Percy in the once off-limits area. Cesar also recommends, "Lift his tail, because that brings pride. When a dog walks with his tail in the air, he is very proud of himself."

When they take Percy out for a walk, Cesar offers Diane another important tip. "Let's say your walks are thirty minutes. The first fifteen minutes he follows you. Then you reward him by letting him smell the grass and letting him pee. So it becomes a reward. We're going to allow it on our terms."

Diane is thrilled that she no longer has to worry about bringing up Percy's rear. "It's just awesome; I couldn't believe it. And with the simple method of the leash, it worked, and I know I'll continue with it. So I'm very optimistic."

The Yorkshire Terror

Name: Scrawny

(episode 115)

Breed: Yorkshire terrier

There is never a dull moment inside the home of Tanya Vener and Alan Medvin. If it's not one Yorkshire terrier, it's another . . . or another . . . or another . . . until there were nine! According to Tanya, "It's kind of like a hobby, not to make money, just for fun."

Alan concurs. "We definitely love every one to death." But there's one member of this frisky pack that's a troublemaker—Scrawny. The puppy got her name because she was the runt of the litter. Alan admits, "Scrawny has always been the special case for me. I had to put her up to the nipple and make sure she got the food. I've always made sure she was taken care of; that's why she is so attached to me and so protective."

For the past two years, Scrawny's protective services included nipping and becoming increasingly aggressive toward people and pooches. Little Scrawny attacks anyone or any dog that tries to get near her precious Alan.

When Cesar learns that Alan and Tanya raised Scrawny from the very beginning, he observes, "The great thing is that you saw her being born, so we can actually go all the way back and find out where you made the mistake, because *you* made the mistake. In the beginning she belonged to you; now you belong to her. It's like a fatal attraction, because from the beginning you felt sorry about her weakness."

As the consultation continues, Cesar suspects there's a more substantial motivation behind Alan's affection for Scrawny. "The dog became the project of your life, so whatever happened to you in the past, you tried to change it within the dog." Cesar learns that Alan's ex-wife took their daughter away from him, and he's had little contact with her over the years. "I cried my eyes out when she left. Poor child was put in foster care three times and I couldn't help her. But I did my best to show her who I was as a dad, and now I have to live with the idea that maybe she'll come around or maybe she won't. Maybe it's too late in life."

Cesar says, "I felt Alan needed to be listened to, because there was a lot of pain. Scrawny became his daughter in his mind, just to fulfill that part that was missing in him." Cesar believes they can still bring balance back into their lives by no longer treating Scrawny like a princess.

When Cesar first meets Scrawny in their kitchen, the Yorkie hovers close to Alan, in full protection mode. Alan says that when she's like this, he picks her up to comfort her. Cesar suggests a different approach. "If the problem is mild, you can ignore her behavior and then see if the problem goes away. But when she is all over you [Cesar imitates a dog that is jumping on people], you can't ignore it, you have to address it."

When Scrawny starts barking at another Yorkie that is getting too close, Cesar takes a step toward Scrawny and gives a loud "*tsst*." Scrawny stops her attack and backs away. "So what I did was instead of saying, 'Oh my God,' I just keep moving forward, and I didn't need to touch the dog physically, but I proved my point. And that is, 'What you're doing is unwanted by me.'"

When it is Alan's turn and Scrawny tries to jump up on his leg, he gently pushes her away. When she tries again, he snaps his fingers and she backs off.

Alan is surprised by the entire experience, especially how quickly Scrawny backed off her dominant behavior. "Cesar made me realize that everything in my life is all intertwined emotionally, not just with the animals but how I come across to other people. I think this consultation started us down a path that we need to work on, so we're going to take it from there and see how it works."

Old Dog, New Tricks

Name: Sasha

Breed: Lhasa apso

"I was dating Lois about nine years ago. Sasha was a little aggressive then, and I mentioned something about it to Lois, and she said, 'Not a problem. The dog stays, you go.' So based on that I realized that if I was going to stay with the lady I had to accept the dog," recalls Barry Rubino. Now, nine years later, Barry and Lois are married, and eleven-year-old Sasha has not become kinder and gentler with age. Lois often gets bitten when she attempts to serve her tiny dog a bowl of food. Sasha also exhibits possessive behavior over her basket of toys. She bares her teeth at anyone who dares to take anything away.

Barry says, "It's very interesting that the old adage is, 'Don't bite the hand that feeds you.' Well, Sasha does."

Cesar begins the rehabilitation with the toys. Sasha holds on to one of her toys, Cesar has another one in his hand. As he slowly moves forward to back Sasha into a corner, he says, "I am doing what dogs do to each other when one dog wants what the other dog has in his mouth. The first thing he does is to block the other dog. I want to corner her, and I'm using a toy to block a possible bite from her." When Sasha tries for the toy in Cesar's hand, he takes Sasha's bone toy away from her. "This is the big deal. She can't touch my bone toy now; this is my toy now. No, *tsst*, no." When Sasha backs away from Cesar, letting him have the toy, he says, "That means she gave up. Now I move on to exercise number two."

Cesar gets a bowl of Sasha's food and blocks Sasha with his feet from getting near it. "I'm on top of the food. This is very typical in the dog world. The bigger dog always gets on top of the thing, and it's the psychological fight going on there . . . *tsst*. My goal is to remove the food just like I did the toy. So by

Follow-up ❧ ❧ ❧

Sasha's owners never could get her to stick with the "new tricks" she learned with Cesar. They feel she is simply too old to change.

getting between her and the food, I claim the food. I own the food, I own the kitchen."

After a few weak growls, Sasha backs away again. Cesar picks up the bowl and pretends that he is about to eat it. "The owners needed to see how that exercise gets done without being bitten by your dog, without also creating any emotional trauma or any physical trauma."

Barry is nearly speechless. "You've done in five minutes what we've not been able to do over the years."

Key Cesar Tip

Owners who have allowed their dogs to rule the house for many years will have to be especially persistent in upholding new rules if they want to see permanent change.

The Good, the Bad, and the Bubba

Name: Bubba

Breed: Maltese

(episode 110)

Six years ago, Heidi and Hal Wasserman brought home an overly pampered three-year-old Maltese. Now at age nine, this adopted "son" Bubba has become an insufferable spoiled brat, especially when it comes to his intolerance for being left alone. To keep peace in their home, the Wassermans have to take Bubba everywhere they go, something that Hal doesn't seem to mind. Hal, who has difficulty walking, simply pops Bubba into his electrified sit-down scooter and motors next door to their office.

But Bubba also makes trouble at the office. According to Heidi, "We have a corporate gift business, and I do have some clients who come into the office. Bubba greets them beautifully, loves them, licks them, but the second they go to leave, he attacks them." Bubba barks uncontrollably and nips at the heels of anyone who has the temerity to leave.

After Cesar arrives, Heidi tells him something a little unexpected. "We have a perfect dog here—absolutely perfect. Except he has a major problem." Cesar is not surprised. "They're saying 'we have *the* perfect dog.' That to me is a red flag. In this case, we have an unstable little dog living this unnatural style of life. Obviously the dog is being empowered every single day of his life to be the pack leader to both of them."

Cesar then explains that the real issue is Heidi and Hal. "You are reinforcing his negative behavior, because every single day you wake up and give him affection first instead of structure. It has nothing to do with the size or the breed of the dog. It has to do with who is behind that dog. And he doesn't think about the fact that you might get a lawsuit. He doesn't know he's hurting your feelings."

The good news is that even with a nine-year-old dog, Cesar believes that it's never too late to begin the rehabilitation process. They begin in the kitchen, where Cesar has a Dog Whisperer crew member leave the area to set off Bubba's nipping behavior. When Bubba starts to bark at and chase the person, Cesar steps in Bubba's path with a snap of his fingers and a loud "*tsst.*"

Cesar explains, "Every time he protests, you have to say something, like having the last word about it." Cesar repeats this process several times, occasionally using two fingers to touch Bubba in the neck to stop the dog in his tracks. Finally, Bubba stops trying to nip anyone who tries to leave the kitchen.

Heidi sees Cesar's results but is unsure. "What's been going through my mind is self-doubt and whether I'm capable of following through." Cesar knows that rehabilitating Bubba will not be easy. "This is nine years of bad behavior, so it's not going to be fixed in two months, three months. This is a year's worth of work."

Nearly one month later, Cesar returns to check on the Wassermans' progress. Unfortunately, Hal feels that correcting Bubba takes too much time and energy, so he's decided that he likes Bubba just the way he is. Heidi, however, totally got Cesar's message. "I have tried very hard to follow what he has taught us and he's a hundred percent right. I'm the one who really needs to be trained. It's all up to me. And it's very hard to teach an old dog like me new tricks." Acting like Bubba's pack leader does not come easy to her. "But I can't be nice, because then he walks all over me."

Follow-up ❀ ❀ ❀

Heidi understands that it's her behavior that makes Bubba unstable. She is now able to stop Bubba's attacks if she gets to him in time.

Behind the scenes

Spoiled Bubba, who was wearing a $300 "smoking jacket" on the day of shooting, had no trouble showing off his bad behavior to the *Dog Whisperer* crew. He gave series producer and segment director, SueAnn Fincke, a serious nip on the heel.

Sadly, Hal Wasserman passed away a few months after the segment was filmed. The episode was dedicated to his memory.

Pesky Paris

Name: Paris

Breed: Chihuahua

(episode 112)

Nelson plays tug-of-war with Paris.

"*The fact that* he's blond and long haired, I thought Paris would've been a perfect name," remarks Nelson Chang, who found the canine love of his life online. "I love Paris Hilton and I thought Paris's name is, it's sort of metrosexual, so he could be a guy or a girl or whatever he wants to be."

Nelson purchased a variety of haute couture outfits for Paris, making the dog something of a celebrity on the streets of West Hollywood. Paris is seldom seen without four little shoes on his paws, even though he is mostly transported every-where by chic handbag. Admirers are constantly coming over to pick Paris up and pet him. However, when these strangers make a move on Paris, he gets aggressive and tries to bite his fans.

There's also trouble on the home front. According to Nelson's significant other, Jhett, "The dog just goes crazy when there are strangers in the house." Nelson adds, "It eventually led on to biting." Feisty Paris has also been known to run into the street and come back only when he feels like it, creating no end of stress for Nelson and Jhett.

During their consultation, Cesar tells them, "This kind of behavior comes from a dog that doesn't know rules, boundaries, and limitations. He's always living in this human world, and the human is the one who's getting fulfilled here. Can you see how selfish that is? Ninety percent of this is about you two guys."

Cesar is surprised that Paris almost never walks anywhere. The dog travels by handbag to the car, then by car to the destination, then by handbag again. According to Cesar, "Dogs are supposed to enjoy the world by walking. They don't migrate in a car." Cesar alerts them to the fact that many of Paris's unwanted behaviors could be tied to the dog's frustration at not getting any exercise. The result is a frustrated, dominant dog that has become aggressive.

One of Cesar's first recommendations is that Nelson and Jhett say no to any strangers who ask to pet or touch Paris. Next, they have to walk Paris, but in a very specific way. "What I'm asking you is to walk in a very formal, disciplined way, where the only thing he can do is to follow you. After five minutes or ten minutes, you'll see that he just gets in the zone automatically. He's going do it on your terms, and that makes you his leader."

Follow-up 🐾 🐾 🐾

Paris is doing much, much better and is even a father now. Nelson thinks fatherhood has helped to "center" Paris. Nelson thanks Cesar for helping them realize the importance of treating a dog like a dog.

Key Cesar Tip

"These guys were providing only affection, affection, affection—instead of exercise, discipline, and then affection. You can earn a dog's trust with food, water, and affection. But you earn his respect by walking with him and giving him structure in his life."

The Little Rascal

Name: Maya

Breed: pit bull

(episode 109)

Eleven-year-old Destiny Blakely wrote Cesar a letter.

Dear Cesar,

This is a day in my dog's life. After a long night of snoring and nursing her kitten, yes nursing her kitten, she wakes up and goes to the bathroom on the living room floor. Then, she wakes her owner, which is me, with kisses, then jumps on me. She started tearing up the trash, digging everywhere, chewing my toys. She was a great puppy but then started being bad for some reason. And sometimes I wish we didn't get that dog. But, I love her. Cesar, please help my dog.

Cesar responds to Destiny's letter and arrives at the home of single mom Athena Blakely and her two teenage girls, Destiny and Arielle. Their busy household includes two dogs, three cats, three hermit crabs, a hamster, small lizards, and an iguana. Maya is definitely the troublemaker in the household. She digs holes in the garden, steals clothes and then refuses to give them up, attacks the broom when they sweep the floor, and is a nonstop bundle of energy.

"And you have no clue what is happening to her, why she's doing all this?" asks Cesar. Athena shakes her head. "She's bored out of her mind!" exclaims Cesar. He finds out that they take Maya on one walk per week. "She's manipulating you ladies, because you're not manipulating her. We need to exercise with dogs, we need to provide the ability to go out and then come back."

Cesar is concerned by what he sees, "We have too many symptoms. We have a hyperactive symptom, we have nervous symptoms, we have fearful symptoms, and we have dominant symptoms. If you put all the symptoms together, it can become a bite. A pit bull is definitely the strongest breed. This is the only breed that can pull thirty times its body weight." Maya is not yet a red-zone case, Cesar cautions, but she's well on her way to becoming one.

Cesar believes the family has to take charge and to start that process with a daily walk. Just before they leave the driveway, Maya starts bucking like a wild horse, fighting Cesar's attempts to put a leash on her. Cesar holds her calmly by the collar and waits while Maya flops around. "We have to stay there until the temper tantrum passes away, and then we can accomplish what we want to accomplish. I'm just holding the collar until she calms down, because the only thing I want is just to put the leash on."

He recommends that for now they keep Maya's head up when walking. "So she doesn't put her nose on the ground. Once she puts her nose on the ground, she's in a tracking mode. So if you control the nose, you control sixty percent of the brain reaction."

Once they get outside the yard, Maya tries to pull, but Cesar keeps the leash short so Maya must walk right next to him. "Your energy is very important, your state of mind is very important. You have to understand that you're not hurting her; you're just asking her to do what you want her to do, which is walking side by side with you. Slowly she's going to get it."

When Athena takes over the leash, she is able to keep Maya near her without much of a struggle. Destiny can't believe the change in Maya came so quickly. "She was bad, but now she's good."

Since Cesar still has concerns about Maya's behavior, he returns three weeks later to check out their progress. He finds that Maya is much less destructive, and the family is now walking Maya four times a week. To increase the effectiveness of Maya's exercise regimen, Cesar brings a gift—a dog backpack. By adding the pack with an appropriate amount of weight, Maya will drain even more energy on their walks. A thirty-minute walk with a weighted pack has

Follow-up ❀ ❀ ❀

Maya did indeed become that "great dog" Destiny hoped for. Maya loves her backpack and is now much better behaved, both at home and on walks. She no longer steals Destiny's toys, growls at other dogs, charges the fence, or jumps on the kitchen counters.

Key Cesar Tip

A high-energy dog that's bored is bound to take out its frustration on its environment or on the other animals and humans around it.

the same effect as a regular sixty-minute walk. Athena is thrilled by the experience. "Destiny very much wanted to walk her, but Maya was always walking Destiny. But Cesar now showed us a way, where Destiny can walk her also. Maya's progressing nicely. She's got a little bit more to go, but I think we're gonna make it. I think she's gonna be a great dog."

Picture-Perfect Pepper

Name: Pepper

Breed: border collie-terrier mix

(episode 107)

Chris Nelson and Scott Smith are professional photographers who've developed a small problem—Chris's dog, Pepper. When Chris brings this seven-and-a-half-year-old pooch to work, Pepper can get ferocious. Whenever clients come to the studio, Pepper barks and continues to bark after they have entered, then he bites at their heels. Considering that Chris brings Pepper to his studio every day, this type of bad dog behavior has to end.

Chris admits he's in a tough situation. "It makes me very uncomfortable, because at some point she's going go after a client who doesn't understand, and I will have to get rid of the dog."

Not willing to part with Pepper, or leave her alone at home all day, Chris and Scott turn to Cesar for help. When Cesar enters the studio, Chris has to hold back the barking Pepper. One of the first things Cesar learns during their consultation is that Pepper goes after people the same way in Chris's home but acts perfectly normal whenever Chris takes her on a walk. In fact, the two often walk down busy streets together, with Pepper off leash! "In neutral territory, you're in control. But in the territories that you own, she really owns them," Cesar explains. "And you are a follower in her brain."

Cesar shows Chris what he did wrong at the very beginning. "When you hold her back, like when I came through the door, that only intensifies her territorial behavior. Now if a client comes through that door, most of the time people get nervous, tense, or anxious, right? So if we are conveying that energy to a dog that is out of control, that dog will go after that human."

Cesar has a crew member knock at the door. As usual, Pepper goes wild and continues to bark as the person walks in, while Chris turns and says, "No!" to Pepper. Cesar tells Chris that he's not acting in a calm and assertive manner when admonishing Pepper. "That's why she gave the last word, '*ruff, ruff*,' barking at you. When dogs take you seriously, there is no last word."

Cesar then demonstrates his method. "My way of communicating with any animal I'm gonna work with is I give the sound "*tsst*" and wait until the animal relaxes, and

Pepper is doing well, although she had a setback after undergoing an operation on two of her legs. Now recovering, she's back on her walks and getting along well with a second dog, which belongs to Chris's fiancée.

Key Cesar Tip

It's always better to use a simple sound of your choice, in a calm-assertive manner, rather than trying to explain what you want to your dog using complicated words and sentences. Communicate your intention simply and clearly. If your energy is calm-assertive, your dog will understand.

then I go and open the door." When Chris tries using the "*tsst*" sound on Pepper, she calms down almost immediately. Cesar points out that it's not the specific sound, but the simplicity of the sound and the powerful, calm-assertive energy behind it that make the difference.

Cesar has Chris and Scott use the same technique to help cure Pepper of her need to be territorial whenever anyone sits on the studio's couch. Scott has a revelation during the session. "Cesar taught us to make the dog be submissive to us, to love her still, but not let her be the dominant one. And that's what I was letting her do. I loved her so much, I just let her be my boss."

According to Cesar, "What happens to dogs like Pepper is most of the time when we can't control their behavior, we keep them in the backyard. We isolate them from society and sometimes we end up euthanizing them, because we don't see any other way. But Pepper was very close to being a well-balanced dog. It's just up to them this time."

Horsing Around

Name: Sophie

Breed: Sheltie-retriever mix

(episode 125)

Rachelle Wyse adores the freedom of the mountains and the company of her loyal horse, Jack. But to be a proper cowgirl, she needed to find herself a sidekick. Rachelle and her roommate, Melissa Sanders, went to a local shelter to rescue a dog. Immediately they picked out Sophie, knowing that she had recently been returned to the shelter and would soon be scheduled to be euthanized.

Once Sophie was home, Rachelle discovered her dog prefers horsing around to horseback riding. "She was relentless. She would bark at my horse Jack's heels and nip. Having Jack and Sophie together has been a nightmare. He's a very patient horse, but he's kicked her twice now. She had a horseshoe mark over her eye. What is amazing is that she doesn't learn from this."

Having grown up on his grandfather's farm in Mexico, Cesar is no stranger to horses. While dogs are predators and horses are prey, these pack-oriented species share some things in common . . . including the fact that they both need a strong and trustworthy leader.

During their first meeting, Rachelle admits to Cesar that she sees herself as Sophie's mom. He tells her, "With horses, you have to represent an authority figure, so the horse sees you as the dominant one, and then you can ride the horse. But somehow in America, we believe that dogs are human." Rachelle talks about why she might treat the two animals so differently. "The mind-set when you have a horse is you don't have a choice not to be in control. There're safety issues and things like that. Whereas I don't think I take Sophie as seriously. My own personal safety isn't as much of an issue with a thirty-pound dog as opposed to an eleven-hundred-pound horse."

Rachelle's ideal situation is for Sophie to stay outside the ring and watch while she works with Jack. She typically exercises Jack by lunging him, guiding him in circles while controlling his pace. It's during this exercise time when Sophie becomes the most aggressive.

As Rachelle walks Jack around the ring, Cesar stays in front of Sophie, backing her away from the ring with a snap of fingers and a loud "*tsst*" every time the dog starts

Follow-up ❀ ❀ ❀

Rachelle worked hard with Sophie but wasn't able to get the results she wanted. Sophie is now living happily with another family.

to move in. "I'm stopping her excitement before it increases. So this way she goes into a different state of mind. Notice how I'm not using her name? Her name is only for a positive experience. Right now it is just hard for her because she's never done it before."

For several minutes, Cesar continues to stay near Sophie, claiming the ring as his space every time she attempts to come inside. Finally, Sophie sits down outside the ring and watches while Rachelle gets Jack to canter and then run even faster around the ring.

Rachelle is thrilled. "I've never seen her lie down and watch. It was just such a relief. I could really focus on the task at hand."

Rachelle lets Jack run free around the ring at the end of their session as a reward. "See," Cesar says, "he works and then he gets rewarded. Freedom is not something he gets just because he is a beautiful horse, he gets it after he works for her. That's the principle of exercise, discipline, affection."

The Lucy Bowl

Name: Lucy

Breed: Dalmatian

Nine-year-old Lucy has a host of neuroses. Most of them show up around feeding time, when for no apparent reason she lashes out with a bizarre aggression toward anyone or no one at all. Her owner, Ron Gertsch, says, "The process is, she'll eat, and then after a while, she'll start growling. If you try to approach her food, she'll lunge at you. The only way I can get her food away from her is to put a chair in front of her and she still got really vicious. If the chair hadn't been there, she would have bitten me."

A Jekyll-and-Hyde case, Lucy can be sweet one moment and aggressive the next. Ron's wife, Caroline Baddour, has also been a victim of Lucy's "Hyde" side. "I was playing a board game on the floor. And Lucy just turned around and bit me right on the bridge of the nose. I ended up getting stitches."

For Caroline and Ron, the key issue is protecting their new baby, Callison. According to Caroline, "She doesn't show any aggression at all toward the baby so far, but there's no way I'm going leave her alone with Callison. I love Lucy, but I don't trust her. I hate to say it, but if we did give her to another home, eventually I think she'd be put down."

When Cesar arrives, he discovers that Ron and Caroline don't really take Lucy on walks and instead just let her run around their yard. Cesar believes that a big backyard is no substitute for a walk. Cesar tells them, "You didn't create this consciously, but this dog has not been properly walked in eight years. So the walk will be an important part of her rehabilitation. But the beauty of dogs is that they move on faster than humans. So if she relapses or doesn't move forward, it's not because she's not capable, it's because the human is not putting in one hundred percent."

Cesar decides to begin Lucy's treatment with an exercise at the food bowl, which seems to trigger the worst behavior. When Lucy starts growling after the food bowl is placed on the floor, Caroline responds with a firm "No!" Cesar remarks, "There's really no reason for Lucy to show aggression. And then your reaction was to be a little frantic about it. 'Lucy, NO!' That won't calm her, because if the mind is too caught up in that zone, then the dog won't really stop."

Cesar demonstrates how a dominant dog would move in on another dog's food by calmly and assertively claiming the food dish with his feet. "This is one exercise right here. I'm not suggesting you do it yet. I'm moving in to the food. Without creating a fight, a dog will use its body to block the other dog from getting close to the food. A dog moves in gently to the food and takes advantage if the other dog doesn't respond." Cesar slowly moves forward until he has successfully blocked Lucy from the food. "Once he is on top of the food, then he gets assertive about it. I'm letting her know that this plate now belongs to me. When Lucy didn't try to strike me, that's when I knew that I was in control of that food."

Caroline understands Cesar's observation that dogs can read a person's energy and body language. "When Cesar said it was his attitude that protected him, that made so much sense. I saw that she respected him. In fact, her whole attitude improved."

But Lucy's problems run very deep, and they'll take time and patience to work out. Cesar instructs Ron and Caroline to keep her away from the baby for at least a year. "This is a dog that needs to be under supervision twenty-four hours a day, seven days a week, until they start removing some of her issues."

Terror Bella

Name: Bella

Breed: border terrier

Bella has spent both years of her life thus far being spoiled rotten by her adoring family, the Francescons. Perhaps that's because she represents something tremendously precious to them.

According to Elisa Francescon, "My youngest sister developed brain cancer and passed away from her disease." Elisa adopted her daughter, Heather, who was already like a sister to her cousin, Elisa's daughter Nicole. "Before she died, she made me promise that I would get the girls a puppy. We gave her the name Bella Angel, because *Bella* in Italian means pretty or beautiful—and my sister was— and then Angel because my sister was that, too."

According to Nicole, in some ways Bella fits in perfectly with this loving Italian family. "She likes spaghetti, she likes meatballs—she's just like us," Nicole says with a giggle. Despite all the attention and love, Bella has developed a nasty side. Elisa says, "She would chase the girls, nip at their feet all the time. As she's gotten older, it's turned into a more aggressive situation, where any person who comes into our house is not welcome." Little Bella attacks almost anyone who comes through the front door. This has become a big problem for a family that loves to socialize and have large, boisterous dinners. "She's the Tony Soprano of the Italian dog world. When the veterinarian tells you that she's a lawsuit waiting to happen, you live in fear," says Elisa.

Cesar demonstrates how to walk Bella for Nicole, Elisa, and Heather.

Cesar identifies with the importance of solid family bonds and he's eager to help when he learns about the Francescons' case. "Dogs can be an important part of our family, but they have to be treated like dogs, not children." When Cesar learns that Bella was given to the girls at the request of Elisa's dying sister, he asks, "Did your sister say that the dog shouldn't have any rules, boundaries, or limitations? Because that's what's missing."

Cesar refers to the moment when he arrived at their door for the consultation, and Bella went crazy barking and lunging at him. Everyone was trying to calm Bella down by talking baby talk and trying to soothe her while she was acting nervous and aggressive. "What happened at that moment is, you're actually telling her that it's okay to do what she is doing." Cesar tells them why he thinks Bella is out of control. "Sometimes we use animals to fulfill something that is empty. Bella represents a lot to your family. But even though you share all this love and all this spiritual belief with a dog doesn't mean she sees you as the authority figure. And, as you see, it creates a monster."

Nicole begins to cry when she hears this. "I feel guilty now that we've done this to her, because I feel like it's our fault that we made her the way she is. It's just because she's so special, I feel bad." The Francescons tell Cesar that they are ready to put the past behind them and move on with his help. Cesar says, "The strategy that we're going to follow is exercise, discipline, affection—and we have to play the Italian role."

Cesar demonstrates how to contain Bella's explosive behavior at the front door. Cesar recommends for the time being that they keep a leash on Bella when they know someone is coming over. "So if she runs to the door, we grab the leash, and then we bring her to the door. She has to learn to greet people in a different way, with manners." When Cesar has someone knock at the door, he makes Bella sit and wait before he opens the door and welcomes the guest inside. Whenever Bella starts to pace or bark, Cesar quiets her and makes her go back to a sitting position. "We don't allow her to become chaotic. We control the explosion when she's only at level one. So we are reconditioning the mind to behave in a certain way."

Elisa is ready to put her new knowledge to use. "Cesar showed us that she needed discipline. So now she's gonna know that she's just as important to us as she was before, but she'll have good behavior."

Elisa says, "I know my sister Laura is looking down and smiling, saying, 'This is the way it should be.'"

Follow-up ❧ ❧ ❧

It's hard for Nicole and Elisa to find time to walk Bella, since they work long hours. They know what they're supposed to do but they haven't been following through, and Bella's behavior still reflects that. Nicole does say that they are being better pack leaders inside the house now and have noticed that Bella is somewhat calmer there.

Behind the scenes

Cesar was touched when the family invited him to join them in celebrating their grandparents' anniversary. "This family became very special to me. My hope is for them to really stay consistent with what Bella really needs, every single day."

Chapter 6

Dominance

Cesar, Tedd, Shellie, and Gus at the herding ring.

Bouncing Bouvier

Name: Gus

Breed: Bouvier des Flandres

(episode 108)

Tedd Rosenfeld and Shellie Yaseen both have high-powered jobs in the entertainment industry and they're used to calling the shots. But when they adopted their second Bouvier des Flandres, fourteen-month-old Gus, the big playful pup soon became the boss of their household. When greeting people, the extraordinarily friendly Gus throws his hundred-pound body at them, regardless of their age, gender, or size.

As Tedd laments, "It's totally curiosity and being friendly, but being a hundred pounds, he can knock people flying. And he's sent Shellie onto her rear end more than one time already."

Follow-up ❧ ❧ ❧

Tedd and Shellie made good on their promise to bring Gus back for regular runs at sheep herding and stayed 100 percent committed to following through on the rest of Cesar's advice. The result is that Gus is a shining success story! From an "impossible" problem, he's turned into such a delightful and well-behaved dog that he's become an official therapy dog for the Love on 4 Paws pet-assisted therapy program. Shellie has even taught Gus how to "whisper" in the hospital.

Gus's instincts play a role as well. According to Shellie, "Bouviers once pulled milk carts and herded cattle and sheep for the farms in Europe. So Gus tries to herd everything and everybody he can. Tedd and I, if we are walking too far apart on the street, he'll try to get us both together because he needs to control the fact that we're his herd."

When Cesar first meets with the couple, he learns that Gus has been bouncing with energy since the day they brought him home. "To control a high-level-energy kid like Gus, you have to really do a lot of exercise," Cesar says. "Gus is in need of being challenged. He doesn't have a job. And when you don't get to use up energy you get frustrated. So the bouncing thing is a negative energy."

Cesar knows the perfect place that can give Gus a job. After working with Tedd and Shellie on their walking technique, Cesar introduces them to the Long Beach herding facility, where owner Jerome Stewart specializes in training dogs to manage a flock of sheep. Cesar recommends that they bring Gus to a facility like Jerome's once a week to help Gus burn off energy. Cesar notes, "This is a great thing for a dog because he gets to be a herding dog. He gets to release a lot of that energy that he has accumulated during all these ten months that he's been living with Tedd and Shellie."

Jerome carefully guides Gus out into a pen that contains a half-dozen sheep. Before Gus's innate herding drive kicks in, there's a danger that he'll go into prey mode and try to attack the sheep. So Jerome leaves Gus's leash on to slow him down and then monitors his movements carefully. Shellie is fascinated to watch Gus's instincts appear to kick in. "You could tell he was trying to figure out, should he follow the flock, should he follow the one that was running away? You could almost see his mind working." Then it happens. Gus begins to swing wider and focus on the sheep that are straying. He starts to round them up. Jerome confirms it. "Now he's herding!"

With a giant grin spreading across his face, Cesar comments, "Gus was able to do it. In a matter of minutes he went from prey drive to herding drive. I couldn't stop myself from laughing because I was so happy for him and, at the same time, I was enjoying the whole scene, such a natural scene. No streets, no cars, no home—just sheep and a dog."

When Gus's session is over, Tedd and Shellie are astonished as they witness a completely fulfilled Gus. Tedd marvels, "I just haven't seen him that active and that happy in a long time. He will definitely go to more herding classes with Jerome."

For Cesar, this is what makes his work so rewarding. "It just doesn't get any better than this day for Gus."

Behind the scenes

Jerome Stewart, a decorated American Kennel Club and American Herding Breed Association herding test and trial judge, has a saying about herding breeds: "A dog with herding instinct and no training can make enough work for nine men to do. A trained herding dog can do the work of nine men. You need to decide which you would rather live with."

Lola

Name: Lola

Breed: Dalmatian

(episode 115)

When Liz Dietz and her husband, Ed Lopez, first rescued then one-year-old Lola, they had no idea what they were getting into. Now nine years old, this demanding Dalmatian practically runs the household, even bullying their easygoing boxer, Capone. According to Liz, "Lola is sort of a princess. You know the lyrics from *Damn Yankees*, 'Whatever Lola wants Lola gets'—this dog is Lola." Lola's biggest issue is that she is out of control on walks. If she manages somehow to slip out of her leash, Lola won't listen to anyone. Now only Liz takes Lola on walks—an exercise she has come to dread.

When Cesar arrives, Ed and Liz fill him in on their belief that Dalmatians are hyper, willful dogs, and that they didn't know that when they adopted Lola. Cesar counters by telling them there are four elements to every dog. "The thing is, you're dealing with an animal first. Then species: dog, then the breed, and then the dog's personality, but you're viewing it backward. You're viewing her as Lola first, then Dalmatian, then species: dog, and finally as an animal."

Cesar wants to see how Liz handles Lola on a walk. Things go badly from the get-go as Liz can't even get Lola to come to her or hold still while she tries to attach the leash. Then Cesar takes over, explaining that if Liz tries to put a leash on Lola when Lola is out of control, Liz is allowing Lola to take the leader role. Cesar demonstrates his pack leader way. "Now I'm going to invite her to approach me, because when you approach an animal, you give it the dominant position. The pack leader never comes to the follower. The followers come to the pack leader."

When Cesar motions for Lola to come to him, she walks right over and he easily slips her head into the slip collar leash. "And she came to me with her head

Follow-up ❀ ❀ ❀

"It's like Lola's a different dog now," says Liz. Lola is much easier to walk—she no longer pulls or runs away. She's also developed a new appreciation for other dogs. Before Cesar, Liz and Ed couldn't have friends bring their dogs over, but now Lola loves to socialize with other canines.

low, right? Head low means submission—head up means excitement, domination."

Cesar informs Liz and Ed that because Lola is a high-energy dog, she needs more than just a daily walk. Luckily, they own one of Cesar's favorite tools—a treadmill. Cesar gently leads Lola onto the treadmill. "The wonderful thing about treadmills is when we are short on time, we can put the dog on the treadmill for thirty minutes and *then* we can take her for a twenty-minute walk." He eases Lola on and off the treadmill several times until she is comfortable with it. Then he starts the treadmill. "Once she surrenders you're going to see that she walks on it." And Lola slowly begins walking on the moving treadmill. Liz is amazed. "I'm just so excited, I can't wait to really work with Lola and take her further and further."

Key Cesar Tip

For high-energy, overly excited dogs like Lola, Flexi leashes can sometimes make the problem worse. Flexi leashes work best for mellow, happy-go-lucky, generally well-behaved dogs.

Psycho Flirt

Name: Flirt

Breed: Chinese crested

Cesar believes that dogs are reflections of their owners. In the case of Flirt, the pint-sized pooch of comedian and actress Barbie Orr, the mirror has been replaced by a magnifying glass. If Barbie is friendly, chatty, and highly energetic, Flirt is an amiable version of the Tasmanian devil, but with a double shot of caffeine.

Flirt is a hairless Chinese crested—a cat-sized canine. When Cesar arrives at Barbie's tiny apartment, he gets a clear picture of what's going on. Barbie is letting her naturally exuberant personality keep Flirt in an excited state. Flirt never has a moment of calm behavior. According to Cesar, "During my whole conversation with Barbie, she didn't slow down one moment to allow me to deliver the information."

When Cesar takes Flirt for a five-minute walk, the change in Flirt is dramatic and nearly instantaneous. The dog obediently walks at Cesar's side without a struggle. "Yes, the dog was hyperactive, but it was easier to convince this dog to go back to his natural state of mind. When Flirt and I had the chance to be with each other without the presence of Barbie, I was able to influence her with my presence alone. Flirt was able to accomplish calm submission." Barbie is astounded at the newly calm Flirt. "You've switched my dog out, right?" she jokes.

Clearly, Flirt *can* become more calm and cooperative, but that means Barbie will have to change the

Follow-up 🐾 🐾 🐾

Things are pretty much the same for Barbie and Flirt.

Behind the scenes

When the *Dog Whisperer* camera crew first started shooting, Flirt leaped around the room like a lit pack of firecrackers. Producer SueAnn Fincke became one of Flirt's victims during filming, when the dog jumped on her lap several times and licked her repeatedly. Flirt was moving so fast that the producers added an onscreen disclaimer, certifying that the footage was *not* sped up.

way she deals with her dog. "Cesar gave me a whole bunch of homework to do. It's supposed to start with me being mellow. I don't see that happening, but we're going to work on Flirt being mellow without mellowing out Mom."

Occasionally, Cesar does come across a situation where the hardest creature to change is the human.

Key Cesar Tip

Dogs are often a reflection of their owners. What kind of energy is your dog getting from you?

The Yap Dog

(episode 104)

Name: Boomer

Breed: Chesapeake Bay terrier

Boomer—the name says it all. Boomer's bark is earsplitting, and he bounces around the house like a ricocheting rubber ball. Above this relentless din hang paintings of Boomer standing serenely and dressed in various clown outfits. It seems artist Christy Thom and her boyfriend, fellow Boomer owner Jody Sherman, have a different identity picked out for Boomer. And it's put a strain on everyone in this relationship. "He figured out that he could get attention from barking and then I think it went from there to him just liking the sound of his own voice. He's a dog that always needs to be in your face, letting you know he's around, wanting to play," says Jody. The neighbors have angrily complained about the nonstop barking, and Jody and Christy are worried they may have to get rid of him if they can't do something to keep him quiet.

Cesar's first question to the couple is whether they see Boomer as a dog or as a human. Jody replies, "Like a furry human." Cesar notes that they are trying to use human psychology on a dog. "When a dog is waggling too much and whimpering and doing all these things, he's not happy, he's anxious. If I share my love when his mind is out of control, then I'm encouraging an out-of-control state of mind."

First, Cesar puts a leash on Boomer to begin the rehabilitation process. Cesar recommends putting the leash high up on the neck where they can have more control when giving Boomer a correction. The moment Boomer barks, Cesar gives a quick tug on the leash, accompanied by a "*tsst*" sound, to give Boomer the message that the barking is unwanted behavior. They also use the same technique to get Boomer to stop barking when someone rings the doorbell.

Boomer is a work in progress, but the key is for Jody and Christy to stop accidentally encouraging unwanted behavior.

Hope for Hank

Name: Hank

Breed: mastiff

(episode 112)

In the twenty years that Marsha Alexander has been rescuing abused and abandoned dogs, she never met a canine she couldn't handle. She had eight-year-old Kalif, a blue Neapolitan mastiff, and English mastiff–shepherd mixes Casey and Louis, each of which tops the scale at over 120 pounds. Then she brought home Hank, a three-year-old, 155-pound mastiff. That's when everything changed.

Never before had Marsha been fearful around an animal until she came across Hank at the shelter. In fact, the shelter worker was reluctant to release Hank to Marsha due to the dog's viciousness. Nevertheless, she brought Hank home determined to turn him around and give him the love and discipline he needs. Marsha has been able to work with Hank, and there is no doubt he has come a long way. But his bad habits have literally destroyed her home. "Hank suffers greatly from separation anxiety. While I was at work, he ate my oak windowsills and my window frames, pulled the paneling off the wall, chewed the furniture up, and ripped to shreds the bed that I had given him. He's taken down toasters. I literally have no furniture in my house now because Hank has eaten his way through the house."

In addition to all of this, Hank has no tolerance for people walking by his gate. He barks and lunges at them. Hank's barking is incessant, intimidating, and seemingly impossible for Marsha to control.

When Cesar arrives, Marsha tells Cesar, "He basically doesn't allow anybody to touch him. And I am desperately afraid that Hank may bite somebody. Not intentionally. It's more like, 'I will get you before you can hurt me,' because all that Hank knows is to be hurt, until he came here."

Hank hangs with his packmates.

Marsha received many admiring calls and letters after the segment on Hank aired, applauding her for her selfless caring for dogs that might otherwise be put down.

Cesar sees Hank as a dog that is extremely fearful and unsure. "His aggression was more of a defense mechanism and he will try to defend himself from anybody taking him away from his environment. It was not because he wanted to hurt anybody."

Cesar believes that draining Hank's energy will help with his separation anxiety, and that means plenty of walks. Cesar is happily surprised to watch Marsha act calmly and assertively when the two of them take Hank on a walk near her home. Cesar needs to give Marsha only a few tips to improve her walking experience. First, he wants Marsha to use a shorter leash so Hank can't stray too far from her. He also recommends that she keep Hank's choke chain near the top of his neck so she can have better control during the walk.

According to Cesar, "Separation anxiety is one of those sicknesses that take a little longer than aggression to be rehabilitated. We need to be consistent with a lot of exercise, because the separation anxiety comes from the lack of exercise. So he needs to walk every day. That's the medication for Hank."

Marsha is relieved by Cesar's prognosis. "Cesar made me feel like I was handling Hank in the proper way. I've seen an improvement in Hank already. I've seen a lot of anxiety disappear, and I've seen a lot of his pent-up energy ease off. I think we're going to be okay."

Humping Daisy

Name: Daisy

Breed: Labrador retriever

Nearly two years ago the Benda family adopted Daisy as a puppy. Since then, they've given this purebred yellow Lab—full name Queen Elizabeth Daisy—the royal treatment. Marlene Benda says, "She's a great walker; she trained with me for the marathon. She loves fetching a ball, she just loves people. There're just a few things we have to straighten out." Marlene's husband, Randy, adds, "I don't know if it's a dominance thing or what she's doing, but she tries to hump my son, Drew, and Marlene when we're sitting around."

Daisy also goes after the Bendas' daughter, Lacee. "She bites our heels and we just have to get away from her," says Lacee. Daisy always has to rush through doors first, and the family has to throw food or ice to lure Daisy away from the door so they can get out without her stampeding them.

Cesar is normally more focused on a dog's energy, but purebreds like Daisy can become frustrated when the inherent nature of their breed goes unfulfilled. "They went and got a yellow Lab because their expectations were that this dog magically is the perfect dog. But this is a dog that is controlling the house. And this is only going to lead them into a very bad family dynamic."

When Cesar arrives, he's curious to hear how the various family members try to deal with the humping issue. Son Drew tells him, "I just go, 'Get off me,' and push her off." Lacee adds, "And we say, 'Bad behavior, bad behavior,' and tell her, 'Get off, Daisy.'"

Cesar responds, "You're removing the animal from you, but you are not following through with the ritual. The ritual is, first you remove the animal from you, then you make sure the animal goes into a lying down or submissive position. Right then and there she has to show submission to the person she mounted. You can see this at the dog park. When the dog that is being mounted disagrees with the behavior, it turns around, bites, and makes sure the other dog goes on the ground."

The session begins in the kitchen, where Cesar puts a leash on Daisy. By discreetly stepping on the end of Daisy's leash, Cesar keeps her away from the door until

Follow-up ❀ ❀ ❀

Marlene reports that Daisy has improved 100 percent. She is walking a great deal with Marlene and no longer jumps on people or charges the door. She tries to hump small children from time to time, but they know how to stop her right away.

she becomes calm enough to remain there on her own. This allows the family to walk in and out the door without a struggle. "Every door is actually an opportunity for you to gain power," says Cesar, while recommending that they should praise and reward Daisy only when she is behaving the way they want.

Cesar then has everyone practice making Daisy wait while they go in and out of the door. They can't believe how quickly Daisy is responding to them. Cesar says, "Consistency is the key to balance. Marlene is already walking the dog the way a dog owner is supposed to walk a dog. I would love the whole family to be connected to Daisy during the walk. They can all share leadership at the same time."

King

Name: King

Breed: rottweiler

When Teresa Valdivieso got a rottweiler puppy for her daughter, Chantel, it was almost as if there were two siblings in the house. Chantel, a ten-year-old professional actress, loves hanging around with her "big brother," King, who now tips the scale at 150 pounds. The problem is that the eighty-pound Chantel is no match for King when they go on a walk. Teresa says, "I actually do not let Chantel go out and walk King by herself."

Cesar has worked with hundreds of rottweilers over the years, and he has a special affinity for this powerful breed that is often unfairly criticized as being violent. After Cesar arrives, he asks Chantel

King walks Chantel.

and Teresa about their earliest days with King. Chantel recalls, "I treated him just like a big brother. He sleeps on the bed with me. It seems that, through all the time that I've had him, he just gets so excited. If I'm playing by myself he'll knock my toys down."

Cesar explains a little about a dog's growth cycles. "The reality is that from birth to eight months is childhood, from eight months to three years is the adolescent stage, and from three years and up is the adult stage. He is an adult, your big brother. But in his reality, he is a rottweiler, he's a dog, he's an animal, he's a very proud guy. So if you ladies try to control a hundred-and-fifty-pound rottweiler with just love, it's not going to work."

When Cesar observes Chantel walking King in the park, he notices that King leans into the girl often, which is what a dog does when trying to put its claim on someone or something. Cesar tells Chantel that she needs to keep King's collar high up on his neck, which will give her more control on a walk.

When Cesar walks King for the first time, he is concerned to see just how powerful

Follow-up ✿ ✿ ✿

The relationship between Chantel and King has become better and better since her session with Cesar. Now she can handle him with ease, and he truly is the "big brother" she always dreamed of. But Chantel heard Cesar's message loud and clear. "I learned that the biggest thing is that I'm the person and King's a dog. And I have to make sure that he knows that I'm in control and that he's not in control. I'm walking him, not him walking me like it was before."

King is when he gets into his excited state of mind. "His reactions were excited, dominant. And to me that is a red flag. The protection part of it is good, the aggression is not. A lot of times dogs solve problems with each other with just eye contact or by body language. But King wants to lunge."

Cesar believes that they need to drain more of King's energy before Chantel can practice being King's leader. Cesar wants Chantel to use her acting skills with King and asks her to pick a favorite superhero. Chantel instantly replies, "Catwoman!" Cesar wants Chantel to act as if she's Catwoman to bring out her assertive side when walking King.

King is not going to have an overnight transformation. Cesar expects it will take at least two months of "Catwoman time" for Chantel to be able to control King on the leash.

Key Cesar Tip 🦴

No matter how old you are, how strong you are, or how much you weigh, if your energy is consistently strong, calm, and assertive, you can be a pack leader to a powerful breed dog. The key is to assert your leadership from the beginning and always remember that you are the human— and your companion is the dog.

Behind the scenes

Chantel has starred in *The Polar Express* and *The Santa Clause 3*.

The Wrath of Opie

Name: Opie

Breed: Labrador retriever

Suzanne Ohanesian simply loves her black Lab. With his oversize tongue hanging out the side of his mouth, Opie seems like the poster dog of the happy-go-lucky canine. That is, until Opie meets another dog. Perhaps worse, Opie doesn't necessarily attack the other dog but turns his fear and aggression on Suzanne, who sports numerous scars from his bites. Now, just taking Opie for a walk around the block induces a lump in Suzanne's throat. *What will happen* THIS *time?*

Suzanne is willing to do anything to solve the problem. When Cesar takes Opie's leash, Suzanne quickly learns that Opie has it in him to change. Under Cesar's calm-assertive leadership, within minutes Opie is walking beside an unfamiliar dog without so much as a whimper. Suzanne is shocked by the almost instant change. Cesar tells her, "This is not about his heart, this is about his mind, and the only way you can control his mind is by you bringing your mind together, making your mind stronger, showing him that you are now this assertive person."

Cesar makes a follow-up visit to Suzanne after discovering she is still having a difficult time with Opie. She admits that she just cannot get over her own fear and dread when she walks him. Again they walk together and Cesar tries to help Suzanne learn to project calm-assertive energy. Cesar tells her, "Right now fear is controlling you, and you know there's more work to be done. But change is a possibility as long as you work on it . . . and it takes courage."

Follow-up 🐾 🐾 🐾

Despite many valiant efforts, Suzanne cannot consistently keep Opie under her control. "Psychologically speaking or energywise, her body was there but her mind wasn't there; it was overwhelmed with fear. She allowed fear to overpower her and it was very important for her to acknowledge that."

Spaniel Hospital

Name: Goldie

Breed: Brittany spaniel

(episode 120)

Spaniel Hospital with Jackie Zeman,
Cassidy, Lacey, and Goldie.

Actress Jacklyn Zeman has starred on the soap *General Hospital* for more than twenty-five years. Lately, however, she's endured a real-life soap opera starring her six-year-old Brittany spaniel, Goldie. In a gorgeous beach home in Malibu, Goldie seems to have an ideal dog's life with a big backyard and two energetic young girls, Cassidy and Lacey, to play with. Yet behind this picture-perfect pup lurks a dog with a dark side. As Goldie's world turns, this is the script for an episode of *Spaniel Hospital*.

JACKLYN ZEMAN
You put Goldie on a leash and you get yanked!

LACEY
She will yank you down the street till you're running.

CASSIDY
So she doesn't get out as much as I know she should.

Goldie acts as if she's in the Iditarod, constantly pulling on the leash. Also, the family causes such a commotion during their neighborhood walks that the other dogs on the street come to their gates barking, which only incites Goldie to bark more. Cesar is used to the young and the restless in his dog pack. Now he's about to enter another world—the realm of Goldie's *Spaniel Hospital*.

CESAR MILLAN

They live in this huge, beautiful home, with a big backyard. But this is a good example of a dog that lives in that environment and is not happy. Dogs don't really have a dream and say, "I want to live in the biggest backyard ever." Their dream is just to move on with their life and to have adventures every day. They can't just live twenty-four hours a day, seven days a week behind walls, because that's not natural for any animal.

Cesar tells the women how important it is for dogs to get exercise, discipline, and affection daily and that it seems like Goldie is getting only affection every day. He also learns about Goldie's aggressiveness toward other neighborhood dogs, particularly females.

CESAR MILLAN

Goldie does not see you as the dominant ones. Goldie controls everybody here. So no other female is going to come and control her females.

Cesar decides the best way to deal with Goldie's issues is to teach her three owners how to be powerful pack leaders on their daily walks. It begins with the leash. Cesar expects a dog to be calm and submissive before he will put the leash on. He also makes sure to go out the door first, then invites the dog out to follow him. Cesar demonstrates how Goldie needs to walk right next to whoever is holding the leash, and that the dog needs a correction whenever she tries to go in front or starts to bark at other dogs. When Cesar hands the leash over to Jackie, Goldie starts pulling again.

CESAR MILLAN

Jackie has a bad habit of looking at the dog, to see what the dog is going to do. She was tense, and dogs don't follow tense energy. So Goldie started pulling her. You need to be in control of her world at that moment. This is why animals will follow you.

Within a few minutes, Cesar has all three owners walking Goldie calmly by their sides.

JACKLYN ZEMAN

I assumed that Cesar would be successful but I didn't expect him to take all of ten seconds.

Still, those changes won't stick unless Jacklyn and the girls practice consistency in their leadership of Goldie. Cesar advises them to stop using their yard as an excuse to skip walks and instead take Goldie on a disciplined promenade around the neighborhood for at least forty-five minutes each day. Her rehabilitation will undoubtedly take time, with plenty of twists and turns along the way.

CESAR MILLAN

This is not the end of this case. This is just the beginning.

Like most soap operas, this one will continue daily, but with the guiding light of her three lovely costars, Goldie's *Spaniel Hospital* should have a happy ending.

Un-crossing Jordan

Name: Jordan

Breed: bulldog

(episode 118)

Bill Herrera decided to adopt Jordan thinking he would be a typical bulldog—a mellow, lazy creature. But Jordan proved this stereotype wrong almost from the beginning. Jordan's main problem is that he gets overly excited pretty much all the time. Jordan jumps all over everyone who comes in the house, licking them relentlessly with his big, slobbery tongue.

Jordan also has a few major obsessions. Whenever Bill waters the lawn, Jordan grabs the hose away and sprays water everywhere. Neighbor Remi Frazin has tried to get a hose away from Jordan, saying, "You'd have to grab on to the hose and use all your strength, because he's a really tough dog." Jordan also goes crazy around skateboards and basketballs—he continually bites the objects and takes them away from whoever is playing with them.

Cesar v. Jordan.

First, Cesar wants to know how often Bill walks Jordan. "I take him for a lot of walks, two or three times a day." Cesar believes that it's not only the breed that determines a dog's behavior. "We have to really understand that energy plays the biggest role when you adopt a dog. You have to make sure that his energy and your energy are equal or that your energy is higher. This way the dog sees who the dominant one is. I just want you to see that we can control excitement, so it doesn't become obsession."

Cesar takes Jordan outside and makes him confront one of the objects of his obsession—a skateboard. Cesar keeps control of Jordan on a leash while he pushes a skateboard down the sidewalk. Every time Jordan makes a move for the skateboard, Cesar gives him a correction by pulling quickly and firmly on the leash. Then Cesar hops on the skateboard and gets Jordan to pull him down the street. After fourteen minutes of skateboarding, a tired Jordan is able to sit next to the skateboard and doesn't try to attack it.

Next, Cesar works in a similar way with Jordan's basketball and water hose obsessions. It takes another thirty-three minutes for Cesar to get Jordan to stop attacking the basketball and nineteen minutes with the hose before Jordan gives up. Cesar says, "He's a bulldog. So that makes him a very, very determined dog and he's gonna do whatever he wants. But I'm a bulldog, too. This is a dog that has never had any kind of limitations, rules, or boundaries, so he's going to put up the worst fight ever. He's making me work for my money. Jordan actually reminded me how important it is to stay calm."

Cesar also notices that Bill tends to get angry whenever Jordan goes into his obsessive mode, but he tries to hide that anger. "Bill did show me that whenever it didn't work at that moment, he just gave up. And he became frustrated, so it was very clear to see him going from a calm guy to a frustrated guy."

Cesar tells Bill that he needs to acknowledge his own impatient nature and deal with it. "Maybe Jordan is here for that reason, so you can achieve calm-assertive energy. If you had gotten a calm bulldog you would've stayed the guy you are right now. There's a reason why Jordan is with you."

Bill realizes that he does indeed need to work on himself. "Being assertive and calm will help me with a lot of things—my work, with friends, and my relationships. I definitely do think that will help me."

Follow-up ❀ ❀ ❀

Bill reports that he can walk Jordan now and control all of the problems that Jordan used to have. Bill's mother, Elisa Herrera, bonded with Jordan once the dog became calmer, and the two were very close until Elisa passed away in March 2005. The knowledge that his mother was able to enjoy Jordan during her last years is a comfort to Bill, who is thankful that Cesar came into their lives.

The second season of *Dog Whisperer with Cesar Millan* premiered in
January 2006 in prime time and quickly became the highest-rated series on the
National Geographic Channel. Episodes were now one hour long instead of a
half hour, and they usually contained two or three separate stories. Because
of the longer duration, stories could unfold in more depth and detail, and there
could be more follow-ups with the dogs and their owners.

    Since the network went "all high-def" that year, so did *Dog Whisperer*.
Shooting the episodes in high-definition video was challenging at first, since
HD cameras are larger and bulkier than the cameras the series had previously
used, so the *Dog Whisperer* crew had to work harder than ever to keep their
intrusions into the action to a minimum. But all involved agree that high def
makes the show even more powerful. When that lightbulb realization happens
for dog owners now, audiences can witness every moment of it.

    There were a few other changes in the second season. Because segments
would be developed more completely, only one story would be covered on
each shooting day; frequently, there were one or more return visits and follow-

ups filmed as well. And this season, Cesar no longer had to sit on the curb before shooting! The production rented a small air-conditioned motor home, which housed Cesar, Ilusion, and whatever members of Cesar's pack (almost always including Daddy, the pit bull) joined him on each case. Also stocked in the RV were a smorgasbord of the various tools that Cesar uses in his rehabilitations—from a collection of his famous 35-cent leashes to skateboards, LandRoller skates, and a bicycle.

In April, during the production of Season Two, Cesar's first book, *Cesar's Way* (cowritten by this book's coauthor Melissa Jo Peltier) was published and spent a year on the *New York Times* bestseller list, ultimately selling more than one million copies in less than a year. Shortly thereafter, the DVD boxed set of Season One was released. All involved in the production of this new, improved second season shared the proud feeling they were a part of something wonderful, perhaps even changing the world "one dog at a time."

Chapter 7

Aggression Toward People

Bandit.

Raging Bandit

Name: Bandit

Breed: Chihuahua

(episode 201)

Lori Ovanessian had always dreamed of getting her thirteen-year-old son Tyler a dog so he could have the kind of warm, loving experience she remembered with her own childhood pets. They found an adorable Chihuahua over the internet—a diminutive male with a masklike mark over his eyes. They named him Bandit. Both Lori and Tyler looked forward to sharing the irreplaceable experience of raising a loving dog together.

Bandit, however, turned out to be the hound from hell.

Follow-up ❧ ❧ ❧

While it began as a case Cesar almost gave up on, Bandit's tale has become one of the Dog Whisperer's proudest success stories. Lori kept to her promise and stopped babying Bandit, and Tyler began to take the lead in managing and disciplining him. With new rules, boundaries, and limitations, Bandit soon learned how to peacefully socialize with houseguests and strangers, and when Lori gave birth to a son in November 2006, Bandit even learned how to be calm-submissive to an infant.

Cesar works with Lori, Tyler, and Bandit.

By the end of the first year, Bandit's extreme aggression had become unbearable. When the family had guests, he'd lunge and bite at their legs. "He's de-socialized us. I used to be a very social person. Now my friends don't even want to come over anymore."

The most tragic aspect of Bandit's aggression is that he focuses most of his attacks on Tyler. "He's bit his lip, his finger, his cheek, his ear," Lori says. Tyler continues, "He's bit me in the leg, bit me in the armpit . . . he almost got my eye." Bandit has turned the wonderful experience Lori had wanted for her son into a living nightmare.

Cesar had already rehabilitated one demon Chihuahua, NuNu, during the first season of *Dog Whisperer*. But when he arrives at Lori and Tyler's home, he sees right away that this raging bandit will be a real contender for the crown of "Meanest Chihuahua Ever." Cesar is surprised to hear that Lori has actually shown dogs in the past, so it's clear she has some leadership skills that she's not using. "I'm his mom," she says of Bandit. Cesar shakes his head. "You're his female. Bandit is saying, 'This is my female that I own and nobody else can get close to her, because I am an insecure, dominant dog.'"

The tone of the consultation turns, however, when Cesar watches Lori let Bandit violently attack Tyler, then goes to comfort Bandit! Cesar is shocked. "As a parent and as a dog behavior specialist, I would never ever in my whole entire life choose a dog over my kids." Cesar sits on the couch next to Lori and blocks Bandit with his elbow when the dog attacks him. Frustrated that a human would dare touch him and not back down to his aggression, Bandit yelps and jumps off the sofa. Lori is visibly upset. "He's biting, so I have to touch. I'm not hitting, I'm just touching," Cesar explains. "But he yelped!" says Lori. "Well, you want me to yelp so it's equal?" Cesar replies. Lori begins to cry. "Now he doesn't know what to do," she says of Bandit, who is wandering around the room looking submissively at Cesar. "You don't like that, do you?" Cesar asks. "No," says Lori.

"Well, then, this is a case that is not going to work. It's not going to work because here we have an owner who doesn't want to allow the discipline you would normally use with your kids."

It's incredibly rare that Cesar gives up on a case, and after a few moments Lori agrees to give it one more try and let go of her "mothering" of Bandit. Cesar tells her it's perfectly possible to discipline the mind without hurting the body. He takes Lori through several exercises on the couch, where she uses two fingers to firmly touch Bandit every time he makes an aggressive move toward Cesar. "Don't hold him back, don't remove him, just a touch will snap him out of it." Newly empowered, Lori catches on quickly. Next, Cesar brings Tyler into the exercise. He tells him to take all the energy he's been using to "hate" Bandit and turn it into assertive, leadership energy. The relief on Lori's and Tyler's faces is palpable. "Now, thirty minutes, one hour doesn't get rid of a year of bad behavior," says Cesar. "But what I want you to see is the possibility that this dog can go back to normal."

Behind the scenes

Bandit's story has another wrinkle to it—a cautionary tale for all who shop for dogs over the internet. Lori found Bandit online from a breeder who said she could guarantee the health of the dog. The breeder flew in from Louisiana and delivered the puppy. For the flight and puppy, the price came to $2,000.

However, not long after Bandit arrived, it became clear he had a kind of mange common in puppy mill dogs. The ASPCA told Lori that she had been defrauded, and fined and punished the breeder. Bandit went through six weeks of treatments to get rid of his mange, and at the end of it all, this adorable Chihuahua had turned into an angry, aggressive, and terrified little pup.

"I think Cesar definitely showed me I was the problem, not the dog," Lori says. "You think that when you give him love and affection that he's going to feel secure, but instead, by loving him and not giving him any boundaries, I made him insecure. He's not going to bite somebody anymore because I'm not going to let him."

Rottie Pups

Names: Tiger and Roxy

Breed: rottweiler

Sisters Janet and Mary Baskharoun came across two abandoned rottweiler pups under the 10 freeway in Los Angeles. They ended up adopting them, naming them Tiger and Roxy. However, in the three months they've had the dogs, they're no longer the cute babies Janet and Mary first brought home. Roxy will bite Janet if she is not getting enough attention, and Tiger will knock the food bowl out of her hand. They both jump on their owners and terrorize Janet and Mary's two-year-old niece, Kyla.

Upon meeting Janet and Mary, Cesar is especially concerned that they may be creating two very dangerous monsters with Tiger and Roxy. "The good thing is we're working with puppies. So it's very easy to redirect them and send them in the right direction. This is not a red zone case yet. Can they become red zone? Absolutely. They have all the symptoms already."

Cesar works a long, hard day with Janet and Mary, showing them the proper energy and routine for a pack leader, teaching them how to apply rules, boundaries, and limitations, and giving them safety tips for monitoring Kyla around the puppies. But for this powerful breed, exercise is especially important. Cesar assigns the ladies two forty-five-minute walks with their dogs daily, in order to help drain their extra energies.

Finally, Cesar asks Mary, Janet, and Kyla to bring Tiger and Roxy to his center so they can interact with a pack of balanced dogs. Tiger, the dog with more anxious energy, gets a backpack to intensify her rehab. Now it's all up to Mary and Janet. It's their choice—they can have a pack of strong, calm rotties or two out-of-control animals.

Follow-up ❖ 🐾 🐾 🐾

Janet and Mary have worked hard at getting Tiger and Roxy under control. They do well with regular walks; however, Janet is traveling a lot, and it's hard to find time for the walks. She has considered finding a new home for one of the dogs but does not want to separate them. Their young niece Kyla picked up immediately on Cesar's tips and started using them. Kyla used to be chased by the dogs, and that's totally changed. Kyla's now the real pack leader of the house. She easily makes the dogs sit and behave for her.

Buddy the Biter

Name: Buddy

Breed: corgi-papillon mix

After their family cat passed away, Linda and Rich King met Buddy, a corgi-papillon mix, in their local shelter. Though timid at first, Buddy soon showed another side of his personality when, that first night, Buddy charged Linda and bared his teeth at her. The Kings took Buddy back to the shelter the next day but were told he'd probably be put down unless they kept him. Since then, Buddy has developed a tendency of randomly attacking feet and biting his owners. Now, after six long and frustrating years, Linda and Rich have seen no improvement.

Buddy's biting has one other serious downside—it escalates when it comes time for Linda to give Buddy his medications. Buddy has ear and skin allergies and must have his meds, but ministering to the little guy has become a nightmare for Linda. "Buddy's behavior scares me a lot. We cannot give Buddy the normal care that Buddy needs."

First, Cesar observes the way Rich and Linda try to coerce Buddy into taking his medicine. Buddy snarls, snaps, and hides behind the couch. "Rich was projecting a very tense, frustrated energy. And that only increases aggression from animals. Linda was projecting a very painful energy, a feeling-sorry energy. So that makes you a very weak individual. So here we have two extremes in one couple. One is very passive, the other is very aggressive. So they have to learn to come in the middle." Instead of trying to overpower Buddy from the top like Rich, Cesar sits down next to Buddy, ignoring him but blocking him physically from running away. As Buddy adapts to Cesar's calm-assertive energy, he begins to relax.

Now that Buddy has submitted to Cesar, it's time to give him his meds. Cesar plays "nurse," laying Buddy on his side and massaging him to keep him calm. Cesar lets Buddy smell the medicine while he administers a loving, relaxing massage. "So the nose smells the product when the mind is relaxing. So then he associates: the smell equals relaxation."

The session ends with Rich and Linda replicating Cesar's technique and, most important, understanding and admitting what they had been doing wrong before. "I'm

Follow-up · · · ·

Buddy has made a remarkable change and no longer has problems with taking medication. Rich has also changed; when he interacts with Buddy, he's less aggressive with his body language. Linda and Rich have made so many improvements with Buddy that they are now often asked for advice about dogs.

Key Cesar Tip

Any event that is new or unnatural to a dog can be made into a positive experience, if it is associated with something pleasant—a treat, a massage, or something else that makes the dog happy. The most important elements, of course, are the patience and calm-assertive energy of the owner.

impressed every time people are willing to change. I'm very inspired by people when they let go, at least for that moment. And they give themselves a chance to project or to become different energy. They can have a dog that associates medication with relaxation. What a comfortable thing to do."

Chip Vicious

Name: Chip

Breed: miniature pinscher

(episode 208)

The Pack family—husband Tom and wife Lisa and teenagers Steven and Natalie—saw an ad for a miniature pinscher and decided to buy Chip. Chip was the perfect puppy . . . until he turned two years old. That's when he started nipping visitors who came to the house. Then he developed a grudge against the kids, especially fifteen-year-old Steven. Chip's nips soon turned into bites that drew blood and even required stitches. But Lisa Pack is adamant—her husband goes before the dog does.

During a consultation with the family, Cesar quickly discerns that it's Lisa who is the source of Chip's bad behavior. The rest of the family reports that Lisa is always saying, "Chip is the only one in the house who gives me unconditional love." But Lisa is in denial. Cesar challenges her to face reality and take a leadership role with Chip. For the sake of family harmony, she agrees.

Cesar works with Lisa first, showing her the way he calmly and assertively corrects his dogs. But during a walk with Sonny, one of the calm-submissive dogs from Cesar's pack, Chip attacks—and Cesar realizes his problems stem from a total lack of social skills, with dogs as well as with humans. He brings Chip to the center for a two-week stay. It takes several days, but Chip finally begins to get along with everybody. The next test is to bring Lisa to the center, to see if she can remain calm and assertive in the pack, even when Chip is trying to manipulate her. To Cesar's joy, Lisa rises to the challenge. Even daughter Natalie is impressed. "It was weird seeing my mom walking through a pack of dogs, like, in control of them all. And in control of Chip. Looks like she's a different person, 'cause she has so much more dominance over all the dogs."

"I am absolutely proud of her, "Cesar crows. "I am delighted that she is showing women that they can change their relationship with their dog and still be in love with their dog."

Follow-up ❀ ❀ ❀

The Packs report that Chip is now a responsible, productive member of their pack—and that Lisa has remained consistent in her leadership behavior.

Can This Marriage be Saved?

Name/Breed: Ted/chow mix

Name/Breed: Wendell/Lab–pit bull mix

(episode 209)

Cesar introduces Wendell to Daddy and Preston in front of Tyler and Patricia.

When nurse Patricia Robbins met Tyler Shepodd six years ago, they fell in love and he asked her to marry him. There was only one problem—Patricia's dogs, Ted, a chow mix, and Wendell, a Lab–pit bull mix. Wendell, in particular, had a history of troublesome, aggressive behavior—so much so, that in the past, Patricia's neighbors had taken her to court. Once Patricia accepted Tyler's proposal and the two set a date, she knew she had to get Tyler and Wendell together. The first meeting became a disaster when Wendell growled and lunged at Tyler. The more Wendell was around Tyler, the more threatening and aggressive he became. Finally, Tyler laid down the law: Patricia would have to choose between her marriage and her dogs. The wedding was canceled. Patricia is torn—she loves Tyler, but she feels very strongly about keeping her dogs. Tyler fears that Wendell will attack someone, and he will lose his home in a lawsuit. In this case, Cesar's challenge is not only to rehabilitate a vicious dog but to save a marriage as well.

Cesar believes that when our animals have problems, they are often reflections of our own unresolved issues. From the beginning, Cesar saw that Tyler was not trustful of Wendell, which escalated Wendell's aggression toward him. Patricia, on the other hand, nurtured Wendell's possessive, dominant behaviors with affection and over-protectiveness. Tearfully, Patricia admits she has not let go of the pain she felt as a girl, watching dogs be mistreated in her family. Cesar encourages her to feel all the feelings, so she can move forward and let go of the past. Right now, she's living in extremes—either totally affectionate or totally out of control. "You need to be living in the middle," he tells her.

Wendell lunges at Cesar at first but soon submits to Cesar's calm energy. Waiting in the backyard with Patricia and Tyler are Daddy and Preston, two calm-submissive pit bulls from Cesar's pack. Patricia is terrified and tearful, thinking Wendell's in danger, but Wendell does just fine. "I see possibilities," Patricia admits at the end of the session.

A week later, Cesar brings Patricia, Tyler, and Wendell to continue their work at his Dog Psychology Center. Once again, Patricia is a wreck, but Cesar challenges her to call up the calm-assertive energy of her job as a nurse. Meanwhile, it's Tyler's time to do some work—to face his fear of pit bulls by walking solo among the pack. Tyler makes Cesar proud. "You are surrounded by thirty-seven dogs, but not one is attacking you. That means your energy is really good. But Wendell senses you don't trust him, so he can't trust you back."

When Patricia enters the center and sees Wendell socializing easily with the other dogs, she has an insight. "He looked very happy out there. And I was thinking that he was going to be scared and running around and shaking and not listening to me, but I see that it doesn't have to be like that."

Follow-up ❀ ❀ ❀

Fairy tales do come true! Patricia and Tyler wed on June 23, 2007, and the two of them—along with Ted and Wendell—are all living happily ever after.

Key Cesar Tip

Never forget that your dog's behavior is always, in some way, a mirror of your own. "I think it makes sense before you marry somebody to fix the relationship that you already have with your dog, because that is going to become an expression of how you deal with people."

Bringing Home Baby

Name: Cosmo

Breed: shepherd mix

(episode 210)

This segment recounts the story of newly married Victoria McMinimy and Armin Rahm and their two dogs, especially Armin's aggressive shepherd mix, Cosmo. As a new husband, Armin has had less time for his dog, and Cosmo's belligerent behavior has escalated. Cosmo has now bitten two people who were simply walking down the street near their home. Victoria is expecting a child, and she is concerned that the dog will be too much to handle and possibly dangerous to the baby. Nine months are ticking by fast, so this dog has to be turned around before the baby arrives.

"The most important thing for me is that the dogs have to be balanced before the baby comes into the house," says Cesar. First, he establishes leadership with Cosmo by walking him alone. Next, he observes Victoria walking him. She passes with flying colors. The source of the problem becomes apparent when Armin takes over. "You're too tense. Come on. Relax," Cesar coaches. But Armin is in denial and acting as if everything is fine. "You have to admit you are getting tense. Yes, you are getting frustrated. Yes, you get angry. Nothing wrong with it. What is wrong is when you don't want to acknowledge this is who you're being." Cesar reminds the couple that dogs see who you really are inside. You can't fool them about your emotions.

Four months fly by, and now there's a new addition to the family—baby Lorelei. Cosmo and Victoria's dog, Boo, stay with friends until Cesar can return. Now they're ready to introduce them to the baby.

Follow-up ❧ ❧ ❧

Victoria says that their *Dog Whisperer* experience has changed all their lives for the better. The dogs are doing great. Cosmo has had no more dog or human aggression issues. Lorelei is twenty-one months old and her first word was "doggy!" Lorelei is already a pack leader. Because of Cesar, Victoria was inspired to become a dog trainer. She will soon graduate from Animal Behavior College.

"Because both of you guys behave as pack leaders, the baby becomes automatically a pack leader," Cesar tells them. Bringing the dogs in, he shows them how to create invisible boundaries around the baby, so that whenever she's around, the dogs are at the highest level of submission and respect.

The Other Woman

Name: Snowflake

Breed: bichon frise

With nearly forty years of marriage behind them, Malcolm and Judi Sitkoff were enjoying a quiet life of retirement, until four years ago, when another female entered the picture. Snowflake didn't take to Malcolm or Judi at first, but gradually she developed a fatal attraction to Malcolm. Her affection was enthusiastically reciprocated, but suddenly, Judi was the odd woman out. Now Judi has actually been forced out of the marital bed by Snowflake, for fear of being bitten in the middle of the night; Judi sleeps alone, in a recliner in the living room. Malcolm does not groom Snowflake, so Judi is left with the job of tending to her toilette. But Snowflake despises the bathing process, leaving Judi's hands covered in bites. Even several walks a day have done nothing to curb Snowflake's vicious aggression toward her rival for Malcolm's attention.

Cesar is shocked when he hears that Judi has been exiled from her own bedroom. "Why does Snowflake have to be on the bed?" he asks. Malcolm replies that he's tried to move her, but she always jumps right back on. "But you don't mean it; that's why she comes back. That's the only way animals don't listen, when the human doesn't mean it," Cesar responds. Cesar demonstrates how easy it is to make Snowflake obey when he projects the energy that says, "I'm not playing here."

"So instead of my wife leaving, she should tell the dog to move?" Malcolm asks. "No, *you.* You're the source of protection," Cesar explains.

The first exercise takes place in the bedroom, where Cesar teaches Judi to empower herself by moving forward toward Snowflake when the dog acts up, instead of moving away. "If you stay five seconds, you're going to psychologically defeat her, because if you don't move, then she is not powerful enough." During the session, Malcolm reveals that ever since he was a boy, he always wanted a dog that was his alone, nobody else's. That's a mistake, Cesar

Follow-up ❀ ❀ ❀

Snowflake is no longer biting Judi. Malcolm makes Snowflake sleep on the floor and takes her for walks throughout the day. The couple is very happy with what they learned and continue to control Snowflake.

responds, because "people don't understand that they're creating an antisocial dog. A dog would rather be part of a pack or a family." Cesar gives the Sitkoffs a homework assignment: when he returns two weeks later, he expects to see that Judi has regained control of her place in the bedroom.

Sure enough, the Sitkoffs are a changed couple when Cesar comes back, and Snowflake is no longer taking Judi's place in Malcolm's bed—or his priorities. "Malcolm is now more proactive, making sure that Judi is his priority. He listened, he got it, and he did it!" Cesar proudly announces.

Behind the scenes

When the *Dog Whisperer* crew arrived at the Sitkoffs' home to shoot, Judi told them they had to postpone because Malcolm had to take an unexpected trip. Then, surprisingly, she gave Snowflake to the crew to take with them—begging them to keep her until Malcolm came home, because she was biting Judi so often.

Attack of the Jindo

Name: JonBee

Breed: Korean Jindo

Actor Scott Lincoln has rescued thirty-seven dogs in all, caring for them, training them, and placing them with friends and family. Then he encountered JonBee. Things started off well among JonBee, Scott, and his wife, Patrice. But as time progressed, JonBee's ferocity became more apparent. When walking the Jindo outside, the Lincolns are able to be affectionate with JonBee and vice versa. But inside the house is another story. JonBee will turn on Scott in seconds, trying to take off his hand for touching him.

JonBee has started to make Scott wonder if some dogs just can't be rescued. "We've had two trainers come out," Scott says. They both told Scott to put the dog down.

JonBee is an example of what Cesar Millan calls a red zone case. Most owners and even some canine professionals believe that these dogs are so dangerous they must be put down, but in more than twenty years of working with such animals, Cesar has rehabilitated hundreds of red zone cases, returning them to normal lives and happy homes. "Scott felt that I was the last resort," Cesar says.

JonBee will turn out to be one of the most dramatic rehabilitations Cesar has ever attempted on the *Dog Whisperer*. In the Lincolns' living room, Cesar holds the leash for several minutes, projecting a strong but very calm energy, while JonBee struggles and tries to attack. JonBee thrashes so hard that his muzzle comes off, but Cesar stays calm. Patrice, however, is visibly upset by the process—not because she fears JonBee will be hurt, but because she is afraid even Cesar will fail. "It's emotional for us because when you rescue an animal, you feel responsible. If you can't care for that animal, then you have to take the animal to a shelter and you know it's going to die." Because of her extremely anxious energy, Cesar asks Patrice to please step out of the room while he works. "Any negative energy while you are dominating or while you are taming a wild animal is not the ideal energy to be around, because the dogs feed themselves from this energy," he explains. "It's all psychological. It's not really physical what I'm doing. It's blocking the mind from achieving the goal of trying to kill or hurt somebody."

Finally, JonBee wears himself out and submits to Cesar. But can Scott accomplish the same thing? "So you're still unsure, you're still nervous?" Cesar asks. "Scared to death," Scott replies. "I'm glad you're being honest with yourself, because that's how you become a target," Cesar says. "They don't want to be touched by negative energy." While Cesar shows Scott how to help JonBee create a calming, positive association with the muzzle, he asks Patrice to tell him all the things she loves about her husband, to increase the positive energy in the room. Gradually, Scott also succeeds in getting JonBee to gently submit.

Three weeks later, Scott reports amazing progress. "From the day Cesar left, there's been no more attacking. You tell him, 'Down,' and he sits and turns over. It's amazing. I can't imagine giving him up, even though now he's home ready. I mean we love him. He's a different dog, that's the bottom line."

Anyone else but Scott and Patrice would have given up. But Patrice is adamant. "I hope people see this and realize it can be done. Dogs aren't throwaways. They're not disposable."

Follow-up ❧ ❧ ❧

Scott and Patrice made a lot of progress with JonBee and were thrilled to live peacefully with him, but when Scott's mother moved in with them, the dynamic changed and JonBee began to show aggression again. The Lincolns found a new home for JonBee where he would be with other dogs and less contained inside a house.

Behind the scenes

Some critics of Cesar viewed the JonBee episode and interpreted his holding the leash while JonBee was thrashing around as abuse or choking. Patrice and Scott were so upset by these "experts" and their erroneous claims that they sent us a letter to clarify their feelings:

> We can testify from firsthand experience that Cesar never hurt JonBee in any way and in fact was willing to risk injuring himself . . . It was only through the use of Cesar's techniques that we were able to help JonBee work through the fear issues he carried from what must have been horrible abuse . . . This is how dogs communicate and what they understand. By asserting his domination and teaching Patrice and me how to do the same, we were able to make JonBee a very special and well-loved member of our family . . . Cesar was able to make him feel safe, freeing him from the pressure of trying to dominate the pack . . . We have never seen, in over twelve years of rescue work, a more courageous, dedicated, loving, and gifted trainer (psychologist) than Cesar.

Jumping Min Pins

Names: Taz and Victoria

Breed: miniature pinscher

The Brown home has been turned upside down by the arrival of min pin siblings Vicky and Taz. Taz began as the perfect dog, but Vicky's aggressiveness has rubbed off on him, and the pair are creating chaos in the home. Vicky has already bitten four people, and since Maria and Steve Brown run a home-based business, they now must meet with their clients away from their house. A vet has recommended the dogs be put down, but the Browns would hate to have to do that. Steve and Maria would also love to walk their dogs together, but the way things are now, the dogs must be walked separately and in the middle of the night.

Early in the consultation, Cesar learns that Maria has always had a fear of big dogs, a fear so deep that she actually would use her children as human shields. She has not let go of the past and therefore projects a very weak, unsure energy around the dogs. She lets them get away with everything. Cesar must concentrate his rehabilitation on empowering Maria, but only after he goes on a vigorous Rollerblading session with the hyperactive min pins, in order to drain their energy. Next, he teaches Maria how to let go of the tension and apprehension she feels while on walks. Daddy, Cesar's trusty pit bull "assistant," helps Maria overcome her fear of big, powerful dogs. At the end of the session, Maria is walking the min pins and Daddy together, and is finally feeling like a powerful woman. "Now I can be an honest dog owner," Maria marvels. "A proud dog owner."

"What we accomplished was to control the dogs in the outside world. I know they have a lot of

Follow-up 🐾 🐾 🐾

Sadly, Maria had a setback with the min pins and, taking a vet's advice, had Victoria euthanized. Cesar was notified only after the fact and was devastated that the family hadn't come to him first, to discuss other options.

homework to do in the inside world. But to me right now, the most important part of this case is that they are committed to walk every day consistently, not at 11 p.m. but at normal hours," Cesar summarizes.

Key Cesar Tip

When you decide to adopt a dog into your home, don't simply give in to a whim or fall for a cute face. You must be honest about yourself, your lifestyle, and your energy level, and do your best to select a dog that can fit within those parameters. Remember, whenever a dog is returned to a shelter, chances are high that the dog will lose its life.

Laker Dog

(episode 213)

Name: Princess (aka Cujo)

Breed: Maltese

Cesar with Jeanie and Phil, and Coco, Louis, and Princess Cujo.

Jeanie Buss, executive vice president of operations for the Los Angeles Lakers, is one of the highest-ranking female executives in professional sports. But the biggest stress in her life comes from dealing with the split personality of her Maltese, Princess. At times, the fluffy dog is cute and cuddly, but often in the presence of company, Princess is hardly a princess. Jeanie's boyfriend and coach of the L.A. Lakers, Phil Jackson, has given her the nickname Cujo because of her gnashing teeth and ferocious barking. Jeanie feels it's her fault that Princess Cujo now tries to attack and bite Laker team members and any other visitors to her office. "I think I need some training," she says.

From the moment he enters Jeanie's office, Laker fan Cesar witnesses Jeanie's inability to control Princess. Jeanie reveals that Princess hasn't been the same dog since she was attacked by two German shepherds in a park. "I feel I let her down because I'm supposed to be her leader and her protector," Jeanie admits. Cesar observes what a powerful leader Jeanie is in a male-dominated profession and suggests that she can best help Princess become less of a Cujo by channeling those same skills toward her relationship with her dog.

To help improve Princess's social skills, Cesar brings along a pack of calm-submissive assistants: Coco, Louis, Nicholas, and Daddy. Princess immediately cowers between Jeanie's legs. "Now I really need you to not be there for her in a nervous way," Cesar tells her. "If she goes behind or under you, just move. Do not nurture insecurity." Now, using that strong energy, Jeanie learns how to stop Princess's barking with just a sound. Jeanie gets it immediately, and Princess relaxes, avoiding, but giving room to the new dogs. When Phil Jackson drops by, he reveals himself to be another source of the problem, by encouraging Princess's aggression and treating it as "cute."

Three days later, Jeanie comes to the Dog Psychology Center to take Princess's rehab to the next level. Cesar lets Jeanie witness Princess interacting with a pack of small dogs and actually becoming curious about them, just like a normal dog. Next, he brings in German shepherd Zeus to help Princess get over her fear of the breed of dogs that attacked her in the park. By Jeanie asserting dominance over Zeus, she proves to herself that she can once again know she is her dog's protector.

Follow-up ❀ ❀ ❀

Princess is markedly better about barking when people walk into Jeanie's office and is much more confident and better behaved when she and Jeanie go places together. She's not totally cured, but Jeanie says the lessons Cesar taught her about leadership have really helped, and she promises to keep working until Princess is 100 percent Princess and 0 percent Cujo.

Behind the scenes

Phil Jackson usually gets stopped in airports and asked by fans, "What's Shaquille O'Neal really like?" Lately, he reports that he's more often asked, "What's Cesar Millan really like?"

Aggression Toward Dogs and Other Animals

Peaches, Dolly, and Eton chill on a bench after their rehabilitation.

Desert Bulldogs

Names: Dolly and Eton

Breed: bulldogs

(episode 215)

Retired in the relaxing California desert, ex–Canadian Football League pro Jeffrey Tafralis and his wife, Susan, live with a menagerie of animals including rescued bulldogs Dolly and Eton, an inherited cocker spaniel named Peaches, and a cat named Claire. Eton and Dolly were best pals at first, but now they are locked in a fierce battle to be the pack leader. They fight all day over food, toys, and attention. The conflict has become so violent—especially when the couple is around—that the Tafralises must keep them kenneled and separated almost all the time. The two bulldogs also team up against Peaches, who wants nothing to do with their erratic behavior.

"So there're three packs in the house," Cesar concludes. "The bulldogs, the humans, then the cat and the cocker spaniel. And the humans most of the time are number three." Because the bulldogs' behavior escalates when the Tafralises are around, Cesar surmises the bulldogs believe they "own" the couple and certainly don't see them as authority figures. In addition, the dogs are bored and frustrated from their lack of activity. "The background of bulldogs is that they're gladiators. So when they don't have anything to do, being a gladiator is their way to drain energy." "Damn, I was hoping it wasn't us," Jeffrey admits sheepishly.

Cesar asks the Tafralises to step out of the picture for the moment and begins by addressing Eton. "This is a red zone case; these dogs will kill each other. So my meaning has to be powerful coming in." Cesar uses his "claw-bite" hand to establish dominance. He does the same with Dolly, who is a little more difficult at first but then submits easily. "I'm very impressed when red zone dogs just give it up. 'Here it is, we just needed rules, boundaries, and limitations, I'm glad you're here.' For me they're going to behave totally different than they behave for the owners, because for five years, these dogs have seen the owners as followers."

Now it's time to bring Jeffrey and Susan into the rehabilitation. Cesar teaches them how to start out their day with a pack walk and to dominate the situation so both dogs recognize the humans as the pack leaders. But with two red zone bulldogs, this case will not be a quick fix. "We need to see Susan and Jeffrey as number one. Then I can show them how to make everybody else number two. But without them committed to the rehabilitation of this family, we can't go anywhere." Cesar gives the Tafralises homework that includes daily forty-five minute walks as the bulldogs' calm-assertive pack leaders.

Follow-up ❀ ❀ ❀

The Tafralises say life is now peaceful because their dogs are truly best buddies again. They play and wrestle, but in a fun way. They haven't had to use the cages and kennels in the garage for over a year, and all the dogs live happily in the house with them.

Three weeks later, Cesar is amazed at the Tafralises' progress. After four or five days, the dogs began to get the message that the humans were the leaders in town. Jeffrey reports he has even been able to walk Dolly, Eton, and Peaches as a pack. Cesar works with them on the still sticky issue of territoriality over the food dish. Because the fights over food are instigated by both bulldogs, not just one, Cesar shows the Tafralises how to make both dogs submit when an altercation begins.

A revealing incident occurs outside that makes Jeffrey realize that Peaches isn't always the innocent bystander when the bulldogs fight. When a neighbor's dog begins to bark, it's Peaches—not the bulldogs—that instigates a rush to the fence. Cesar wants the Tafralises always to relate to their dogs and the cat as a pack and not give favoritism to anyone who breaks the house rules. "Every time I am invited to work with aggressive dogs, it gives me a great honor to show people that it's not the breed, it's the humans not being able to exercise discipline on a daily basis."

Embarrassing Bikini

Name: Bikini

Breed: bull terrier

(episode 217)

Christine and Ferrell Burton have three championship bull terriers—Chanel, Turbo, and Bikini. Despite all her blue ribbons and accolades, Bikini has a dangerous dark side: when Christine is walking her and they encounter a larger breed of dog, Bikini seems to turn from a mild-mannered puppy into the Incredible Hulk. Christine can barely control her. Bikini's aggression has become not only dangerous but embarrassing as well. "I'm an American Kennel Club obedience judge, I'm a Therapy Dogs International evaluator, and I'm a Canine Good Citizen evaluator—and then I have this outbreak of improper behavior. And I don't know how to fix it," Christine admits.

After more than twenty years of working with dogs, Cesar Millan has discovered that just because a dog is well trained in obedience techniques doesn't mean it's necessarily psychologically balanced. In fact, Christine may be so anxious about her own failure to control the behavior that she is passing that state of mind on to Bikini. Her own embarrassment may be intensifying the problem. "When a human goes into a nervous state, fearful state, embarrassed state, the human can't come up with the right solution because she's taking it personally. It's really not about you. It's about the dog."

Christine, Ferrell, and Cesar go outside to work hands-on with Bikini, borrowing a neighbor's calm dog to play the role of one of Bikini's antagonists. When Bikini passes the dog, she goes nuts. "She started chomping her jaw just to get close to him, like a Pac-Man coming after this dog. She just wanted to make that dog disappear." Cesar's solution is to teach Bikini how to socialize with strange dogs by meeting them the way that "real" dogs meet each other—by smelling. But Bikini will have to be the one to submit and let the other dog smell her first. "Because she doesn't want to meet, she wants to attack," Cesar explains as he puts Bikini through her paces, "we have to create *a meeting*. Smelling each other is what they

Follow-up 🐾 🐾 🐾

Bikini was adopted out, but her new family did not have the time to give her the corrections and walks she needs. She still shows dog aggression.

do. A meeting means no challenge, and it calms the brain down." This is one of the many ways Cesar mimics what works in the wild dog world to help a domestic dog that is unstable.

Christine and her husband are amazed at how naturally Bikini relaxes. Finally, Cesar works with Christine, helping lessen her anxiety and become once again the confident pack leader Bikini can trust.

Key Cesar Tip

Just because a dog gets A's in obedience doesn't mean that dog is psychologically balanced, any more than a degree from Harvard means a person has it all together.

The Fabulous Life of Prada

Name: Prada

Breed: Pomeranian

(episode 213)

In 2004, Toni Gray-Jarosz and Zach Jarosz watched their two Pomeranians, Prada and Gucci, suffer through the same mysterious illness. After Gucci passed away, the couple began to shower an outrageous amount of affection on the depressed Prada, trying to make up for her loss. Toni spends more than $100 a week on toys, giving Prada a new one every day. Prada accompanies Toni to work and is rarely left alone for more then a few hours. She has all the trappings of a privileged human life—a cashmere blanket and gourmet home-cooked meals. But two years later, Prada has become a vicious prima donna. If she does not get her way, Prada throws herself on the floor, kicking and barking, until she gets what she wants. She growls and snaps at people and throws a fit if Toni pays attention to anyone else. Toni has become concerned lately because Prada acts friendly and lures people in, then growls and lunges at them as if to bite.

Cesar challenges Toni to move forward from the past, because she can't help Prada by trying to fix everything by spoiling her. "That is only to make yourself feel better. You couldn't help Gucci. You have to let go and say, 'I still love Gucci, but I have to let go.'"

Watching Toni try to take Prada for a walk, he sees how Toni's hysterical energy is making an already excited Prada crazy. He uses a toy in a positive way, offering it to Prada but giving it to her only after she becomes calm-submissive and has accepted the leash. He gives Toni homework simply to practice this new way of being.

Four weeks later, Cesar returns to work on the aggression issue. He brings along Lhasa apso Luigi, one of the calmest members of his pack. Prada goes crazy at first, lunging and barking, but Luigi simply ignores her. After a moment, Prada realizes this behavior will

Follow-up ☆ 🐾 ☆ 🐾

Toni can now bring Prada to work with her and let her play with the other dogs there. Prada is getting regular walks with Toni's husband, and Prada really enjoys them. Toni has cut back the new toys for Prada to once every three days.

get her nowhere, and she goes into a relaxed-submissive mode. Cesar wants Luigi to act as a role model for the couple as well. "You ignore the behavior when it's mild," says Cesar, "but when it's intense, you have to address it."

"Seeing how calm she was with Luigi, I think there's hope for her to act like I think a dog should," a relieved Toni observes.

Key Cesar Tip

Humans who spoil dogs are not doing the dogs any favors. Usually, the behavior is simply to make the human feel better.

The Battle for Eppie (episode 211)

Name: Eppie

Breed: Staffordshire bull terrier

For the first few years of her life, Heather Mitchell's dog Eppie seemed like a normal, social dog. But three years and several moves later, Eppie hates and wants to attack every dog she sees. Heather now lives with her boyfriend, Nate, in a bohemian neighborhood where off-leash dogs are an everyday occurrence. For Heather and Nate, Eppie's daily walks have become a paramilitary operation. One person takes the role of a scout, fully equipped with dog mace, as the other walks behind with Eppie.

When Cesar takes the couple out for a hands-on walking session, it's clear that Eppie is always in charge—pulling on the leash and charging out in front of them. Cesar shows them how to snap the leash to the side or tap Eppie on the hindquarters with a foot, to correct her when she begins to pull. "If I touch her to the side, it breaks that concentration. But if I pull back, it only intensifies the behavior."

Learning how to correct Eppie the moment she begins to turn aggressive becomes even more vital when Cesar and the couple run the gauntlet of the dogs in the neighborhood. Cesar shows Heather and Nate how to ask Eppie to ignore the dogs she'd been aggressive with before. When Eppie's energy changes and she becomes calm-submissive, the other dogs automatically calm down too. "The whole neighborhood is being quiet because they're passing the information to all the other dogs about how to behave or how to be with the dog that is passing by. And so it becomes a chain reaction."

By the end of the session, Heather is as changed as Eppie. "You really have to get in there the first second the dog even thinks about being aggressive . . . because if you don't, it's just going to escalate and there will be a fight. So I think Cesar did a really good job of showing me the signals that Eppie was trying to give me, that I wasn't understanding, before she actually took aggressive action."

Follow-up ❧ ❧ ❧

Nate and Heather report that Eppie is greatly improved. Walking her with a backpack has made a world of difference. Nate does a lot of running with Eppie, and it works to calm her down. The couple got married on May 12, 2007, and Eppie was the ring bearer at their wedding.

Canine Confidential

Name/Breed: Tina/pit bull mix

Name/Breed: Isis/pit bull

Burl Barer is an investigative crime journalist and novelist. Judi Faye is a Broadway diva. The two met on the internet and it was love at first instant message. That was, until Burl's dog Isis met Judy's dog Tina. Isis, a pit bull, and Tina, a pit bull mix, are dangerously aggressive toward each other. Judy and Burl are as much in love with their dogs as they are with each other, so leaving the dogs at home is not an option. A future together may not happen if the dogs can't get along.

Right away, Cesar suggests that the couple introduce the two dogs to each other in a different way. "When you put two dogs together, it's best if they move forward instead of facing each other. So the ideal way of introducing dogs that live in different homes, especially when they're not raised together, is to walk them together without seeing each other first. They're next to each other but they're not looking at each other." A lightbulb goes on for Burl, who has had experience dealing with criminals and antisocial human personalities. "Whenever I'm dealing with a sociopath, I always move to the side of him. When I move to the side, it seems to calm him down." Cesar agrees. "Without the eye contact, there's no fight."

After meeting the two dogs, Cesar determines that Isis is a red zone case, and that while Burl handles her well when they're alone, he's never given her limits in the outside world. Removing Burl from the equation and muzzling Isis, he brings her into Judy's backyard, where Tina waits. Cesar works on having Isis submit to Tina, allowing Tina to smell her. Next, he gets the two to walk next to each other as a pack, teaching Judy to do the same, acting as a calm, relaxed pack leader. When Burl joins the group, Cesar reminds him to approach the dogs in a nonemotional way, just as he would one of the criminals he works

Follow-up 🐾 🐾 🐾

The dogs are doing beautifully. They play together side by side and cuddle together on the couch. Judi and Burl are now living together in blissful harmony with their dogs in lovely Van Nuys, California. They've had more people recognize them from being on *Dog Whisperer* than when Burl was on *Good Morning America* promoting his books.

with. "The thing I found most fascinating," Burl observes, "was those exact same techniques that I use in my field with criminals are the same techniques that he uses with the dogs: reducing aggression, bonding by approaching them from where *they're* coming from, which is—they're animals."

After a successful session, Cesar advises the couple to walk their dogs side by side every day, leaving Isis's muzzle on for the time being. With time and persistence, both Burl and Judy hope the dogs will no longer be obstacles to their budding relationship.

Animal Killer

Name: Buddy

Breed: Lab-Staffordshire mix

Kim and Greg Benson found Buddy, their Lab-Staffordshire mix, through Petfinders.com. The Bensons enrolled Buddy in dog-training classes, where he learned very quickly and excelled above the other students. But buried deep inside the sweet and loving Buddy was a dark side. The Bensons discovered that Buddy had a knack for stalking and killing small animals. He would sneak up on squirrels, cats, opossums, and Chihuahuas before pouncing on them and shaking them to death. Though the death toll has been low, there have been way too many close calls.

Cesar and his rabbit assistant rehabilitate Buddy's deadly predator instincts.

The Bensons are talking about expanding their family. Can they trust Buddy around a baby? "If we had one wish, it would just be that Buddy could just get along with all creatures," Greg says with a sigh.

From the moment he arrives, Cesar picks up on the fact that although Buddy can be submissive to the Bensons at home under relaxed conditions, he does not perceive them as consistent or reliable pack leaders. "Pack leader is when you control the animal in the outside world. Notice I am not talking about Buddy; I'm talking about an animal. If you control the animal, you control instincts. Friendship doesn't equal leadership. It equals love but doesn't equal leadership. Once you're the pack leader, you control instincts and genetics."

Since Buddy is an animal that has tasted blood already, this will be an intense rehabilitation. Cesar uses a prototype of the "Illusion collar," a training device designed by Cesar and Ilusion that helps keep the collar high on the neck. The collar gives Cesar maximum control over Buddy, particularly when he brings him to meet today's "special assistants"—a rabbit and a guinea pig, currently waiting in cages. Buddy immediately tries to lunge at the small prey, and each time he does, Cesar gives him a

Greg suspects that sometimes Buddy still thinks about attacking small animals, but he and Kim have learned how to walk him and stop that behavior from escalating. They have not had any problems since they retrained themselves in how to handle Buddy.

Key Cesar Tip

"It's important to remember that dogs are absolutely natural predators, and that's why we are seeing some dogs that have this hunting desire. This is how Mother Nature is designed. Predators and prey."

split-second correction—a quick snap of the leash. Next, Cesar puts Buddy on his side, asking him to submit to the rodents. "Buddy's working really hard and trying to ignore the scent and the sight of them," Cesar observes. "We have four options in animals: fight, flight, avoidance, and submission. What we have right now is a submissive position with avoidant state of mind, which is blocking the brain from going into a fight mode. So because the animals are not sensing any challenge from the predator, they can behave calmly, curiously, and relaxed."

Next, Cesar removes both the rabbit and guinea pig from their cages, and works with Buddy, waiting for him to relax, submit, and give the smaller animals their "space." "A pack leader has to tell his follower that this rabbit is now part of our pack. So right now we're making the rabbit and we're making the guinea pig the dominant ones." Eventually, the guinea pig's squeaking becomes a signal for Buddy to relax and not to prepare for an attack. By the end of the session, Buddy, the rabbit, and the guinea pig are all on kissing and snuggling terms. After a little practice, Kim is actually able to accomplish the same thing with Buddy.

But Cesar believes the Bensons need more work inside the house in establishing leadership. A week later, he returns to monitor their progress. From the moment he enters the home, Cesar can sense that the couple is feeling more empowered. "He definitely pays more attention to us since you were here," Greg remarks. Today, Cesar will challenge the family by having them walk Buddy next to two small dogs from his own pack, Luigi and Scarlett. With some intensive coaching from Cesar, Buddy and his owners are able to run the gauntlet of the neighborhood dogs.

By the end of the day, the Bensons are brimming with pride—for Buddy and for themselves. "We have always known that Buddy is a great dog, but now that Cesar has given us these tools, we know he will really be able to reach his potential of being a perfect dog."

Spike in the Heart

Name: Spike

Breed: German shepherd

(episode 209)

When Ande and Frank Endewardt and their four-and-a-half-year-old twin girls lost their beloved ten-year-old German shepherd, Blake, the whole family fell into a depression. Six months after Blake's death, they adopted another German shepherd, Spike, who was trouble from the very first day, when he tore apart his crate. He also tore free from a chain leash supposedly strong enough to contain a 250-pound dog. For six weeks, Spike spent his days at Obedience Plus in Pasadena and was trained twice a day. During this time, he bit a fifteen-year-old boy named Josh. Ande was horrified and tried to return Spike to the German shepherd rescue but never heard back. He now stays in the backyard and can't really leave because he is too aggressive to walk on a leash in the neighborhood. Ironically, Spike is sweet with and protective of the twin girls but is aggressive with almost everyone else . . . including the family cat. The twins sleep with Ande and Frank, but Ande must sleep with the dog tied to her wrist because she fears he may kill their cat or escape.

From the first, Cesar sees that the Endewardts have been living in the past and in denial, trying to act as if Spike is Blake, as if he'll respond the same way as Blake did. First, Cesar works with Spike, using his own dogs, Coco the Chihuahua and Daddy the pit bull, to help teach him to be calm-submissive around other dogs. By the end of the day, the family has had the uncommon experience of seeing Spike be calm and submissive.

Fifteen days later, Cesar returns to the Endewardts to check on Ande's progress and to face the unresolved issue of the cat, Tinkerbell. When Cesar reconnects with Spike, Ande begins to cry when she sees Spike immediately melt into a sweet, relaxed dog. "The look on his face when you looked at him—he was another dog, he was a different guy," she whispers. "That's what we have to bring. We have to bring a different state of mind to where the cat is," Cesar tells her.

The Endewardts have been using an electronic collar on Spike, so Cesar instructs Ande how to use it properly to give him corrections when it looks as if he's going to kill the cat. "This is all psychological, 'cause we are bringing the cat toward him. So if

Follow-up ❀ ❀ ❀

The Endewardts did their best with Spike, but his aggression toward the cat became too much for them to handle. They feel Cesar's advice was correct, but with their hectic lifestyle, they did not have the time to give Spike what he needed to truly become balanced. Spike was given to a rescue where he was adopted by a new family without children.

Behind the scenes

Some viewers criticized Cesar after this segment showed an electronic collar being used on Spike—a collar that the Endewardts were already using. Cesar clarified his position that he almost always uses the tool that the owners feel most comfortable and confident with, but he believes it is his job to take the time and reacquaint the owner with the proper and safe use of that tool. In regard to electronic collars in general, Cesar believes they have their place in certain rehabilitation situations but should never be used as a long-term solution to a behavioral problem. They are best used under the guidance of a canine professional.

he pays a little bit of attention to the cat, then we're going to give him a correction." After a good deal of repetition, Cesar accomplishes his mission: "Calm-submissive dog, calm-submissive cat."

However, Spike is a red zone case, and Cesar cautions Ande that she will have to be entirely consistent in his rehabilitation if it is going to stick. Perhaps, Ande prays, "there can be a day where there will be harmony in the house again."

Three's a Crowd

Names: Pete, Dax, and Nixa

Breed: German shepherd

Brigitte Englahner first fell in love with German shepherds eighteen years ago, and now she has three. With her first, Pete, everything was fine until Nixa's arrival. Pete tried to take control, lunging at her and once even biting her shoulder. But Nixa quickly flipped things around, and Pete was no longer top dog. The arrival of Dax caused more complications. Initially, Pete growled at Dax when he came near. This behavior soon escalated, and every time Dax was in Pete's line of vision, Pete would attack. Brigitte knew something had to change when she found Pete on the ground, with Dax at his throat and Nixa at his back. For six years, Brigitte has been playing musical chairs with the dogs, alternating them between the rooms of her house to ensure that Pete and Dax never have contact.

Cesar's challenge is to see if Brigitte can turn her hostile dogs into a true pack. But early in the consultation, he sees that she has been in a little bit of denial about her part in the problem, even when Pete turns his aggression on her. "In order for us to influence the mind of an animal, it has to give us one hundred percent respect. So when an animal charges you, that represents to me he doesn't one hundred percent respect the human. He doesn't do that to the pack leader."

After meeting Pete, Cesar determines he is a fearful-aggressive type. It is relatively simple for Cesar to get control of Pete, but more problems arise when he puts all the dogs together. "There were two packs in this household: one was Pete and the other was Dax and Nixa. That is a fight waiting to happen. In order for them to coexist, they have to be one unit."

Cesar takes all the dogs for a vigorous Rollerblading session—the first time they've ever been comfortable working together as a unit. Part of the problem was clearly lack of focused activity for these energetic, working breed dogs. "This pack needed to migrate, not just track. Tracking is excitement. Migration is about being focused, being one unit." Brigitte is overjoyed when she too is able to walk them all as a unit. But Cesar tells her, though the dogs may be ready, she still needs more work on her own leadership skills.

Follow-up ❀ ❀ ❀

Sadly, Pete passed away from cancer several months after Cesar's visit, but Brigitte reports that two is not a crowd in her household anymore. She has upped the amount of exercise that Nixa and Dax get every day, and now she can take them everywhere with her. She takes riding lessons and they run alongside the horse while she rides. Brigitte reports that the dogs have never been happier and she no longer has any problems with them.

Finally, Cesar brings Brigitte and her three shepherds to the Dog Psychology Center for some advanced power-of-the-pack training. Brigitte is able to witness how, after an initial outburst, the usually aggressive Pete peacefully submits to the pack and allows them to get to know him. "Now there is hope," says Brigitte.

Bad Bearz

Name: Bearz

Breed: rottweiler

Kelle Taylor adopted Bearz from a shelter in the summer of 2005. The rottweiler was very sick and considered dangerous, but she nursed him back to health. As he got healthier, Bearz also got stronger and pushier. He tugs on the leash so much that Kelle has been pulled to the ground on more than one occasion, skinning her knees. She has to wear gloves to protect her hands from the leash and has resorted to walking the rambunctious rottweiler at night. Bearz likes to chase after buses and motorcycles, and he hates garbage trucks. He also vents his aggression on shopping carts. As luck would have it, there is a surplus of shopping carts in Kelle's neighborhood.

"He feels safe with you, and he trusts you, but he does not respect you," Cesar says. "Pulling you all around? That's disrespect." When he jumps on the people in Kelle's building, she interprets it as love. Cesar, however, sees it as dominance and disrespect. Because Kelle encourages such behavior, it's only become worse, and with a 110-pound rottweiler, will eventually become dangerous. When Cesar sees how ferocious Bearz gets around shopping carts, he realizes how serious the situation is. "This is as bad as it gets."

First, Cesar has to establish leadership with the disrespectful, dominant Bearz. It's important to take Kelle out of the equation for a moment. "Kelle is a source of *owning*. The shopping cart is a source of prey drive. So it was easier for me to deal with prey drive when he had nothing to own." Cesar repeatedly corrects Bearz when he begins to attack the cart. "I start touching parts of the body. I find out that between the rib and the leg was just the point for him to snap him out of it. So I start touching that part, and from that point on, I decrease the aggression to only excitement." After many repetitions, Bearz's behavior has visibly

Follow-up ❀ ❀ ❀

Kelle has made good progress on the walk but still has trouble controlling Bearz around other dogs.

changed. "Now I'm using only *sound* to control him. But in the beginning, I used physical touch, no sound. If I'd used sound when he was in that state of mind, sound would have meant nothing."

It takes Cesar much longer to train Kelle how to be a pack leader. He goes back to the basics: how to master the walk, how to make simple corrections, and calm-assertive energy. "I'm getting that he's always been in control of me, and now I have found a way to control him," Kelle says.

Fears and Phobias

Fella, now not so frantic.

Frantic Fella

(episode 217)

Name: Fella

Breed: Jack Russell–Italian greyhound mix

Single mom Cindy Steiner and her ten-year-old daughter, Sidney, brought the winsome Fella home to their Los Angeles apartment complex, even after learning he had been fearful of the other dogs at the shelter. When Cindy came back from work the next day, she heard some barking as she approached her door but thought nothing of it. The first complaint came two months later—neighbors had called the apartment manager to say that Fella barked all day, every day, when Cindy went to work. After several months, the manager laid down the law. Though she liked Cindy and Sidney personally,

Follow-up ❀ ❀ ❀

Fella is still doing fabulously. He will announce when someone comes to the door but he never barks during the day anymore.

Key Cesar Tip

If your dog has separation anxiety, make sure you begin the day with vigorous exercise, to put it into a resting state for the moment when you leave. Never make a production of leaving or coming home; no touch, no talk, no eye contact for the last and first minutes you spend in your home. And make sure your dog is in a calm-submissive state—not over-excited or barking—before you close the door behind you.

unless something was done about the dog, she would have to evict them. Cindy and Sidney fear losing their home—but they also realize that to return Fella to the shelter might ultimately result in his death.

After the consultation reveals that Fella also gets fearfully aggressive toward other dogs, becomes territorial in the car, and gets only fifteen minutes or so of exercise a day, Cesar realizes this isn't only about Fella's separation anxiety. The problem relates directly to Cindy and Sidney's failure to take strong leadership positions in the home. "Fella has a very boring life. Fella has to wake up with a challenge. This is not a case about a barking dog. This is a case about a dog asking for help."

First, Cesar addresses Fella's aggression issues by bringing in two canine role models: the calm and submissive Coco and Luigi from his pack. Within a matter of minutes, he has the three of them walking happily together. The next thing Fella needs is a serious exercise program to help drain some of his anxious energy. Cesar instructs Cindy on the correct and safe way to bike with the dog. He puts them on a strict daily exercise program for two weeks, which they must follow before they can even begin to tackle the separation anxiety.

When Cesar returns, Cindy admits that her half-hearted excuses for not walking Fella in the past were selfish, and she's already seeing the results. "Everyone is remarking about how calm he is, how he listens to me." "I love to come back and see that a person is committed to the change," says Cesar. Now, for the real work, teaching Fella to be comfortable with separation, which is not a natural condition for dogs. If Fella begins the morning with a vigorous workout, he is more likely to be in a resting mode. Once that's accomplished, Cesar teaches Cindy and Sidney how to make the moment of departure less traumatic by constant repetitions of putting the dog into a calm-submissive state, then leaving for a little while. "So you are setting him up to understand the concept of being behind walls or being without you. We have to condition the mind to become solitary sometimes. So you begin with ten minutes at a time, and then the next day you go fifteen minutes, and the next day you go twenty minutes." He teaches the women not to make a big production of leaving or of coming back; to ignore Fella for a short while, and to lessen the excitement in the apartment.

Three months later, Cesar returns to find two empowered pack leaders and a much less frantic Fella. Even the neighbors agree. "I would ask, them, 'Did you hear the dog?'" Cindy reports. "And they're like, 'No, we haven't heard him in months.'"

Scared Sonny

Name: Sonny

Breed: German shepherd mix

Cyndi Reynolds is a gentle, bighearted counselor for adults with special needs. She and her coworker/roommate, Kelly McKenna, helped rescue a litter of feral German shepherd puppies from a field near their home. Cyndi adopted one of them, Sonny, but Sonny's first experience with his animal control rescuers had been so traumatic that from the very first day, he was terrified of humans. Though Sonny gets along well with other dogs and is the star of his local dog park, he goes berserk when he sees unfamiliar people. When Cyndi brings him to the center where she works, Sonny cowers under her desk.

"When we walk through the center, he'll see the developmentally disabled clients who attend this program, and he'll start barking at them. A lot of times, they might try to go up and pet him, and he'll bark and try to run away," Cyndi says with a sigh. "Then he'll just run straight into my office, which is where he hides under the desk for most of the day."

Right off the bat, Cesar asks Cyndi how she approached Sonny when she met him for the first time. "Well, he was so scared that he was shaking. He was in a crate. And I left him in the crate and kind of reached in and just petted him on the head."

Cesar informs Cyndi that although she had the best intentions at the time, she was inadvertently nurturing Sonny's fear, by petting him and giving him affection when his mind was unstable. "The best thing you could have done that day is to let him go through the shock. Once he gets hungry, he gets out of the kennel. Then you provide food. And food becomes affection. Then you're associated with food and with affection." Cesar reminds Cyndi that by feeling sorry for Sonny, she was sending him weak energy, which made it even less likely that he would trust her. "Love was never intended for us to create instability or to nurture instability. Love is supposed to end instability."

The lightbulb goes on for Cyndi at that moment. Because she works in psychology with special needs patients, she recognizes that feeling sorry for people does them no good when you want to help them move forward. It's the same with dogs.

Cesar watches Cyndi try to bring Sonny out from under the desk. Despite her coaxing, he shuts down and just lies still. "Do you see yourself asking him a favor?" Cesar asks. "See, that's not making you powerful. What they teach you around horses is you have to have a perception of what you want to happen. If you don't, the horse hesitates." Cesar demonstrates by bringing Sonny out with very little hesitation. "When you have an animal that completely shuts down, there is no other way. You just have to bring him and get him out, bring him and get him out. And then the animal learns that there is no other option."

Cesar coaches Cyndi in walking with Sonny, telling her to imagine that she's with one of the clients she works with, not a scared dog. "That made a lot of sense to me. And I was able to find a place to go, inside myself, to be that way with Sonny." The more confident Cyndi becomes, the more Sonny appears visibly secure.

Cesar returns three weeks later to see how Cyndi and Sonny are doing. He discovers that Cyndi's clients are also taking an active part in Sonny's rehabilitation! Sonny no longer hides from them, and Cesar watches as they take turns leading Sonny around the rec room. Sonny's confidence grows—as does the clients'. "Talk about a dog that is of service. He's not a dog that should be afraid the rest of his life. Cyndi is another angel here."

"This is my best day," he says with a tear in his eye. "This case will stay in my heart forever."

Follow-up ✿ ✿ ✿

Sonny is doing much better and interacts with the clients in the program without getting scared. It's been a win-win situation for both Sonny and the clients.

Behind the scenes

Tragically, a few months after filming the *Dog Whisperer* segment, the church where Cindy's therapy groups were based burned to the ground. Cesar and MPH donated some computers, office equipment, a TV, VCR/DVD players, and DVDs to help get the new center off the ground.

Key Cesar Tip

Feral dogs are often fearful of people. When working with a frightened dog, it's always best to hold back and follow the "no talk, no touch, no eye contact" rule until the dog becomes comfortable with your presence.

Spooked Hootie

(episode 201)

Name: Hootie

Breed: Australian shepherd

Competing in agility courses with her dogs is a passion for Pam Marks. Four-year-old Hootie is the fourth of the prize-winning competitors she has handled. But Hootie's promising career stalled after a traumatic incident turned an ordinary fear into a phobia.

"Hootie was a year and a half old," Pam recalls. "He had been running for six months, already had some ribbons, and was working on some titles." But one day, after a

Cesar helps Hootie overcome his fear of children.

trial, Pam and Hootie were getting ready to go home when six teenage boys on skateboards thundered past him on the sidewalk. Hootie was incredibly traumatized by the event. "He was just shivering. He was a wreck after that incident."

Ever since then, Hootie's extreme fear of children has become greater than his love of agility. If he sees a child or teen in the crowd during a competition, he'll stop, panic, and bark.

From the moment Cesar arrives, he senses that Pam's reaction to the alleged trauma may have been as much to blame as Hootie's. Sure enough, when Pam recounts the incident, she reveals that she still feels terrible about putting Hootie in that situation. "Once somebody feels responsible or guilty for whatever happened, it creates this sense of not letting it go," Cesar tells her gently. Pam begins to realize that not only does she feel responsible for the initial trauma, she's also been anticipating problems herself every time she sees a child or teenager when Hootie is with her. She begins to cry. "Oh, Hootie, I'm so sorry," she says. "I'm letting it go now."

Now that Pam is ready to let go of the past and relate to Hootie as a dog, not just as her "child" that she's trying to protect, Cesar brings in two very special assistants to help him with the rehabilitation, his sons Andre and Calvin. "Because kids created a traumatic experience for Hootie, only kids can remove traumatic experience. Now, these kids are not just any kids. These are *my* kids."

Cesar wants Hootie to have a positive experience with the boys, one small step at a time. Calvin and Andre employ Cesar's "no talk, no touch, and no eye contact" rule, while Cesar lets Hootie discover their scents with his nose. By letting Hootie come to the boys instead of the other way around, he's not threatened by them. Next, the boys do exercises and movement around Hootie, while still not addressing him directly. "It's important that you make it clear that whenever you want a kid to help you to rehabilitate a dog, the kid has to be ignoring the dog in order to be around the dog," Cesar explains. "Although he's nervous, this is the most relaxed Hootie's ever been with a child next to him," Pam observes.

Next, Cesar progresses to a much tougher challenge—putting Hootie through an obstacle course where Andre and Calvin lie down on the course. "The kids became obstacles. He jumps over the kids. First, he does it on a leash." Hootie is reluctant to start but soon he begins to relax around the boys' presence. By the end of the session, Hootie is running the full course at the top of his form, jumping over Andre and Calvin as if they weren't there at all. "The most magnificent thing is he's jumping over them without a leash on. There's just no way I would've thought that was ever possible," Pam marvels.

"She was seeing the picture more and more. And then slowly you see how she detached herself from that victim part of her," Cesar observes. "From the bottom of my heart, I want Pam to remember this day, just the same way, with the same intensity, that she remembered that day when Hootie became traumatized."

Follow-up ❀ ❀ ❀

According to Pam, Hootie has made a dramatic change—what she describes as an improvement of 70 percent to 80 percent—in his reactions to children when he is competing on the agility course. If he does react, Pam introduces the children to him and he relaxes. Hootie often doesn't even notice a child walking by him. As for her relations with her other agility dogs, Pam reports, "I am finally the pack leader in my own home."

Behind the scenes

When the *Dog Whisperer* crew arrived at Pam's house to shoot, they encountered two Roomba robotic vacuum cleaners running nonstop. Pam explained that living with four Aussie shepherds, she has an ongoing fight to control the dog hair.

Maddy & Me

Name: Maddy

Breed: terrier mix

Using a box of pizza crusts as bait, budding music video director Molly Schiot rescued a stray white terrier mix from a miserable life living under a freeway. She washed her and cut off all of the dog's matted hair and the patches of fur with gum stuck to them, naming her, appropriately, Maddy. After an initial period of shyness, Maddy turned out to be the sweetest dog Molly ever could have imagined.

There was just one hitch. Somewhere in her past, Maddy had developed an intense fear of men. Molly often tries to introduce the petrified pup to men, but Maddy cowers and does everything to get away from them. She even freezes up when the men offer her treats. Molly wants Maddy to feel comfortable around men, because, not only does it make her sad to see her dog so upset, it also puts a huge crimp in Molly's social life.

During the consultation, Cesar shows Molly how to make a fearful dog relax—by not sharing talk, touch, or eye contact, and allowing the dog to become curious and explore you. By holding a treat and acting casual—as Cesar puts it, "acting like the popular guy in high school that all the girls want. I'm playing hard to get"—Cesar helps Maddy relax and take food from his hand. Cesar suggests that Molly teach her men friends to be similarly "cool" when they meet Maddy and not make the first move toward her.

A week later, Cesar returns to work more with Molly and Maddy. They practice walking in Molly's neighborhood, and Cesar shows Molly how to remain calm and assertive when encountering things that make Maddy nervous, such as passing cars and garbage trucks. Molly is a quick study. "Once I felt at ease and kind of relaxed, then that's when she was most at ease and relaxed, and then it was just easy," she explains. But the real test is to help Maddy overcome her gender phobia. Spike, a friend of Molly's, agrees to meet them at a local market. Cesar says, "Spike owns four dogs, so he's a dog lover. But Maddy didn't know that. The only thing Maddy knew is everybody feels sorry for her. And nobody knew how to block her fear." Following Cesar's instructions, Spike is able to give her a gentle massage while she sits calmly at his feet. She only gets nervous when Molly gives her worried eye contact, and Cesar must point out that Molly needs to live in the moment and let Maddy change. "Molly saw today the power of living in the now. We were in the store, Spike, Molly, myself, having a great conversation, not really worrying about what happened the other day, or what happened in the past. We were creating a different relationship between Spike and Maddy. And that's all that counts."

Follow-up 🐾 🐾 🐾

Molly reports that since that day, Maddy is a changed dog "who has developed a personality of gold."

Country Dog, Scaredy Cat

Name: Booker

Breed: vizsla

Booker, a vizsla, lived in the quiet countryside of California, until Michael Forbes adopted him and transplanted him to busy downtown Long Beach. From the moment Booker first hit the city, he was terrified. With his tail between his legs, Booker cowers and cringes and does everything he can to escape the urban sounds and sights. Strollers, suitcases, carts, and garbage bags are among the many things that turn Booker into a trembling ball of fear.

Keeping Booker's tail up creates a more positive experience.

Michael believes Booker is "unfixable" and will never be able to overcome his fears. But Cesar has other ideas. "So what would you like to accomplish today?" he asks Michael. "I would love to see him be able to go for a walk down Pine Avenue with his tail up, paying attention to me, and then beyond that, if I could get him to Rollerblade with me, that would be like heaven." Cesar responds that he would like to Rollerblade with Booker first, then work on the walk. "And you actually think you can Rollerblade with him?" the skeptical Michael queries.

"Booker was probably the weakest in his litter," Cesar explains. "It's easier for dogs that are born in the weak state of mind to become traumatized just by different environments. From the moment he arrived in the city, Booker became uncomfortable with his surroundings."

Since vizslas are hunting dogs, it's in their blood to love a good chase. Cesar successfully redirects Booker's flight motion into a moving-forward motion, with a high-speed Rollerblading blaze through the bustling streets of Long Beach. "So we drained some of that energy before we went into a walk motion."

Booker definitely is more relaxed after his blading session. But his tail still seems to automatically go between his legs. Cesar holds up Booker's tail to send a different, more confident signal to his brain. Then he invents something new—a double-sided leash, one end to hold Booker's head up; the other side to keep his tail high and proud. Amazingly, it makes a difference. Booker is suddenly able to navigate the mean streets of Long Beach with much more confidence. "When I was holding the leash the way Cesar showed me, it was really a new experience," says Michael. "He wasn't scrambling for cover constantly. He was just sort of standing there beside me. I was excited about that, that's way different."

Though Booker's insecurities won't go away overnight, both Michael and Cesar have hope now. "Low-self-esteem dogs do take a little longer than any other dogs because we have to build self-esteem. But I can see a successful rehabilitation between Michael and Booker, because Michael wants what is best for Booker."

Follow-up ❧ ❧ ❧

Booker is better when he's alone with Michael but is still fearful when he's out on the streets. Michael feels that Booker may have been born with some mental problems that can't be fixed. Michael has accepted that this is the way Booker is and loves him anyway.

Key Cesar Tip

Dogs with low self-esteem (extreme fear for no apparent reason) require patient owners who choose calm, steady leadership over sympathy and coddling.

Hardwood Hell

Name: Josie

Breed: Labrador retriever

When Jennifer and Shane Smith remodeled their home and added a beautiful new hickory hardwood floor, everyone in the family was thrilled with the results—everyone, that is, except their chocolate Lab, Josie. Josie refuses to walk on the floors unless the Smiths put down rugs. Their young son, Sebastian, has hardwood floors in his room now, and Josie won't go in to play with him. Josie's home has now become her hardwood hell.

This isn't the first time Cesar has played peacemaker between a dog and a floor. But the family watched the previous season's segment about Kane, the Great Dane that was afraid of shiny floors, and say Cesar's methods didn't work for Josie. Early in the consultation, however, Cesar learns that the family has always been inconsistent in disciplining Josie. She also has a habit of barking when they are in the yard, but they don't always stop her. "In their natural habitat, the pack leader is in charge a hundred percent of the time." Josie senses this lack of leadership. Simply put, the Smiths haven't been following through in helping Josie get over her fear of the floors.

Cesar takes Josie through the house slowly and calmly, and after an initial protest, she easily submits. "Josie was born to be a follower. The minute I take control, she says, 'Okay, I follow you. I was waiting for you to tell me what to do.'" After a few more trips around the floors, Cesar is ready to hand the reins over to Jennifer. Things are a bit rocky at first. "Notice when you don't ask permission, she comes, but when you ask, she hesitates?" Cesar asks. "So in order to help animals when they have problems, it's best not to negotiate. Just do it."

Jennifer admits that she has a lot of work to do but promises to follow through.

Follow-up ❀ ❀ ❀

The Smiths report that they have not been able to get Josie used to the hardwood floors on their own. Since this is their beloved dog's only problem, they have decided they can live with it.

Chapter 10

Territorial/Possessive

Kerrie, Cesar, Mary Jo, Cinnamon, and Chocolate.

Too Much Cinnamon

(episode 202)

Names: Cinnamon and Chocolate

Breed: dachshund

Mary Jo Stirling passed on her family's love of dachshunds to her daughter, Kerrie. Their first dog, Chocolate, was the ideal pet. When they rescued another dachshund with a broken leg, they felt this new girl, whom they named Cinnamon, would be a wonderful companion for Chocolate. They had no idea that Chocolate and Cinnamon would mix in a recipe that would be much too spicy. Once Cinnamon's leg healed, she proceeded to take over the house and began to terrorize Chocolate, trying to keep her from her toys and food. She's hurt her sister dachshund and nearly tore her ear off on one occasion.

Follow-up ❖ ❖ ❖

Mary Jo reports that the dogs are doing great and that Cinnamon finally listens to her. She has become more disciplined herself in making the dogs behave, and even the techs at her vet's office have noted the big improvement.

Behind the scenes

Mary Jo told *Dog Whisperer* producers that the highlight of the experience was when Cesar was showing her how to "reclaim her bed"—and sat down in bed next to her! Her friends still tease her about it.

Cinnamon also is fiercely protective of Mary Jo. If anyone—especially a man—tries to approach Mary Jo in the house, Cinnamon attacks.

During the consultation, Mary Jo admits that she's lax on leadership. She doesn't walk the dogs regularly and prefers to nag them and give them time-outs when they disobey. Cesar explains that this approach may work with kids, but it doesn't cut it in the animal world. Since Cinnamon is a rescue dog, Mary Jo has been feeling sympathy for her, but that has only been fueling Cinnamon's dominant behaviors. Cesar also notes that both Mary Jo and Kerrie are low-energy and passive. "They'll view you as the energy you share, so if your shoulders are down and your head is down, that's who you're being at that moment. And as you see, they show you no mercy. You show weakness, they show dominance. Even though you rescued them, they don't see you as having rescued them. They see you as providing shelter, but you're not providing leadership."

Cesar's first recommendation is for Mary Jo and Kerrie to take a lot more walks with Chocolate and Cinnamon. Aggressive dogs need extra exercise to vent their frustrations. Next, he works with both women to build up their confidence so that the dogs know they mean it when they say no. Finally, he enlists the help of a crew member to approach Mary Jo on her bed, where Cinnamon's possessiveness is at its worst. He shows Mary Jo how to stop Cinnamon's possessive aggression before— not after—it escalates.

"Today we gave power back to who should own the power, which is the human being. The human being should tell the dog what to do," Cesar states at the end of a successful session.

The Lady Is a Tramp

Name: Lady

Breed: Dalmatian-German shepherd mix

Karolynn Hill considers Lady to be the child she never had. Karolynn's mother, Floriece, however, does not feel in any way "grandmotherly" toward the dog. When Lady was young, Floriece got so fed up at her constant barking that she would bark back at her. "I could tell she didn't like it," admits Floriece. Now, five years later, they don't get along at all. Lady constantly barks at the elderly woman, as well as the gardener and any other visitor who comes along. She is possessive and will not let anyone near Karolynn, even Karolynn's other dog, Fluffy.

During the consultation, Cesar gently admonishes Floriece for teasing Lady and asks her to be willing to move on from her bad feelings about the dog. Floriece knows that Lady can sense that she doesn't like her and grudgingly agrees to try to have a more positive attitude. Cesar defeats Lady on her own turf, by chasing her around the yard, dominating her, until she tires out and surrenders. After a successful "pack walk" through the neighborhood with Lady and Fluffy, Cesar returns to empower Karolynn as a pack leader and to work with Floriece on her animosity. "I needed to make sure Floriece sees her daughter in control of two dogs, the dogs that they can't control, right? I want her to see that picture, and I want her to maintain that picture in her mind, because that's the only way Lady can have a chance to be seen as a normal dog."

Cesar's goal is to get Floriece and Lady to relax around each other. Because Floriece loves her piano, Cesar challenges Floriece to think of Lady as a piano.

Follow-up 🐾 🐾 🐾

Karolynn reports she came home recently and found Lady and her mother happily relaxing together in the backyard. Lady and Floriece now get along fine. Karolynn walks Lady every day and is thrilled with how well her dog is behaving.

Key Cesar Tip

"Teasing a dog is a very common mistake," warns Cesar. "It can make a dog aggressive, dominant, or fearful of humans, and it destroys trust, which is vital in human-dog relationships. In a pack, dogs play, but they don't tease each other. You do something or you don't, but you don't tease."

With Lady in a calm-submissive state, Floriece is able to let go of the past and pet her. Both Karolynn and Floriece are thrilled. "In the past, if I had touched her like that, she would try to bite me. But today she looked up at me, 'Let me see who this is,' as if she would've done something to somebody else, but she saw that it was me. So it gave her a new feeling toward me. And me toward her," Floriece says.

Dominance

Chapter 11

Insane Dane

Name: Hudson

Breed: harlequin Great Dane

(episode 204)

Ron and Amber Oberman adored their Great Dane pair, Calvin and Violet. The four of them lived blissfully together until Calvin developed bone cancer and passed away. Violet and the Obermans were overcome with grief. To fill the hole in their hearts, they adopted a Great Dane puppy who was Calvin's spitting image. But the puppy, named Hudson, did not fit into the family the way Ron and Amber hoped. From the day he arrived, he began bullying and harassing Violet and making her life miserable. He wouldn't let her relax, eat, sleep, or even relieve herself. Once he grew into a horse-sized, ebullient adolescent, Hudson's behavior escalated to uncontrollable, even with Ron and Amber. He ate a sofa from the inside out and has claimed much of their furniture as his own, refusing them a place sit. He has taken over their bed and won't even allow them room to turn over in their sleep. To top it off, Hudson—now one and a half years old and weighing 140 pounds—is a terror to walk. He even gave Amber a concussion when he took off after another dog and pulled her into a tree. The Obermans have hired three trainers, but to no avail.

When Cesar sits down with the Obermans, he immediately gets to the root of the problem. It goes all the way back to the death of Hudson's predecessor, Calvin. "When a dog senses that there's no leadership in the house, he immediately takes over," Cesar tells them gently. "He doesn't know that he's a replacement. He doesn't know that you lost a loved one. He just knows that when he came into the house, everybody was mourning the dog that passed away. Mourning makes you weak in the animal world."

When Cesar works with Hudson, his behavior improves so quickly the Obermans can't believe it. With the snap of a finger and a dose of his calm-assertive energy, Cesar is able to stop Hudson from following Violet up the hill and preventing her from relieving herself. The Obermans are speechless, but Cesar explains it simply: "This dog is a very easy case. Hudson was born to be a follower. That's why he gave up the position right away. He didn't *want* the position!"

Now it's time for Cesar to teach Ron and Amber how to take back their house. One of Cesar's techniques for helping his clients become more calm-assertive is to channel the energy of a person they associate with confidence and power. For Amber, it's her mother, who has the persona of a very confident, dominant Italian woman. For Ron, it's Bruce Springsteen, "The Boss." Using their newfound assertive identities, Ron and Amber are amazed to watch Hudson respond to their commands and walk next to them on the leash, instead of pulling them all over the neigh-

Behind the scenes

When filming this episode, Cesar snapped his fingers and got Hudson to submit instantly. When National Geographic Channel executives watched the segment, the network complained that "the change happens too fast!" "What can we say?" the producers had to admit. "That's Cesar."

borhood. Although the solution is simple, it took Cesar to show the Obermans the light.

Amber declares, "You know, I feel that we can take control now of our destiny in the house and that he's not going to run things anymore. I just feel that we're going to be in control. Which is the way it should be."

Persistent Pasha

Name: Pasha

Breed: Lab-beagle mix

(episode 210)

Bradley and Gala Minkoff cannot understand why their four-year-old dog, Pasha, is not able to be around other dogs. Pasha pulls on the leash, and she bucks and strains to get at another dog that is nearby. She is very dog aggressive, tries to bite people who are jogging and snarls and growls when approached by children. Even though Bradley walks Pasha three times a day, she is still hostile and aggressive. Although Pasha is bad with neighborhood dogs, she is very good with their other dog, a golden retriever named Harley, although she is consistently humping him as well as Bradley's legs. She also sleeps between Bradley and Gala in their bed—causing the obvious problems there.

"It's not that the dog has a problem. It's that the dog lives with humans who don't know how to control a dominant mind," says Cesar. As Cesar discovers, Bradley is a passive guy who'd rather take direction at work than tell anyone else what to do. But Bradley is willing to try to change for the good of his dog. "I guess we're just gonna have to suck it up and go to it," he says with a sigh. "That's my man," says Cesar. "For the time that I'm here, just give me one hundred percent."

Tackling the first obstacle, Cesar teaches Bradley and Gala how to reclaim their bed, using calm-assertive leadership with Pasha. Next, he puts them through the paces of mastering the walk—walking Pasha, instead of Pasha walking them. He uses a prototype of the Illusion collar, to keep the collar high on the neck where they will have more control. Once both Gala and Bradley are comfortable leading Pasha, Cesar teaches Gala to walk as a true pack leader, with Pasha and Harley. Though Pasha protests at first, Gala succeeds. She is soon able to correct Pasha when a stranger passes by. But Pasha's biggest challenge is facing a neighborhood Australian shepherd. When the two dogs succeed in walking side by side, the

Follow-up ❀ ❀ ❀

Bradley and Gala no longer have any problems with Pasha on the bed or in the house. Walks continue to be a struggle for Bradley, however—perhaps because he doesn't practice them often enough.

Minkoffs are amazed. "It really gave us some confidence to walk, to feel relaxed, not to be in fear that something was going to happen, to know that we were in control on the walk."

For his part, Cesar is impressed at Bradley's change of energy. "You're definitely not acting like the passive guy I met on the couch."

Key Cesar Tip

"A walk! Who would have thought that a dog could actually become normal just by walking?" Cesar stresses again that walking has a deep primal meaning for a dog, and that by truly mastering it in a calm-assertive fashion, you are unlocking the door to a better human-dog relationship.

Sparky and the Service Test

Name: Sparky

Breed: terrier mix

(episode 207)

Within one five-year period, Abbie Jaye (AJ) Shrewsbury endured a series of unfortunate events in her life, one after another. Her beloved dog Scooby died, followed closely by the deaths of her father and mother. In between, she suffered four miscarriages. Even an optimistic, can-do woman like AJ couldn't stand up in the face of this unrelenting series of tragedies. She developed debilitating panic attacks that

Cesar corrects Sparky.

medication didn't seem to help. The result has been that the formerly outgoing AJ has retreated into her home. "I'm forty-five years old," she says, tears in her eyes. "I don't want to live the rest of my life this way."

Surprisingly, AJ discovered there was one medication that worked wonders without side effects—her seven-month-old terrier mix, Sparky. Sparky had joined AJ and her dog Ginger after Scooby's demise, and AJ soon discovered that simply having Sparky near her not only lessened her anxiety but sometimes even prevented panic attacks from occurring. "If I could bottle the feeling I get when I'm with him and just drop it over the Middle East, there would be peace," AJ says. "Because that's what he gives me, a deep sense of peace and calm." AJ's psychiatrist suggested that Sparky be trained and officially certified as a psychiatric service dog—a dog that helps people with psychiatric disorders in much the same way that a Seeing Eye dog helps the blind. "If Sparky could be certified as a service dog," says her husband, Charles, "it would mean I'd get my wife back."

In order for AJ to take Sparky wherever she goes, Sparky must pass a series of standardized tests administered by a professional. Though he sails through the first two, AJ worries that Sparky may not pass the final "public access" test, which involves remaining calm in public places—because he is already difficult to walk and is fearfully aggressive toward other dogs.

When Cesar arrives to consult with AJ and Charles, he is impressed and moved by the woman in front of him. "She's a survivor. She's also very positive, and that's what drove me to really want to help as much as I can."

It doesn't take long for Cesar to get to the root of the fear-aggression displayed by both her dogs, Sparky and Ginger. AJ admits to him that she has a fear of "dogs that are in the news"—Akitas, rottweilers, and especially pit bulls. Cesar points out that she has passed that fearful way of being on to her dogs. "You are the source." Cesar tells AJ he wants to bring her to his center, to experience interacting peacefully with a pack of pit bulls. He explains the concept of using calm-assertive energy to achieve balance, among both animals and humans. "Interesting," AJ observes. "If you could teach me how to be in a calm-assertive state, I wouldn't even have this disorder or need a service dog."

The real work in AJ and Sparky's rehabilitation comes a few days later, when Cesar brings them to his turf, the Dog Psychology Center, currently housing forty-seven dogs, including twelve pit bulls. "I have a pack of pit bulls who can change anybody's mind. And these are guys who were once dog-aggressive." Ironically, it's one of his burliest pit bulls, Popeye, that immediately gravitates toward AJ and warmly welcomes her into the group. But Sparky is still defensive. "Here I was being judgmental about certain breeds and then in a group of fifty dogs, I had the only aggressive dog."

After Cesar works on integrating Sparky peacefully into the pack, he does the same with AJ, teaching her to walk among and play with a group of large, boisterous dogs while remaining calm and assertive. The climax of the visit comes when he throws AJ a private "pit bull party," having her sit among and learn to manage twelve pit bulls at once. "When somebody tells me the worst-case scenario of their life, I know this is what they need to do, to confront that fear. I know that the only way fear will go away is if you actually live that scenario." After her life-changing experience with the pit bulls, AJ concurs. "This is better than any therapy I've ever had in my life. This day is going to stay with me a long time."

After one more day of extensive work at the center with the whole family—AJ, Charles, Ginger, and Sparky—it's time for the scruffy little terrier to take his service

Follow-up 🐾 🐾 🐾

The story of Abbie Jaye Shrewsbury and Sparky is one of Cesar's proudest success stories. The episode generated a huge response and a slew of much-needed publicity for psychiatric service dogs. Shortly after the segment was filmed, AJ went back to work as an organic chef and a volunteer for the blind. The change in her is amazing, and her panic attacks are rare these days. The upbeat, energetic whirlwind that is AJ frequently pops by the *Dog Whisperer* production offices to drop off a batch of her original raw food snack bars and "grawnola," or just to say hello. Sometimes Sparky is with her, proudly wearing his service vest. Sometimes, she comes on her own. "It just keeps getting better and better," AJ writes. "And all of this was made possible by meeting the Dog Whisperer. I am forever grateful."

test. Tensions are high at the pharmacy where AJ will have to demonstrate Sparky's calm-submissive new attitude to Rick Belmonte, the handler/specialist who administers the service test. But Sparky passes with flying colors. Cesar is ecstatic! AJ presents Cesar with a framed drawing she did of Popeye, the dog who taught her to love and trust pit bulls, or rather, to trust her own ability to remain calm and assertive, no matter what.

The Pig and the Pug

Name: Boo

Breed: pug

Psychologist Charlene Fuller is an expert in understanding human behavior, but when it comes to her three-year-old pug, Boo, her master's degree is no help. When Charlene relocated from Florida to California to live with her sister, Denise, she brought Boo along with her. On a whim, Charlene brought Denise a surprise—a baby potbellied pig named Papa. After a rocky start, the pig and the pug now play outside together, eat together, and share "family time" in front of the TV. However, Boo isn't so polite with human guests who come to the house. He greets them by jumping all over them and won't let up. He also acts overly friendly in this way on a walk. But the worst

Boo.

problem of all is that Boo is an escape artist. He darts away if Charlene lets up on his leash. At the house, if she opens the door, he tears off and is blocks away before she can follow him. Charlene is petrified that he'll run into traffic and be hurt or killed.

At her first meeting with Cesar, Charlene reveals that since she moved to Southern California, she hasn't been walking Boo as much. Cesar sees the root of the problem right there: "He's bored. Because he is an active type, and he doesn't get enough physical activity, it makes sense for him that when he see an open door . . . wham! That's why he shoots right out." To make matters worse, Charlene has been filled with guilt about neglecting her pig and pug. "Guilt is weakness in the animal world," Cesar explains. "Animals just know that you're in a 'down' state of mind, so somebody has to run the show." Cesar's challenge is to help Charlene connect with the "primal leader" inside her. The kind of leader both her animals will respond to.

When Cesar enters Charlene's backyard, he makes the acquaintance of both pig and pug in the proper way. Boo immediately tries to dominate him. "Did you notice how I addressed myself to Boo?" Cesar asks Charlene. She responds, "You immediately let him know that you were in charge. You stuck your finger out and let him know." Cesar nods. "I want him to meet me, but not by jumping on me. So he knows exactly what position I want to play in his backyard."

The crux of the visit is for Cesar to teach Charlene how she can control Boo at the front door. Ilusion helps out by playing the role of a friend coming over for a visit. When Boo prepares to rush forward at the sound of the doorbell, Cesar takes control of the space between the pug and the door. He addresses himself to Boo until the pug shows a calm-submissive posture. Only then does he greet his "guest." "Whoa," Charlene responds, awestruck. "I have never seen him back down like this."

Suddenly, Charlene has a life-changing insight. "I realize in every relationship I had, that has been my downfall. I didn't know how to be the leader and be assertive and say to a person, 'Don't disrespect me. Don't treat me this way.'" "This was the day for her to get a clear understanding of what is going on with her life," Cesar notes. "So when you stop being a victim you become that new person, that person who was always there hiding behind fears and insecurities and hesitations."

With her newfound knowledge, Charlene practices being a firm-assertive leader. And Boo immediately responds. Cesar further coaches her to channel a powerful hero from her own life—Rosa Parks. "She was strong and silent," Charlene muses. "She stood her ground." With the image of Parks in her mind, Charlene's control of Boo becomes easier and easier. "What I experienced, what Cesar has helped me through, is personal, spiritual growth that I will transfer right into my life, and I'm telling you, I'm a woman with a master's!"

Cesar is pleased with the day's work. "She was thirsty for knowledge, and today was the day. Now, it's not up to the pig or the pug. It's not up to Papa. It's not up to Boo. It's up to her. They need her."

Follow-up ❀ ❀ ❀

Charlene took Cesar's advice to heart, and as a result, Boo gets three good walks a day and is no longer running away. He still enjoys his time with Papa the potbellied pig, who is now 150 pounds.

Key Cesar Tip

A dog that consistently runs away is almost always a dog that's bored.

Taming Major Jones

Name: Major Jones

Breed: German shepherd

(episode 212)

Marlo Emmert is Fillmore, California's biggest animal lover. A senior citizen, she makes a habit of rescuing any abandoned or abused animal or bird that crosses her path. But when she rescued Major Jones, she met her match. He's a huge, ninety-three-pound German shepherd that's never been socialized and won't submit to Marlo on a leash. He even bit a friend of hers who tried to help with a prong collar. She risks injury every time she tries to take him out.

Cesar arrives to help Major Jones surrender to the leash. Going into the dog's backyard, Cesar lets the powerful dog fight and try to reject the leash, while he remains calm and relaxed, holding him. "The more he fights, the more he drains energy. This is how he has won in the past. This is from being cooped up for a while. He just needs to run that energy out and then it will be much easier to make him understand that the leash is actually a friend." Once Cesar gets Major out of the gate, he takes him for a long run to try to drain his frustrated energy. "Major is not an aggressive dog; he's an excited, frustrated dog."

After Cesar and Major finish their workout, it's time to teach Marlo how to get the dog into a calm-submissive state in order to walk him. Marlo starts out nervous, but she's a fast learner. But the ultimate test for Marlo is to handle Major Jones where his behavior has been the worst—going in and out of the gate into his home territory. Sure enough, once they approach the gate, Major begins to fight. "This is very

Follow-up ✿ ✿ ✿

Marlo has helped Major Jones develop social skills; he now sits and waits patiently for his dinner, and he no longer jumps on her. He gets regular walks, and Marlo is thrilled with how Cesar taught her to handle Major Jones on the leash.

Behind the scenes

In addition to dogs, Marlo rescues birds. She has dozens of parrots and exotic birds in cages in her yard, and the film crew faced an unusual level of bird chatter while shooting.

typical," Cesar explains. "The brain goes right back into what he has always done here. Dogs don't rationalize. They just react." Marlo doesn't back down, and a miracle occurs—Major submits. "I would pay to see this," Cesar exclaims, watching the fragile woman take charge of the powerful shepherd. "You know, Marlo is going to be an inspiration for a lot of women. Tears came to my eyes. With Miss Marlo I have no doubt that she will follow through."

Drop It, Sugar!

Name: Sugar

Breed: beagle

(episode 218)

With an empty nest and a longing for a lovable four-legged companion, Ray and Lynda Forman adopted Sugar, a three-month-old beagle. But Sugar has proved to be anything but sweet. She chews on anything she can get her paws on and is known for pulling things off the tables and counters. When grandchildren Carly and Sam come to visit, Sugar terrorizes them and tears their clothing. The wheelchair-ridden Ray suffers from MS and can't move away fast enough when Sugar's temper turns sour. And when a door is open, Sugar is no stranger to bolting! To her, it's an invitation to the outside world. Ray and Lynda are worried for their safety and the safety of their grandchildren.

Cesar prepares Ray for a walk with Sugar.

Right off the bat, Lynda admits to Cesar that she has no clue how to apply discipline. She's been trying to use treats and cookies as bribes, to no avail. Cesar explains that in the dog world, they don't negotiate with treats. Although Ray, using his scooter, and Lynda, using a bike, take Sugar for at least an hour of exercise a day, she won't urinate outside and she spends the whole time "tracking," not walking in migration mode, which Cesar recommends to keep dogs balanced. Ray admits that he is frustrated by his physical limitations. "Remember, you don't have to be physical as much as the mental part," Cesar tells him. "Just the fact that you are projecting the right energy toward that dog—she feels it."

Cesar begins the rehabilitation by reclaiming the Formans' living room from Sugar's madness. Using mild touch at first, then simply energy, he is able to make Sugar drop all of the many items she's used to taking for herself—a cup, the newspaper, and Lynda's cell phone. He stresses that owners should never pull something out of an animal's mouth, but instead, use their leadership energy to get it to drop it. Sugar even waits patiently until Cesar lets her know it's okay for her to move toward her favorite

Follow-up ❀ ❀ ❀

Sugar has made amazing progress! She no longer runs off with the TV remote or cell phones. When she has a lapse, Ray and Lynda simply tell her, "Drop it," and she complies. They no longer give her treats for bad behavior, and they are taking her for regular walks.

Behind the scenes

When filming the segment, Cesar was most impressed with Carly, the Formans' young granddaughter, and how easily she picked up his techniques. He called her a beginning *Dog Whisperer*, and that statement made a big impression on her. Since then, she has become an excellent dog trainer and Sugar idolizes her! Carly also has shared with her class at school what she has learned.

treats. Sugar behaves so well, it's clear that all her bad behavior was simply masking her extreme boredom and lack of rules and boundaries. "She's saying, 'Look, we have to move! We can't just stay in the house doing nothing,'" Cesar explains. "So the dog learns that by being mischievous she can actually have some kind of activity!" After a little practice, the Formans and their grandkids also succeed at the exercise.

Ray's motorized scooter is, to Cesar, the perfect piece of equipment to allow a senior citizen to match the speed of a younger dog. So is Lynda's three-wheeled bike. They simply have to learn to walk Sugar like pack leaders—making sure she's focused straight ahead and not becoming distracted during the exercise. Cesar is thrilled with the ease of this case, especially the change in Ray. "What I would really love Ray to get this day is that when he's in a pack leader mode, he can totally forget that he has MS. This dog is going to keep them young!"

Greta & Hoss

Name/Breed: Greta/Akita

Name/Breed: Hoss/Akita mix

Lori Lober rescued Greta, a stray pregnant Akita, from the side of a freeway and helped her bear her litter of puppies. Lori and her husband, Bob, found happy homes for most of the pups, but they decided to keep Greta and her son Hoss as part of their family. As Hoss grew, his dog aggression grew with him. If he sees a dog outside the window, he throws himself at the glass, and has already broken a large picture window. The Lobers' dog walker has mapped out a route for walking Greta and Hoss that avoids all of the neighborhood dogs. If Hoss goes after another dog, Greta goes after Hoss in an attempt to correct him. Greta is also touchy around the Lobers and snaps if Bob tries to brush her. As an attendee of Cesar's seminars, Lori is familiar with the responsibilities of owning a "gladiator breed" like an Akita. But she just isn't quite sure how to keep Greta and Hoss from destroying their house or fighting each other.

Cesar's first insight into the Lobers' situation comes when Lori talks about how, after four years, Greta still won't let them groom her. "She's a magnificent dog," Lori rationalizes. "We just . . . respect her boundaries." "Does she respect yours?" Cesar asks pointedly. With the aid of two calm-submissive members of his pack, Cesar shows the Lobers how to reclaim their picture window—by owning their own space and blocking dominant behavior. "What I'm doing is blocking the possibility of excitement or dominance. So if you block, the mind has to go somewhere else. So the tool here is not a leash. It's your energy and your body language." "Will we have to keep doing it, or will he eventually learn?" Lori asks. "Over time *you* learn, and that's how he learns. So if I learn to be calm and assertive, my dog can only be calm and submissive, that's it. There's no other way." According to Cesar, "Bob and Lori will have to reclaim dominance over every area of the house for their dogs to change."

In order to get Greta to submit to the grooming brush, Cesar puts her on the treadmill to get her mind to relax and focus on something else. The Lobers are stunned when she immediately lets herself be brushed, with no hesitation whatsoever. "Literally, I have not been able to do this for years," Bob marvels. "You know, I keep saying, live in the now, because you keep wanting to go back to the past. So if the now is tell-

Follow-up ❀ ❀ ❀

The dogs are doing fantastically well. Greta gets brushed all the time with no more problems. Now Hoss sits at the entrance to what used to be "his" window room and waits for permission to enter. When people come over, the Lobers tell them, "No touch, no talk, no eye contact," and they say it really works. Not long after the taping, Hoss had to be rushed to the vet for a medical emergency, and Lori was able to get him there and keep him calm throughout his recuperation. She credits it all to what she learned from Cesar. "It's just night and day," Lori says.

ing you brush the dog, brush the dog, simple as that," Cesar replies.

Finally, Cesar works with the Lobers and the dogs' walker, Lori Scarlett, for a lesson in mastering walking two powerful breed dogs. The Lobers are overcome by the change they see in their dogs—and in themselves. "This is a commitment that we've made," Lori remarks. "And with these tools, we'll be able to keep them calm and submissive, which is how they should be."

School for Shelties

Names: Jake and Nugget

Breed: Sheltie

Megan Traver, a schoolteacher, was so happy with her eight-year-old Sheltie, Nugget, that when an opportunity arose to get another Sheltie, two-year-old Jake, Megan jumped at the chance. The first ride home was a nightmare. Jake was anxiously barking in the car, snapped, and bit Nugget. Megan bought a larger car so she could keep Jake in a cage while driving, but the endless barking continued. Megan lives in an apartment and takes the dogs to "doggie day care" at her parents' every weekday so they can run in the yard and have company, but the two out-of-control Shelties have made her parents' lives miserable as well.

Since Jake arrived, the dogs have developed other issues: barking madly at the hair dryer and the vacuum, making getting ready for work and cleaning house nightmarish experiences. The irony is that Megan handles a classroom full of rowdy seventh and eighth graders every day—but her own home is out of control.

When Megan calls in Cesar to put her through his intensive "school for Shelties," the first thing he learns is that Megan has been using affection to try to manage her dogs' behavior. "Something Megan shared with me is that, 'Every time I go into a relationship with a real human being, a boyfriend, I choose the one I want to rescue. I choose the one I feel sorry for.' I always say in my seminars that you can't rehabilitate unstable men—or dogs—with affection."

Megan's new discipline begins with mastering the walk, which she does in record time. Her next challenge is to use a calm but firm attitude to create a calm-submissive state with her dogs before she turns on the hair dryer or the vacuum cleaner. Cesar notices during this exercise that it's actually bad boy Jake—not teacher's pet Nugget—that responds right away to her shift in energy. "So they both have to be addressed, not just Jake. We can't just put all the load on one dog when it's two dogs making the same mistake." Another piece of the puzzle comes together when Cesar points out that it's Megan he has to address more than Jake, in order to keep her confidence up. She needs to learn how to "own" her space, the hair dryer, and the vacuum cleaner, not give them up to the dogs' barking.

Follow-up ❀ ❀ ❀

Things are 75 percent better with the dogs, but they are both still works in progress. Jake barks in the car for thirty seconds but then calms down. When Megan wants to dry her hair or vacuum, she has to put Jake and Nugget on the bed and have them lie down and stay. Their behavior is much better, but Megan has to correct them all the time, or they will go back to how they were before Cesar came. Megan is recovering from having two knee surgeries and is looking forward to being able to walk longer with the dogs.

Finally, Cesar works with Megan and her Shelties to ease the barking situation in the car. The key, Cesar tells her, is to make sure both dogs are totally calm-submissive before she starts to drive. "Before the dog goes in the car, the dog has to be calm-submissive. Then we did step number two, which is to invite Jake into the car instead of him inviting himself into the car." With minor corrections, Jake is suddenly a model citizen on the road. With her new calm-assertive personal power, Megan begins to think she'll start attracting more balanced boyfriends, not the "rescue cases" she's been accustomed to.

"Before Cesar came, I was thinking that I was going to have to see it to believe it, that Jake could ever get better. And now I know that I have to believe it to see it."

Yorkie 911

Names: Winston and Oliver

Breed: Yorkshire terrier

Police officer Tom Cusson has faced some stubborn crooks on his beat, but none as difficult as his two Yorkies, Oliver and Winston. These doggie delinquents are making the lives of Tom and his wife, Valerie, unmanageable. Two-year-old Winston's MO is to attack every plant that crosses his path. He goes after the hedges in the front of their house and the vines in the backyard. Other problems arise in the presence of one-year-old Oliver. If Oliver tries to eat Winston's food, Winston bites him, and the same goes if Oliver accidentally nudges Winston while he is asleep. At night, Valerie and Tom have to take turns sleeping downstairs to stop Winston from barking. Going for a walk is another challenge. If the dogs see Tom and Valerie put on their shoes or jackets, both dogs start yelping, barking, and running around. On the walks, Winston attacks his own leash, any plants they pass, and Oliver.

The Cussons reveal that discipline with the Yorkies has not been their strong point; they end up either yelling or begging the dogs to calm down. Cesar reminds them that neither is an effective leadership approach. Tom breaks down, finally admitting, "It's just that they're so small; I see them as babies. I'm really emotional when it comes to kids and animals. I have a soft spot for people who can't defend themselves. That's probably why I'm a police officer." Cesar reminds him that instead of giving in to the Yorkies, he can use the same leadership skills he's developed as a police officer to bring back balance to his home. "You're a police officer. If you're going to stop somebody from doing a bad behavior, and that person is already in Level 8 or Level 10, you can't come at Level 2 to try to stop the behavior."

Cesar demonstrates this principle and how it applies to the dogs, beginning with discipline inside

Follow-up ❀ ❀ ❀

Winston and Oliver are much better. They don't have separation anxiety anymore, and they listen when the Cussons speak to them. Overall they walk better on the leash and are much more mellow. Winston still starts to go for the plants, but they know how to control him. When Valerie and Tom are the pack leaders, there's peace in their house.

the house and then graduating to the great outdoors, where the dreaded shrubberies lie in wait. Valerie, Tom, and their son, Dylan, have to go back to basics, but under Cesar's tutelage, they begin to regain control. Police Officer Tom, who was the softest touch in the household, finally is able to apply his law enforcement training to his care for his beloved pets. "Basically you need to be the top dog in all situations, and that's a principle we apply all the time at work. They call it 'command presence,' and you have to have that command presence to let people know that you mean business, and obviously the dogs need the same thing."

The Escape Artist

Name: Chula

Breed: Shiba Inu

Jack and Rita Stroud fell in love with Chula, a two-year-old Shiba Inu, because of her foxlike appearance. She proved to be a very intelligent but stubborn dog. She ignores her owners, even when they call her by name. During walks, Chula constantly pulls on the leash, but her most frightening issue is a tendency to bolt out any open door at home. Rita and Jack worry that Chula could get lost or be hit by a car.

During the consultation, Cesar is shocked to learn that the Strouds take the very high-energy Chula for a walk only once a week. "Dogs are supposed to go out every day," Cesar explains. "If our parents kept us in the house and let us go out only once a week, most of us, once we saw a window open or a door open, would take off." He also notices that the Strouds let Chula claim the furniture and do whatever she wants, but then they complain that she doesn't listen to them. It's clear they have to go back to square one with Chula, learning how to master the walk and project calm-assertive pack leader energy, in order to cure her of her life-threatening escape habit. Armed with new information they had never considered before, the Strouds are fast learners. So is Chula. Cesar teaches the Strouds how to use nothing but their calm-assertive energy to keep Chula sitting right in front of an open door—without bolting!

"It was a wonderful feeling, standing there looking at that open door, and I wasn't in panic mode of, "Shut the door!" It was a fantastic feeling to see her just standing there looking out," Rita marvels.

But the Strouds are new at being pack leaders, and Chula's escape artistry can still be a threat to her

Follow-up 🐾 🐾 🐾

The Strouds are ecstatic over their new leadership skills and the corresponding changes in Chula. Rita writes: "It is truly a blessing to be able to have the door open without fear that Chula will run out . . . It was just amazing how Cesar was able to help us and teach us what we were doing wrong, causing Chula's problem. We are walking her daily and what a difference! Everyone who knows her is just as amazed as we are . . . Thank you all for helping us to be pack leaders."

life. To tide them over, Cesar brings in a technological aid—the Global Pet Finder—a tiny GPS tracking device set in a collar that sends an immediate alert to an owner's cell phone or computer if a pet runs away. With this combination of Mother Nature's energy and high-tech support, Cesar believes Chula will remain at home with the Strouds "for a long, long time."

Wild Things

Name/Breed: Lucy/Boston terrier

Name/Breed: Hank/French bulldog

Name/Breed: Betty/pug

Actress and model Denise Richards has owned three dogs since they were puppies. Her canine clan includes Lucy, a six-year-old Boston terrier, Hank, a six-year-old French bulldog, and Betty, a five-year-old pug.

Denise Richards with rascals Hank, Lucy, and Betty.

Betty is great with Denise's kids, but she is terrible when people come to their house. Her aggression has even escalated to bites, and Denise realizes she's vulnerable to lawsuits. Betty is also overprotective of Denise and seems to act more aggressively around people when Denise is home. Lucy and Betty compete to be the alpha dog. They have bitten each other and have even drawn blood. Betty must be fed separately because she tries to eat both the other dogs' food. When any person is eating, Betty stands right next to him or her and barks incessantly. Hank is aggressive toward Sam, Denise's oldest daughter, and treats her like a dog. He even tries to hump her!

Denise has a dog walker, who walks the dogs for one hour each day. The dogs are fine on the walks, but when the leashes come out, the dogs go crazy with excitement. It's very difficult just to get the dogs out the door.

"Everything Denise mentioned has to do with being territorial or dominant, so the only way we can get rid of that is if we act dominant or territorial toward them." Cesar says, "The root of the problem was that Denise treats them like babies, but even babies need rules, boundaries, and limitations."

Cesar works with Denise to teach her how to become firmer with the pack and how to focus her discipline on the specific dog that causes any specific problem. He brings in golden retriever Sonny, a calm-submissive dog from his pack, to help assess the severity of the situation. The female dogs welcome Sonny, but Hank charges him. When Sonny gets excited, Hank attacks, then the girls follow suit. "One of the things that I needed Denise to observe is that becoming panicked or frantic about controlling the situation is not the key." Since Betty tries to bite people when they leave, Cesar and several crew members help Denise test how much she's learned about pack leader behavior. "I'm so excited and I learned a lot from one session," Denise concludes. "I'm so affectionate with them; just shifting my thinking is going to be a bit tricky for me. With the two kids and three dogs, it's very chaotic in my house, so it'll be nice to have some control over them."

Obsessions

Brady waits for his pool time.

The Soggy Doggy

Name: Brady

Breed: Labrador retriever

(episode 201)

Most yellow Labs love the water, but Jim and Roxie Livingston's yellow Lab Brady is obsessed with it. When he was a puppy, Jim and Roxie, their kids, and grandkids laughed as Brady jumped and splashed, but now, at six years old, he is maniacal about diving into the pool and taking it over, driving everyone else out of the water. In fact, he is so aggressive at times—hurling himself into the middle of a group of the Livingstons' small grandchildren—that it's become unsafe to have them in the pool when he is around.

Brady's attention-getting behavior is definitely the worst around Jim. When Jim comes home from work, Brady jumps in the pool and refuses to come out. Brady whines and whimpers until Jim pays attention to him. Their vet suggested that they let Brady swim until he wore himself out, so Roxie and Jim tried his advice. Eight hours later, the Livingstons pulled Brady out of the water, his feet bleeding from all the swimming.

When Cesar arrives, it becomes clear that there's a division in the household. Roxie Livingston is the disciplinarian in the family, but Jim considers Brady more of a pal and an equal. He hates to give him rules, and that's the root of the problem.

"When my clients put friendship first with a dog, they can't accomplish what they want." Cesar explains that friendship is great, but dogs need structure before love. "So when we don't create rules, boundaries, and limitations, we can make the brain become obsessive. They aren't born with obsession. They develop obsession, living with humans who don't give them limits."

Now that he's established the source of Brady's instability, Cesar is ready to don his wet suit. First, Cesar makes Brady sit outside the pool gates until the dog relaxes. "Until he goes into that relaxed state of mind, I'm not going to invite him in." Cesar splashes in the water while Brady watches, shaking with anticipation and envy. "Tsst. This is the time that you don't feel sorry about them. You don't comfort them, you don't say it's okay, you don't give cookies. You just let him go through it. The water activity is going to be on my terms, not on his terms." Finally, Brady relaxes and Cesar lets him in.

The session hits a snag, however, when Cesar dives into the pool and an overexcited Brady follows without being invited. He removes Brady from the pool area and walks with him until the dog's mind is once again calm-submissive. Then Cesar tries again, climbing into the pool while Brady watches from just outside the gate. Cesar explains his strategy: "Let's say you're going to be into the pool for one hour. The first thirty minutes, he's outside the pool. And then the next thirty minutes he comes with you into the pool. But you invite him in." Finally, Cesar invites Brady in the pool with him. "Look how nice he's swimming!" Roxie cries. "He's swimming with a purpose." "I wouldn't have believed it," says Jim. "I'm still having a hard time believing it. Cesar's a miracle worker."

Follow-up 🐾 🐾 🐾

Jim and Roxie worked tirelessly to set limitations for Brady around the pool, and their perseverance paid off. Ever since, Brady has displayed perfect pool etiquette—even around splashing and excited grandkids.

The Chow Hound

(episode 205)

Name: Nugget

Breed: blue tick hound–Great Dane mix

Russ and Nancy Briley adopted Nugget from a local shelter when he was just two months old. As the pup grew larger, so did his appetite. Nugget developed a taste for soccer cones, dish towels, the wood from his owners' box spring, rugs, and even the family trampoline, which resulted in emergency surgery for the dog. With home accessories turning up in pieces and the carpet being trashed, the Brileys have decided that it's time to get some help. "He almost passed away," Russ states solemnly. "And we're very, very concerned because we obviously love the dog. He's got his problems, but we don't want him to die."

The Briley family learns how to walk Nugget properly.

Early in the consultation, Cesar discovers a shocking fact: because he pulls on the leash and is difficult to control, Nancy has been walking Nugget only three times a week. "When a dog destroys a house and chews things, it's just like a physical exercise. When you get a dog that is a working type and you don't have any activity to share, it develops issues, like the one you have. You have destructive behavior because you're not utilizing his energy in a positive manner. Walking is like Prozac but without the side effects."

The mellow, low-energy Brileys seemed overwhelmed by Cesar telling them that they should be walking high-energy Nugget a minimum of forty-five minutes twice a day. "I didn't really think that the family was going to be able to pull it off. They seemed to be too calm." Patiently, Cesar takes the Brileys through the basics of the proper walk—leaving the house before the dog, walking with him next to or behind them, with the dog paying full attention to the pack leader, not the environment. Since Nugget hadn't been walked in two days, at one point Cesar takes him for a two-block run, just to drain his excess energy and help him to focus.

Today, Russ and Nancy get in three hours of walking every day with Nugget, and it has made a world of difference. Nugget no longer eats rugs and items that are unhealthy. They say he is entirely better and he gets along well with other dogs and people. He now waits for the front door to be opened for him. With commitment and patience, the family that Cesar had doubts about worked together to take back their home—and save Nugget's life.

Key Cesar Tip

The walk is serious business for dogs. If you aren't committed to walking a dog every day, for as long as his specific energy level requires, then you should rethink your choice of a pet.

Once the whole family has experienced walking Nugget correctly, Cesar takes advantage of the dog's exhaustion to test him around objects he normally would devour. To everyone's—even Cesar's—astonishment, Nugget not only ignores the objects, he turns his back on them. Under Cesar's firm leadership, Nugget's common sense kicks in. "That's just amazing to me," says Nancy. " 'Cause yesterday he would've been eating all those things. And half those thing he did try to eat yesterday." Russ jumps in. "I can't believe that everything was controlled by just a walk. And it makes me feel bad because I haven't really participated as much as I should in the walking, and now I'm going to make a big point of doing it."

Matilda's Madness

Name: Matilda

Breed: English bulldog

(episode 203)

John and Mia Coveny's adorable English bulldog Matilda was only a puppy when they first
noticed that she had an odd, obsessive reaction to the skateboards that passed by their
window. They thought it was cute and wondered
if she might someday grow up to be a dog that
could perform tricks on a skateboard. When they
bought one, however, the moment Matilda laid
eyes on it she began screeching like a banshee
and proceeded to attack the skateboard, biting its wheels until her mouth bled. Now, when
Matilda sees the neighborhood boys riding their
boards down the street, she tears after them,
biting at their wheels. Her attacks aren't harm-

Cesar and kids work on Matilda's skateboard obsession.

ful to the riders, but mostly to Matilda who forgets her pain in her mission to destroy
the skateboards. The Covenys are worried that Matilda may seriously hurt herself, or
someone else, with these brutal attacks.

Cesar is curious about getting to the roots of Matilda's misplaced mania. "We have
a case here where the owners saw a behavior earlier and thought it was cute. And then
they suffer the consequences later on in life."

Early in the consultation, Cesar begins to get the picture of who is really in charge
in the Coveny household. The director of the episode asks the Covenys if Matilda
can sit between them, on the middle of the couch. Mia responds that Matilda probably "won't cooperate" with that request. "She just seems like she wants to sit at
the edge. I don't know," Mia responds, pointing to the far end of the couch, where
Matilda is lounging. Cesar is puzzled by this response. "You mean, she can make
these decisions?" "Um, yeah, she's very smart, she can decide for herself," John
replies. As Cesar probes more deeply, he begins to see other areas in which the

After six weeks of consistent work, John and Mia were able to take Matilda out in their neighborhood and sit at sidewalk cafés without any "wheel attack" incidents. Matilda had a setback when the couple went on vacation and after they moved, but they report that when they work with her consistently, she always gets better.

Behind the scenes

Being on *Dog Whisperer* made the Covenys famous. They get stopped on the street and distant friends and family from other states and countries have been calling them.

Covenys have been humanizing Matilda and allowing her to dominate them. They admit that they are worried that she gets excited by cats and squirrels, yet Mia likes to point out these same things to her when they're walking. "We like her to be aware of the names of things," says Mia.

"You notice you're contradicting yourself, right?" says Cesar. When you point out the cat, you're telling her to get excited about it, when there is already an instinctual side of her that becomes excited about small creatures." Mia also admits that she feels bad when John tries to discipline their dog. It's clear that Mia gives Matilda no boundaries at all, treating her like a small child. And John seems to give halfhearted discipline. No wonder Matilda has been allowed to become obsessive.

Outside, Cesar begins by determining the degree of Matilda's fixation toward the skateboard. Climbing on his own skateboard, Cesar sees that Matilda goes after it immediately. "She does exactly what a bulldog would do to a bull—attack, grab the neck, bring him down. But she's redirecting this powerful way of being to a skateboard."

But Matilda seems to be responding willingly to Cesar's corrections, so he immediately calls in his son Calvin to help with the rehabilitation. Every time Matilda makes a move toward Calvin on the skateboard, Cesar gives her a tap on her hindquarters. "At the moment she's about to move forward, you see that my body moves to redirect her." When two neighborhood boys pass by with their own skateboards, Cesar ups the ante by having them join the effort. With the constant repetition of being surrounded by three boys on wheels, yet having to submit and stay calm-submissive, Matilda begins to get the picture. Cesar ends the exercise with a relaxed Matilda lying in front of three skateboards and managing to ignore them all.

The Covenys look on in awe. "I can't believe I would ever see Matilda Coveny lying down with three skateboards upturned in front of her," says Mia. But now it's time for the couple to try to replicate Cesar's technique. Cesar works hardest with Mia, since she is the one who has had the toughest time with the concept of discipline. When she sees that all it takes is a tap to snap Matilda out of her obsession, she is amazed and motivated to change. "I wasn't asserting control and I realize that I've been too permissive in my behavior toward Matilda and need to set more boundaries," she admits. "Mia really stepped up to the plate. She listened. She took my positive criticism," Cesar says proudly.

Key Cesar Tip

For some purebred dogs, obsessive behavior can be a sign of natural instincts run amok. Frustrated dogs may gravitate toward the inherited behaviors of their breeds as a way to release anxiety.

Spin, Poodle, Spin

Name: Teddy

Breed: standard poodle

Rhonda and Alan Levy got
Teddy from a breeder when he
was just ten weeks old. With his
work as a certified therapy dog
and his skill at playing soccer,
it seemed that Teddy would
be the perfect pet. But at nine
months, Teddy developed a
quirky but dangerous habit.
When a car zooms past Teddy
during his walks, he immediately tries to chase it. His leash
prevents him from catching the

Cesar challenges Teddy to a soccer match.

car but turns him into a Tasmanian devil, spinning out of control. The Levys hired a
trainer and the spinning stopped, but only when in the presence of the trainer. The
trainer suggested the Levys try a shock collar, but even on the highest setting it left
Teddy unfazed. Rhonda enjoys walking Teddy but fears for his life, not to mention her
own, when cars pass him on the street.

During the consultation with the Levys, Cesar learns that Amanda, the family's
other standard poodle, has no trouble controlling Teddy in the backyard when she
wants to take the ball away from him. The Levys, however, have to beg and cajole to
achieve the same effect. Cesar explains that Amanda is simply exerting her dominant
energy—something the Levys will have to learn to share with Teddy if they want to
correct his dangerous behavior with the cars. Alan immediately makes the connection
between becoming a better leader to Teddy and being a boss at his job—it's all about
being direct and assertive. Cesar takes the Levys on a walk with Teddy and illustrates
how to correct his behavior at the very instant he starts paying attention to a car, not

waiting until after he starts to spin. The transformation is remarkable, and Cesar leaves the session believing the Levys get it.

"They just have to put into practice what they learned today. The way to pull the leash. The way to hold your shoulders. The way to keep your head up. The way to feel energy. They have to go back into instincts."

Snoopy the Sniffer

Name: Snoopy

Breed: beagle

(episode 211)

Nancy Madrid brought home an adorable beagle puppy, Snoopy, to live with her husband and fifteen-year-old son Andrew as well as their nine-year-old Chihuahua. When Snoopy was six months old, the family moved to a home in a rural area where all types of animals made their way into the backyard. With his nose to the ground, Snoopy began meandering through the yard letting out loud, high-pitched yelps and whimpers, so much so that the family thought he

Snoopy surfs!

was hurt. Snoopy does this constantly for hours on end. The Madrids have tried giving him time-outs, tying him up, making him sit, and putting him in a crate. The only thing that seems to calm him is "surfing" on a boogie board in the pool. Snoopy's incessant sniffing and yelping is torture to the ears, and the Madrids are beside themselves.

Cesar's challenge with Snoopy is to turn his obsessive behavior into healthy behavior. First, to drain Snoopy's anxious energy, Cesar takes him on a vigorous Rollerblading session around the neighborhood. Once Snoopy is in a calm-submissive state, Cesar demonstrates how to apply appropriate discipline. Nancy begins to understand that discipline is all about energy. "I would get so frustrated with him, repeating myself over and over again. Then just doing it that one time—when he actually just stopped—felt so good. I knew then that we had realized what Cesar was talking about." But Cesar knows this isn't a one-day fix. He puts the Madrids on a strict rehabilitation program for the next month, consisting of structured walks and runs balanced with playtime. They take Cesar's advice of using a backpack to help him drain more energy and to walk with a purpose—something that will prevent him from zigzagging and sniffing on the walks. The family is amazed at his transformation, and his sniffing behavior has lessened considerably.

Finally, Cesar returns to show the family how to put Snoopy's natural sniffing instincts to better use. He teaches them how to do a mini-search-and-rescue game in their backyard, with Snoopy sniffing out his favorite toy. "This story is a done deal," says Cesar happily. This family just needed to know what direction they should take."

Follow-up ❀ ❀ ❀

Snoopy is sniffing much less, but the Madrids have opossums and raccoons in their yard that are temptations he sometimes can't resist. He does go swimming a lot, giving him the exercise he needs, which goes a long way toward keeping the sniffing under control. A new puppy they've added to the family has also helped Snoopy become a much less obsessive sniffer.

Key Cesar Tip

Beagles have a long history as working dogs. Their unique sense of smell makes them excellent trackers. They're even used to sniff out contraband at airports.

Rock Dog

Name: Punkin

Breed: Rhodesian ridgeback–pit bull mix

Art student and teacher Amanda Yates started training her adorable puppy, Punkin, to play ball when he was just six months old. She tried to teach him how to chase and retrieve tennis balls, but he was not a fast learner. While on walks on neighboring trails, she would throw rocks and Punkin would chase them. The behavior was cute and funny at first, but she had no idea it would turn into an obsession. Since then, Punkin has become a rock freak. Whether on

Punkin and the object of his obsession.

the trails, at a dog park, or at the beach, Punkin searches until he finds a rock and fixates on it. Once Punkin has a rock, he scratches at it or chews on it . . . often until his mouth bleeds. He even refuses food if he's keyed in on a rock. Punkin will attack other dogs—and even his owners—if he suspects they are coming after his rock. Amanda realizes Punkin's "cute" behavior has become dangerous.

"It's unusual, it's unnatural. No dog in its own natural habitat becomes obsessive to anything," Cesar tells Amanda. "A pack leader never allows obsessions or insecurity or instability. Dogs develop that symptom only when they live with us."

Cesar and Amanda adjourn to a local park, where Punkin's obsession always surfaces. Using a physical correction, then deescalating to a simple assertion of dominant energy, Cesar spends forty-five minutes establishing a firm leadership position with Punkin. But when Amanda tries to replicate Cesar's methods, Punkin lunges viciously at her. Cesar realizes that Amanda has become the unwitting source of Punkin's obsessive behavior. "It will be very helpful for him to have a little vacation away from you, so he can thoroughly go into a retreat, so to speak," Cesar tells Amanda. "As much as you love him, you also have brought on this obsession. Unconsciously. By him not having you around, the source of the obsession is not there." Amanda understands that she's got work to do, also. "Meanwhile, I'll go to yoga and calm myself."

Cesar brings Punkin to join the forty or so dogs at his Dog Psychology Center, all of which are calm and balanced. Punkin seems to fit in right away—but at playtime, he finds himself in a dirt lot filled with many tempting rocks. Thanks to the power of the pack, however, Punkin immediately notices that no one else seems to care that they are playing in a veritable rock garden. "My pack never worries about the rocks, never cared about the rocks. He is the only case that we have being neurotic about rocks." The pack influences Punkin because his natural drive is to adapt and fit in with every-one else. And though he seems a bit unsure, he doesn't take the bait. "This is really good right there. If he doesn't go after the rock today, the chances of him rehabilitat-ing himself are huge."

The pack also influences Punkin in learning to be patient and have good manners at dinnertime, and in following the rules of ball playing. The pack at the center are so balanced and responsive to Cesar as their pack leader that forty dogs can all play with the same tennis ball without a fight developing. "The pack has rules, boundaries, and limitations. The pack is not obsessive about the ball. When we begin playing with the ball, fine. And when we end, it's fine as well. The point is, the pack leader makes the decision."

Two weeks later, Cesar reunites Punkin with Amanda. She is ecstatic as she watches Punkin play with a ball, starting and stopping on command, taking food in between exercises, and totally ignoring rocks! But Punkin isn't the only one that's changed. Amanda has been doing her own homework as well, and she shares her newfound wisdom with Cesar. "Having a dog is not just about you and what you want from the dog. Being a pack leader really is a lot of re-sponsibility and you have to be vigilant all the time. That's your job and, once you realize that, then you'll get the companionship that you want from your dog and you'll get a healthy, happy dog. But you can't just expect the dog to give you love and get love from you when it has its own needs and its own desires."

Follow-up ❁ ❁ ❁

Punkin now prefers tennis balls to rocks. He has an occasional craving for rocks, but when corrected he is fine.

TV Dog

Name: Contessa

Breed: shar-pei

Linda Maglia's two-year-old shar-pei has a very unusual problem. She is aggressive toward the television set! Contessa is normally a very sweet, calm dog, but she becomes overly excited when any TV show with animals appears onscreen. In fact, the show she's most obsessive about is *Dog Whisperer*! While it's on TV, Contessa gets so overwrought that she jumps at the television and tears at the very expensive wallpaper. Linda has to TiVo all television shows with animals and fast-forward through the dog parts.

Cesar immediately sees that Linda has been catering to Contessa's dominance and has unconsciously taken a follower position. When they go into the television room, he watches Linda become even more unsure of herself. "If you go into that area where you have problems without a plan, the dog is going to sense that you don't know what you're doing. So once we went into the TV room, I immediately sensed that Contessa was getting excited—even with the TV off." When *Dog Whisperer* comes onscreen, however, Contessa goes nuts, demonstrating that she has more will than grace.

Cesar reminds Linda that corrections have to take place when obsession begins at Level 1—they can't wait until the dog is already at Level 2. He begins with a firm physical touch when Contessa gets excited, and within a few minutes has reduced his corrections to a mere *tsst*! Linda is amazed to watch her video-addicted pet become a polite audience member in such a short time, and after trying it herself,

Follow-up • • • •

Linda reports that Contessa is much better now. She still loves her Cesar fix on TV, but Linda can quickly correct her and they can watch TV in peace. They have added a new dog, Nin, to their pack, and Contessa has adjusted well to it.

sees that setting rules and boundaries for her pet isn't such a hard thing to do, after all. "What Linda learned today is how simple is communication with animals," Cesar muses. "She can share love the same way she can share dominance."

Other

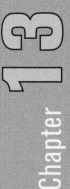
Cesar and his pack teach Storm how to be calm and submissive at feeding time.

Cookin' Up a Storm

(episode 214)

Name: Storm

Breed: Newfoundland

The Blatti family got Storm when he was just eight months old. Since then, he has grown into a massive three-and-a-half-year-old bear. His appetite is the only thing that hasn't grown—Storm is the world's pickiest eater. Gloria Blatti has tried out many foods on her dog, but he refuses almost everything. After numerous trips to the vet and no solid answers, Gloria found some expensive cookies that seem to whet Storm's appetite. She spends more time cooking for Storm than she does for her own family, in an endless quest to find that one perfect meal. But even then, getting him to eat is still quite tedious.

Gloria reports that Storm loved being at the center. Storm was doing great and eating normally after he came home; however, since Gloria got a new dog named Emmy, Storm has not been eating as well. Still, it is an improvement from before meeting Cesar.

Behind the scenes

When Gloria moved to a new home around Christmastime, Storm sneaked out of the backyard and was temporarily lost. When Gloria's daughter, Jillian, went looking for him, she saw him running toward a man—who turned out to be Cesar! Cesar just happened to be shooting another story in Gloria's new neighborhood. He was shocked to see Storm running to him out of nowhere. Clearly, Storm had good memories of his time with the Dog Whisperer.

Cesar's first observation is that Gloria's doting on Storm may be part of the problem. She pushes food on him all the time so he never gets to experience the natural sensation of "working for food" that dogs crave. Gloria agrees to let Storm go to boot camp at Cesar's Dog Psychology Center.

From the moment Storm arrives, it's clear he has to relearn how to be a dog. He doesn't know how to interact with the pack and stumbles over things with no sense of his own space. "He doesn't have good social skills, as you can see. The first step for him in learning to be a dog is to recognize rules, boundaries, and limitations among his own kind." Cesar creates an exercise program to help Storm work up an appetite, including treadmill walking and Rollerblading, ending with a nice swim in the pool. Then he has Storm come to the food, not the other way around. From watching the rest of the pack, Storm learns how to wait calmly and submissively at mealtime, then chow down like everybody else. When the Blattis see him twenty-one days later, he's a different dog. But Gloria will have to stop catering to Storm's every whim. "My suggestion for Gloria was this: cook whatever you want to cook for Storm, liquefy it, and put it as a gravy on simple, dry food. She has to exercise Storm, then she can feed Storm." He cautions her to feed him only two cookies a week.

"I felt great when I saw Storm eat. And I'm gonna try to be really different with him now and see what happens," Gloria promises.

Buford's Blind Date

Names: Buford and Honey

Breed: boxer

Bonita Mozzor is a doting "mother" to Buford, a seven-year-old boxer. Buford's former "wife" was a pit bull–boxer mix named Daisy May. Buford and Daisy were, as Bonita calls them, "soul mates." They were always together and always got along. But since Daisy May died of bone cancer, Buford has been sulky and depressed. Bonita has desperately tried to find Buford a friend, but he aggressively rejects any other dog she brings home.

Cesar arrives at Bonita's colorful Studio City home to play a role that's a new one for him—doggie match-maker. But introducing a new dog into a household can be a tricky assignment, and Cesar wants to make sure Buford's next romance is a lasting one.

During the consultation, Cesar gets a pretty good idea of who rules the household. Bonita admits that Buford listens to her "some of the time," and that

Cesar presents his "blind date" winners, Honey and Buford.

she'd rather Buford be happy than have any house rules to follow. "You know he's not a human being," Cesar tells Bonita. "He's a dog, right? There's nothing wrong with being a dog." Bonita responds with a gasp and covers Bulford's ears. "Don't talk about him like that! He's *not* just a dog." "Okay," Cesar says. Then he sighs. Right away, he knows that this will be a different kind of case. "Some people want to change. They hire me because they want to change. It was very obvious to me that she was not here to change anything. My strategy with Bonita is to be more patient."

"Okay," Cesar says resignedly. "I just want to know where you're coming from, that's all. So I can bring the right dog into your household. We're not going to change you. I'm going to pick for him, based on how you behave. It's just that the environment here is that dogs can pretty much do whatever they want. So we can't have an excited-type dog. We can't have a hyper-type dog. We can't have another dominant-type dog. We have to bring the most calm-submissive type of mind."

A few days later, Bonita and Cesar meet at Boxer Rescue in Los Angeles, where he examines the dogs there, checking for the right energy level. "Make sure you are in a very calm state of mind when you go to shelters. Dogs in shelters don't go for long walks. So you're going to deal with very frustrated dogs. That's why you have to stay quiet so you can see who they are. The most important tip is to understand what energy your dog at home is, and what role he plays in your household. And then go and get another dog that has a lower level energy than the dog you already have."

Cesar settles on Honey, a caramel blond with beguiling brown eyes—and most important, a calm energy. Cesar first takes this boxer bachelorette around the block near the shelter to walk off her pent-up energy. Then it's time for her to meet Buford, who's donned a tux and black tie for the occasion. Bonita can barely contain her excitement, but Cesar tells her that Buford's got to meet Honey like a dog, not like a person. "From that point on, I asked Bonita to stay away from us so I can influence Buford and Honey, so they can have their relationship based on what I want." Guided by Cesar, the new couple progresses from suspicion to affection—doggie style—which involves smelling, mounting, and nuzzling. Cesar is thrilled. "This is when things get done the right way. This is really good, I'm very happy. Look at this face. He's the happiest dog on earth."

When the honeymoon is over, they return to Bonita's house. There, Cesar has to put the brakes on Bonita's enthusiasm for the new match, so that Buford will not feel that his dominance in the household is being threatened by Honey. "The challenge I'm giving Bonita is to go two weeks without the whole hugging, kissing thing. She can do it to Buford, but not yet to Honey. That's gonna show us how committed she is to having two boxers under one roof. To me this is a match made in heaven. In order to keep it real on earth, it's up to Bonita to play the leadership role."

Follow-up ❀ ❀ ❀

Bonita reports that the romance between Buford and Honey is growing stronger every day. Buford the boxer finally got his second chance at true love.

Behind the scenes

In keeping with the *Dog Whisperer* show tradition of not taking itself too seriously, editor Vicki Hamel cut the Buford piece as a parody of the syndicated reality series *Blind Date*, complete with thought balloons and sexy music. Though the cartoon balloons never made it to air, viewers can find this lighthearted original version of Buford's story on the Season Two *Dog Whisperer* DVD boxed set, or watch it on the international edition of the show.

What a Drag Dog

Name: Leo

Breed: basset hound

Linda Raffle recently faced a change in her lifestyle when she sold her business, and her beloved basset hound Luke died at the age of thirteen. She thought he was irreplaceable . . . until she met twelve-week-old bassett hound Leo. Now Leo is ten months old and he is running the house. Though Linda gives him constant attention, he never obeys her. Lazy Leo uses his lethargy to control her life. When Leo hears the hair dryer, he gets depressed and will not get off her bed. Linda has to carry him down the stairs so she can leave the house. When they return from walks, Leo runs away from the house and ignores Linda's pleas for him to come home. He makes her drag him back—it's the only way to get him to move.

Leo simply doesn't want to walk.

"You have to realize that it's okay to see Leo as animal, dog, breed, name," Cesar gently tells Linda, "not just name, basset hound, human." Grudgingly, Linda nods. "He's my child," she admits. Linda reveals to Cesar that she was a powerful boss of more than 138 employees and a strong mother to her kids. Cesar challenges her to bring those same skills to her relationship with Leo. First, she has to stop carrying him downstairs. "When we keep carrying him and carrying him and carrying him, we are conditioning him that that's the only way to be."

Next, Cesar teaches Linda how to master the walk, using his two calm-submissive dogs Luigi and Coco. Asking Linda if she used a sound to get her kids' attention, she reveals she has a powerful whistle. Applying that to Leo has immediate results. "This case was actually very easy for me. Linda's a bright person. It didn't take a lot for her to understand that the energy that she was projecting internally was the message that

Follow-up ❀ ❀ ❀

Linda reports that Leo is perfect on walks these days. He no longer drags on the leash and has been cured of the issues addressed on the show. Linda now leaves Leo alone and he behaves well, but she's trying to break him on one last bad habit—chewing toilet paper.

she was sending to Leo. You can't hide your feelings in front of animals. They know exactly how you feel inside."

"What he did with me today was put me back in the situation as though my kids were young," a relieved Linda reports. "And it's really exactly how I raised and took care of them. I am the person in control. Leo's not in control."

Sunday in the Park with Cesar

Name/Breed: Duke/Doberman mix

Name/Breed: LuLu/Pomeranian

(episode 207)

Cesar, Emily, and fight instigator LuLu at the dog park.

Cesar works with LuLu to create a calm and balanced group of dogs.

The neighborhood dog park should be a place for canines and their humans to get away from it all, relax, play, and socialize with friends. A former dog walker himself, Cesar is all too familiar with the altercations that can turn this peaceful place into a battlefield. In this special segment, Cesar takes his viewers on a trip to a Laurel Canyon park in Los Angeles, to learn the right behavior and proper etiquette so that all canine outings can be fun and conflict free.

Follow-up · · · ·

Karen and Duke have made a lot of progress. Karen has kept his aggression under control but continues to work with him as it is an ongoing challenge. She cherishes her memory of working with Cesar and is committed to helping her Doberman make even more improvements. Emily says that LuLu is still a work in progress, due to her own chaotic lifestyle and lack of "quality time" to give to LuLu's rehabilitation.

First on Cesar's list is Karen Maish, who's been forbidden to bring Duke, her two-year-old Doberman mix, to several dog parks. While Karen would like to enjoy a relaxed outing, Duke would rather start dogfights. But these are no ordinary dogfights; Duke can get several dogs going at each other.

While Karen tells Cesar that Duke just "snaps" without any warning, Cesar shows her how to read his body language as a predictor of his aggression. "When the tail is down, they're going to become targets for others. When the tail is up, it's just like a rattlesnake kind of thing. Can that create a fight? Yes. So the only position that is not gonna trigger the fight is the one in the middle, when the tail is right in the middle. When it's up, they're keying on somebody. Submissive dogs don't get in trouble. Tense, dominant dogs get in trouble."

When Duke's dominance turns into aggression, Cesar jumps in to break up the fight, using his hand as a "claw" and putting Duke into a submissive position. He cautions dog owners never to try to break up a fight on their own and always to rely on a professional to handle such risky situations. However, remaining calm and assertive, no matter what your dog does, is essential for every owner. Karen says, "The big lessons that I've taken away from today are calming down when there's a situation and knowing how to read your dog."

Owner Emily Kerns has a smaller problem. Her eight-month-old Pomeranian, LuLu, thinks she is the queen of the dog park. She charges the other dogs, but when they turn on her, she doesn't know what to do. Whenever LuLu gets into trouble, Emily always rushes in to scoop her up and rescue her from the situation. Emily had no idea that by doing so, it was only making things worse. Cesar demonstrates how Emily can use her calm-assertive presence to reassure LuLu and prevent a fight, not pull her out of the situation and risk making her "prey." "You're just letting them know that the human is here to set the rules, the boundaries, and the limitations. The dogs cannot do it."

LuLu's problem behavior begins even before she encounters other dogs. Cesar works with Emily and LuLu to make sure the dog is calm and submissive before she enters the park. "It took just a few techniques from Cesar for her energy to change, for her behavior to change," says an impressed Emily. "I didn't think anybody could get my dog to change that quickly."

Key Cesar Tips

Cesar offers some vital dog park rules for all owners:

1. Make sure your dog is spayed or neutered, has all the necessary shots, and is in good health. Under no circumstances should you bring a sick dog to a dog park!

2. Do not use the dog park as a substitute for the walk! If you drive to the park, leave your car a block away and take your dog on a vigorous walk of at least thirty-five minutes to drain some of her energy. Never take an overexcited dog to the park.

3. While at the park, don't "punch out" on your calm-assertive leadership. Be aware of your dog at all times and take responsibility for her behavior.

4. A calm-submissive dog will not attract another dog's aggression—but an excited dog, a weak, timid dog, or an aggressive dog can become a fight magnet.

5. Know your dog! If your dog has poor social skills, is overly fearful or dog aggressive, or if you have not yet established your calm-assertive leadership with your dog, find a more controlled way to introduce it to the company of other dogs, such as playdates with one or two other dog owners.

Katrina Dogs Part I

August 2005. Hurricane Katrina devastates America's Gulf Coast, causing more than four hundred thousand to flee and leaving more than thirteen hundred people dead. But there are tens of thousands of other victims left behind—the dogs of Katrina. Separated from their owners—running wild through the streets in packs, or cowering inside abandoned homes—these dogs have been through a trauma as devastating to animals as it was to people.

Lab mix rescued from Hurricane Katrina.

Cheri Lucas, the founder of the Second Chance at Love Humane Society and a longtime associate of Cesar's, volunteers to help place some of the hundreds of animals flown in from New Orleans to a holding center in Torrance, California. She brings three of the most traumatized dogs to Cesar's Dog Psychology Center: an insecure female rottweiler mix with wounds and serious skin problems and infections caused by the flood; a very anxious male Lab-dachshund mix; and an aggressive male Akita mix.

While Ilusion places ads on the Internet, searching for the dogs' owners, Cesar begins to introduce the dogs to his pack, deciding not to name them for the time being, in the hopes that they will soon be reunited with their rightful humans. His first problem, however, is that not one of the animals is neutered. "That's not going to be very easy for the whole pack, because they are sending the scent of mating, and that sends everybody into mating time mind-set. That's why it's so important to spay or neuter your dog. We have to do it for their well-being." For this reason, in addition to the dogs' traumatized states of mind, Cesar must be extra mindful as he brings the new dogs into the compound. Even the aggressive Akita must learn to be calm-submissive in this pack.

As the dogs from the Big Easy adjust to the California coast, their photos go out on the Internet, in the hope that someone, somewhere, is praying for them to come home.

Katrina Dogs Part II: The Homecoming

Lab mix Scrappy is reunited with owner Lois Davis.

Cesar has been rehabilitating three dogs rescued from Hurricane Katrina at his center. The female rottweiler, male Akita mix, and male Lab mix are doing well under Cesar's care, but all must be spayed or neutered. While the search continues for the dogs' original owners, veterinarian Dr. Debra Oliver donates her time and services and treats the Katrina dogs free of charge. Finally, with the help of the *Dog Whisperer* team and Pasado Animal Rescue, a "Katrina miracle" occurs—the owner of the Lab is found and the dog now has a name—Scrappy.

Cesar, Ilusion, and the *Dog Whisperer* team travel to Louisiana to reunite Scrappy with his owners, the Davis family. It is a tearful reunion for all involved.

Follow-up 🐾 🐾 🐾

The female rottweiler rescued from Katrina was adopted by *Tonight Show* director Ellen Brown, who named her Dee Dee. Ellen says Dee Dee is doing well but still has some issues with timidity, which Cesar believes will go away the more people practice "no touch, no talk, and no eye contact" when they interact with the dog. Second Chance at Love founder Cheri Lucas found a happy home for the male Akita with a family that has kids.

Pups on Parole

Cesar preparing a pack walk with the inmates of Pups on Parole.

In early 2005, Rachel Vosko and Lori Kearse, in association with Heaven Can Wait Sanctuary, launched Pups on Parole, a program at the Southern Nevada Women's Correctional Center that rehabilitates dogs and prisoners. The dogs are literally marked for death unless they are adopted. They are brought to the correctional center for their last chance at life. Only forty of the six hundred women at this maximum security prison are allowed in the program. They care for twenty dogs—one dog for every two cellmates.

Cesar arrives at the prison to do a two-day intensive hands-on workshop with the women in the program. Working with a captive—but enraptured—audience, he shows them how to help a fearful shepherd mix walk tall; a fear-aggressive chow mix relax, and an unsociable Chihuahua learn how to play better with others. His inspiring seminar ends with Cesar teaching all the women in the unit how to walk together with their dogs as one big pack. "I know dogs want to be together. They want to be part of a pack, a balanced pack. Hopefully today I created the awareness of becoming one whole unit to work

Follow-up ❀ ❀ ❀

The women on the Pups on Parole unit took Cesar's lessons seriously. Today, it's a daily routine for all the inmates and all the dogs to walk together as a pack.

together." Though the women are skeptical that Cesar can pull off making a calm-submissive pack out of twenty troubled dogs, they are amazed and inspired by his results. "They can be a pack as long as we're a pack and we act like pack leaders," one inmate observes. Says another, "It's a chance to give back. I mean, we're doing something bigger than we are, saving lives. And it's phenomenal. I've gotten a chance, a second chance to do a good thing."

This powerful segment shows how the power of the pack can work miracles for both wayward dogs—and wayward humans.

Behind the scenes

Cesar was so moved by his experience with the women of the Pups on Parole program, that the Dog Psychology Center donated a treadmill to the program, to underscore the importance of exercise in bringing balance back to troubled dogs—and people.

Cesar's Toughest Cases (episode 219)

For twenty years, Cesar has dealt with all types of canines, with problem dogs ranging from stubborn bulldogs to nasty little Chihuahuas to powerful breeds with red-zone aggression. In this episode, we feature several of Cesar's toughest cases. Matilda the skateboard-munching bulldog proved to be so difficult that Cesar brought in his son to help. Jordan fixated not only on skateboards, but on sprinkler hoses and basketballs as well. Eton and Dolly couldn't stop attacking each other. Josh the Maltese was such a nightmare his nickname became "the Grooming Gremlin." Vicious Min-Pin Chip wanted nothing to with anyone other than his owner, Lisa. And just when Cesar thought he was done with vicious Chihuahuas, Bandit stepped into the ring. Emily was a pit bull with severe dog aggression. Perhaps the most vicious of all was JonBee the Jindo dog. He was submissive outside but aggressive as a rattlesnake inside the house.

This special episode of *Dog Whisperer* showcases how Cesar deals with each of these unique issues.

The Power of the Pack

Cesar Millan's Dog Psychology Center is both home and refuge to nearly fifty dogs, boasting canines from celebrity clients to those deemed "unfixable" to dogs belonging to the Millan family itself. The pack is a vital tool and helps Cesar in rehabilitating a wide variety of problem dogs. Punkin's severe rock obsession was chipped away by the pack. Three Hurricane Katrina dogs were given a place to stay and to work through the problems that befell them during that devastating Gulf Coast storm. Maria Brown was aided in her training by Daddy, perhaps the most famous member of Cesar's pack. Abbie Jaye was rehabilitated with the help of a private party with a pack of pit bulls. Prada, a pampered Pomeranian, was shown the way to calm submission by Luigi, another member of the pack. With the help of Preston and Daddy the pit bull, Cesar saved a marriage. The pack even taught picky Storm how to eat and Nicky how to be friends with other dogs.

Cesar's dogs make a truly unforgettable pack and Cesar himself believes his pack teaches him new things every day. In this intimate and revealing episode, witness some memorable moments and experience the power of the pack.

Season Three

Introduction

During the third season, the *Dog Whisperer* team hit the road to find troubled canines across the country. Cesar found himself everywhere from the fields of Nebraska to the boroughs of New York City, with stops in Texas, Mexico, Georgia, Illinois, and Pennsylvania along the way.

This season, Cesar encountered many people who were fans of the show but couldn't figure out how to apply Cesar's techniques to their own dogs. Every episode of *Dog Whisperer with Cesar Millan* has this disclaimer: "Techniques presented during this program are informational in nature. For advice concerning your dog's problems, please consult a professional." This is because Cesar bases his rehabilitation strictly on the dog in front of him, and he wouldn't want viewers to use the wrong methods just because they had seen them on the show.

In order to fill twenty one-hour episodes, the *Dog Whisperer* producers cast the net far and wide to find unusual and unique issues for Cesar to tackle. These episodes included a fearful animal-testing dog, an out-of control firehouse Dalmatian, stray dogs from Tijuana, a tough-as-nails bulldog, and a young girl named Maureen who became an inspiration and gift to everyone who came under her spell.

Aggression Toward People

Australian shepherd Kobe.

Out of Bounds

Name: Kobe

Breed: Australian shepherd

Just three days after the Hoffman family brought Kobe home, the puppy got into a tragic accident and lost an eye. That was five years ago, but since then, Kobe's aggressive behavior has escalated. At this point, the Hoffmans walk on eggshells and live in isolation, because Kobe lunges at guests in the house and has already bitten three people. According to Jill Hoffman, "Most people are even afraid to come to the door." Her son Jason adds, "I'm kinda scared for Cesar, actually. I hope he can handle this one."

When Cesar speaks with the family, he senses one key problem. "They didn't completely let go of the traumatic experience Kobe had. The humans actually encouraged him to be more unstable because they feel sorry for what happened five years ago."

With the Hoffmans watching nervously from a second-floor balcony, Cesar approaches the backyard gate where Kobe awaits. As soon as Kobe starts barking, Cesar makes a quick assessment. "He challenged me when I came into his territory, but he was insecure when he challenged me. You can't back away from an insecure dog if you really want to help him."

Cesar decides to rehabilitate Kobe based on the dog's breed. "I'm going to herd him. I'm going to use a strategy that he's familiar with. So I'm going to become an Australian shepherd, a Mexican-Australian shepherd." For the next several minutes, Cesar dashes around the backyard in an attempt to herd Kobe. By the time Kobe submits to Cesar near the back porch, the winded dog shows no signs of aggression.

To help get a handle on Kobe's overprotectiveness at the front door, Cesar moves everyone inside to participate in an entryway exercise aided by one of Jill's friends. When the friend rings the doorbell, Kobe starts to bark and run to the door, but Cesar steps in front of him and backs the dog away with a firm "*tsst.*" When it's Jill's turn, she struggles with the timing of the correction. After several tries, Jill is able to make Kobe back away from the door and sit quietly while she invites her friend into the house.

Cesar gives the family homework that includes taking Kobe on long walks every day and no longer letting him control the house. Jill says, "I feel so empowered that we're going to be able to have a dog that's going to be normal, and we're going to work really hard at making him be the best he can be."

Follow-up ❀ ❀ ❀

Cesar made a return visit to show the Hoffmans how to make Kobe behave around other dogs. When the family continued to have some troubles weeks later, the show's producers arranged for a dog trainer familiar with Cesar's methods to continue to help the Hoffmans. Jill continues to walk Kobe every day but still has challenges with him.

The Overprotective Guard Dog

Name: Buster

Breed: blue heeler mix

(episode 302)

In the rural farming community of Juniata, Nebraska, three dogs help protect the home of Aimee and Justin Burch. Two of the canines—Chihuahua Mickie and papillon mix Jackson—perform their dog duties as expected. Buster, a blue heeler mix, also known as an Australian cattle dog, does more than just take a bite out of crime. According to Aimee, "I did not realize Buster would be biting everyone who drove into our driveway. Most everybody I know does not come to my house without calling first." The Burches' good friend Scott Anderson is one of Buster's victims. Buster has chased Scott several times and bitten him as well. "I usually end up in the back of my truck or running for the house," says Scott.

Cattle dogs like blue heelers were originally bred to herd livestock, not houseguests. Cesar tells them, "This is a good example of a dog that is territorial. But blue heelers target the cattle's heel and they wait until you turn around. So it's territorial combined with being a cattle dog."

When Cesar heads outside to meet Buster, he brings along a tennis racquet as well as a plastic bottle filled with rocks. "The racquet is just to protect myself from him charging me. I shake a bottle of rocks whenever he moves away from me, and that only intensifies his retreat behavior." Although Buster does take a few lunges at Cesar, within three minutes the dog has completely backed away.

Scott arrives in his truck, triggering another outburst from Buster. Cesar shows everyone how to make Buster back off when he goes into attack mode. When Buster uses his doghouse as an attack launching point, Cesar holds the racquet at the door of the doghouse, and when Buster lunges, the only thing he touches is the racquet. "I'm just moving the racquet around. I'm not shoving it in. I want to psychologically challenge him. When you can't control an animal physically, it's best if you do it psychologically,"

Follow-up ❦ ❦ ❦

The Burch family reports that Buster is getting regular walks and no longer pulls or challenges them. They are still working on his issues with people who come to the door—but these days, he's more bark than bite.

explains Cesar. Cesar suggests that Justin and Aimee firmly say no each time Buster tries to bite the racquet, until he gets the message to stop the behavior.

Scott takes the tennis racquet, goes back to his truck, and tries this technique himself. Within two minutes, Buster has backed away, and Scott enters the house without getting nipped. Aimee is thrilled. As they stand outside before Cesar leaves, Aimee starts to cry. "It's just a relief to know that we'll be able to have people over, have a normal life. And he's still a good dog." When Cesar tells Aimee, "So pretty much what you have to do is to buy a whole bunch of racquets and give one to everybody who comes here," she replies. "We'll keep one at the mailbox."

Blood, Sweat & Tears

Name: Butch

Breed: English bulldog

(episode 304)

When Texans Chap and Amy Reed answered an ad for Butch in their local newspaper, they discovered that the English bulldog had recently been attacked by two dogs, and his wounds were infected. "There wasn't one place on Butch's body that did not have a wound or a sore on it because of the attack," says Amy. It took two months for the Reeds to nurse Butch back to health. After another two months, their former convalescent turned fiercely aggressive. Because Butch is such a loud sleeper, Amy moved his bed from the Reeds' bedroom into the kitchen. Butch didn't take this relocation well. When it comes time for bed, Butch plays possum until the Reeds try to coax him into the kitchen. Then he growls and tries to bite both Chap and Amy. Although Chap owns a golf cart, it is now under Butch's command. When Chap attempts to drive the cart, Butch attacks Chap's feet. He has also left nasty scars all over Chap's legs.

Cesar and Chap work on Butch's hose issue.

When Cesar arrives, Amy admits that they coddled Butch during his recuperation and let him do whatever he wanted, so now he sees them as weak. Chap tells Cesar that when Butch gets out of line, "I'll hold him down, get on top of him, stare him eye to eye, stare him down. Every other dog I've owned, if you stare the dog down, that dog will submit." Cesar replies, "But that's a different breed. Bulldogs are a fighting breed, so they have an extra boost. That's why they can go into a zone where they don't feel the pain anymore. They'd rather die than surrender." Cesar informs Chap that he can't control Butch's anger by being angry himself.

When Cesar starts to work with Butch in the living room, he slips a leash over the top of the dog's neck to gain maximum control. When Cesar leads Butch to the kitchen, Butch goes into a violent rage, and Cesar has to calmly and assertively hold Butch down while the dog battles. "Like a good bulldog, he's going to put up a fight,

Follow-up ❀ ❀ ❀

It took twenty-six days before Chap was finally able to control Butch at the golf cart. Chap and Amy became Butch's grateful pack leaders until the dog died of a heart attack. Amy wrote to the *Dog Whisperer* team:

We will always be so grateful and appreciative of the opportunity that MPH & Cesar Millan gave to us by helping our family to make Butch a happy, well-adjusted dog. With Cesar's help we all became happy, Butch the happiest. Cesar gave our family unit hope and a goal. Our goal was reached and we never reverted back to our old ways. Within the past four months, Butch has not had to be submitted once. A look or a calm-assertive command was all it took. He had become the perfect dog. Cesar taught us all, including Butch, how to respect each other and how to become pack leaders so we could live happily ever after. What a reach for a star dream that actually came true!

that's why they are bulldogs. But we want to create limitations so they no longer live in that state."

After Butch submits to Cesar inside the house, they head outside to face another Butch enemy, the dreaded garden hose. When Butch grabs the hose, Cesar shows Chap and Amy how to safely place a thumb in the corner of Butch's mouth in order to get him to release the hose. But after Cesar starts to put the hose near Butch again, the dog bites him. "I got bitten today because I went over the limit. That was my mistake. I don't have a problem making a mistake, because that's how I learn."

Butch's rehabilitation continues at the golf cart. When Butch starts to make a move to protect the cart, Cesar physically challenges Butch in exactly the same way another bulldog would physically challenge him—by "biting" Butch on the neck with three fingers. "That's what bulldogs do, they chest each other back. The farther away he gets, the less powerful he becomes. And I'm taking my time so I can defeat him at his game."

Under the blazing Texas sun, Cesar worked inside and outside the house for three hours to achieve a calm-submissive Butch. But Cesar emphasizes that it's not quantity but quality that matters when you're dealing with a dog. "Today was just to show you the possibilities. I think repetitions of this day will create what you really want. Because it was repetitions of what you did before that created a bigger monster."

Freeing Sara

Name: Sara

Breed: shepherd mix

(episode 305)

"At first it was just barking. Sara would just bark at people. But now she's charging people head-on," says a worried Gina Felix. Gina brought Sara home from a local Texas shelter as a companion for her other dog, Sam. The two dogs get along great, but when visitors come to call, Sara turns into a biting machine. "Sara has bitten my mother twice. She bit an air conditioner repairman on his calf, and Sam bit his heel. The fact that Sam may be influenced by Sara makes me scared." Gina's life now revolves around Sara and she says that if Cesar can't help her, "Then this is going to be my life until Sara passes away. So I'll deal with it."

Gina watches Cesar work with Sam and Sara.

When Cesar meets with Gina and her mother, Monna, he tells them, "I'm going to be in Dallas for one day, so you better show me all your dirty clothes. Y'all better tell me the truth." Gina admits that she's not her dogs' pack leader, and she lets them walk in front of her for most of the walk. Monna confesses that she lets Sam jump all over her when she comes to visit.

During the consultation, Sara and Sam have been locked up in the back bedroom, the only place Gina dares to keep them when having company over. When Cesar opens the door to that room, the dogs begin barking ferociously. Cesar picks up that the dogs aren't as aggressive as they are fearful. "How did I know? I heard the way they were barking, and the way they were barking was saying, 'We're insecure, but this is how we solve insecurity. Most of the time people surrender to us, so we are insecure, dominant dogs.'"

After a couple of minutes, both dogs calm down and Cesar brings them out into the living room. Cesar notices that when Sara's cycle of aggression begins, she's actually going through the motions of guarding Gina. At that moment, Cesar gives Sara a

Sara is doing a lot better. Occasionally she still barks at people in the house, but most of Gina's friends can now pet her. She isn't charging people like she used to. But even though Gina went to a trainer to help her with the walk, Sara still walks in front of her. Gina now believes she chose a dog with more energy than she has, but she's committed to Sara's exercise program and is thinking of taking her to agility classes.

correction and tells Gina, "I stop the brain at Level 1. That's the rules. So she almost broke the rules, and I addressed it right away. And then I stayed there until she surrendered and then she realized, 'Oh, what he wants is for me to surrender.'"

Cesar tells Gina what she needs to do in order to achieve balance in her house. "You have to be in control every single second," he says. "That sounds like a lot of work," Gina replies. Smiling, Cesar tells her, "Well, life is work, lady."

The Art of Dexter

Name: Dexter

Breed: rottweiler–shepherd mix

(episode 312)

Four years ago in the Windy City of Chicago, Dexter, a rottweiler–shepherd mix, joined artist Mary Jane Duffy, her boyfriend, Shiro, and their other dog, Marnie. Then the troubles began. Dexter spins and barks whenever he encounters dogs, bikes, Rollerbladers, skateboarders, or runners on their walks. Mary Jane is constantly on the lookout to prevent a potential fight. Mary Jane has now become fearful of her own dog, which has prompted Dexter to start biting her. Dexter is in the red zone, and it's only getting worse.

Cesar bikes with Dexter.

Since Dexter didn't have such severe issues when he first arrived, Cesar sees Mary Jane's own fear and insecurity as a big part of the problem. He encourages her to apply her artist's training to her dog's rehabilitation. "We have to project and to create in the mind what we want from the dog and what we want from us. Just like a painting. You create it in your mind first, and then you start painting and say, 'Ah, that's how I wanted it.'"

Since Mary Jane's dream is to someday be able to walk Dexter muzzle free, Cesar takes him out without it, using the Illusion collar to retain greater control. He begins by addressing one of the main triggers of Dexter's unwanted behavior, enlisting the help of two skateboarding neighbors. Using his calm energy, he gradually gets Dexter to settle down a little. Next, he brings in Daddy the pit bull to assess the level of Dexter's dog aggression. Everything goes well until he passes the leash to Mary Jane, whose split-second hesitation causes Dexter to explode again. Cesar decides to exercise Dexter, to try to drain some of his frustrated energy.

A more tired and relaxed Dexter does better with Mary Jane, but he still goes berserk at the sound of the skateboard, so Cesar goes back to the muzzle. "If he bites, he

Follow-up ❁ ❁ ❁

Mary Jane has worked hard on helping Dexter through consistent exercise—she even began running with him two and a half miles, six days a week. She has made improvements in several areas and says that he is much better, but sometimes she still feels overwhelmed by his issues. As a result, Mary Jane will be bringing Dexter to Cesar's Dog Psychology Center soon. That event will be taped and the results presented during the *Dog Whisperer*'s fourth season.

wins," he explains. Gradually, Mary Jane begins to become more calm and assertive.

Three days later, when Cesar returns for a follow-up session, he finds Mary Jane calmer and more relaxed but still frustrated that she can't get the same degree of control over Dexter that Cesar has. Taking Dexter for an energy-draining bike ride around the block, he sees such an improvement in the dog's attitude that he invites Mary Jane to jump on her own bike and join them. "He likes it when we're moving faster," Cesar observes. "It's easier to keep the mind of a dog focused when speed is present, but it doesn't matter if you change the speed if your energy is not different."

Acknowledging that Dexter's rehab will be a long-term project for Mary Jane, Cesar leaves her with one more tool to work with—a two-leash technique for walking together with her boyfriend, so they can share control over Dexter. Even though she knows she has her work cut out for her, Mary Jane is finally hopeful about Dexter's future. "I am a visual person, so I can pull up that image of him just walking calmly at my side and not reacting to things, and if I can visualize that, then I believe that it will happen."

The King Kong Story

Name: Nasir

Breed: South African boerboel

Grammy Award–wining recording artist Patti LaBelle is no stranger to big dogs, having owned rottweilers and Cane Corsos over the years. But three years ago, Ms. Labelle's manager gave her a South African boerboel named Nasir. Patti showered Nasir with affection as a puppy, but as he grew bigger and more aggressive, she began to fear him. Nasir has chased Ms. LaBelle off her own patio and broken through a screen door to get at her. Susan Rosetti, Patti's senior dog handler, called every boerboel rescue organization to find Nasir a home, but everyone recommended euthanizing him. Susan placed him

Patti LaBelle with Cesar while Nasir barks in the background.

in three different homes, but he was returned each time. Susan is willing to take Nasir if he can be integrated successfully into her own pack, but even she is concerned about the 150-pound dog's aggression.

When Cesar arrives at Patti LaBelle's Philadelphia home, he sits outside Nasir's kennel, offering his back so the dog doesn't feel threatened. But Cesar immediately sees that aggression isn't Nasir's problem—it's insecurity. "Everybody gets intimidated by the size," he explains. "They don't get to feel insecurity. They don't get to feel nervousness. They just see aggression. But size doesn't mean anything." Cesar explains that insecure dogs can also become very dangerous because they can attack for no reason at all. "He needs to be reborn with the pack so he can gain back common sense." Ms. LaBelle is thrilled that Cesar invites Nasir to make the cross-country trip back to L.A., but before they go, she gets to enjoy the beautiful experience of hand-feeding her dog for the first time in his and her lives.

"I didn't know you were a little nervous, baby. I really didn't know. I had no clue for

Follow-up ❀ ❀ ❀

Susan reports that although Nasir keeps her on her toes, she is able to be Nasir's calm-assertive pack leader.

three and a half years," Patti tells Nasir, tears in her eyes. "I'm blaming you for things that are not your fault. I'm sorry. I swear to you, I'm sorry."

Patti's trainer, Susan Rosetti, and Nasir make the drive to Los Angeles. At the Dog Psychology Center, Nasir actually becomes a calming influence to all the other dogs. "We really need Nasir because his energy creates a lot of peace." Cesar trains Nasir to pull a cart—giving this working breed a much-needed "job" to do. "There're so many options we can have before we think about euthanasia," Cesar says of Nasir's progress. "We have to learn to redirect energy. We can't just say animals are aggressive, let's kill them. Because Nasir is showing us, 'Look, you can't just kill me because I'm big and have developed aggression. Just show me what to do with that energy!'"

After nearly two months at the center, Cesar feels Nasir is ready to return to Philadelphia and be integrated into his new pack—Susan and her boyfriend, Bobby, plus their five cats and three dogs. Nasir is fine, but one of the couple's dogs, Pete, has an excited, dominant energy that Cesar points out may cause problems. He coaches the couple on how to keep an eye on the group to defuse tensions before they arise. Finally, Ms. LaBelle arrives to do what she's not dared do in three years—walk her beautiful boerboel and wish him well in his new life. "Thank you for Cesar," Patti LaBelle looks up to the heavens and proclaims, "Hallelujah! Thank you."

The Trouble with Titan

Name: Titan

Breed: rottweiler

Engineers Julie Souders and Bo Istrate adopted Titan, a two-year-old rottweiler, from the Lancaster, California, pound, but four years later, the 120-pound dog displays aggression to strangers when they try to touch him. He is also aggressive when people turn away from him when he smells or nudges them. If strangers ignore him, Titan will leave them alone, but Julie and Bo want to trust Titan and not be afraid of people approaching or touching him.

Titan tries sheep herding.

Cesar witnesses Titan's aggression from the moment he arrives, when Titan lunges at a *Dog Whisperer* production assistant. He learns that Julie and Bo don't walk Titan much, and when they do, they take only specific routes that avoid possible triggers to Titan's aggression. Instead, they play tug-of-war games with Titan which, Cesar points out, will only intensify his dominant instincts. Bo and Julie also admit they haven't let him socialize with other animals, for fear that he'll attack them.

Cesar takes Titan outside and uses his calm-submissive dogs Louis and Sid to assess Titan's social skills. Titan doesn't attack them, but his unstable energy causes Louis to run away, which brings out Titan's prey drive. Cesar decides Titan needs a more intensive course in canine social etiquette and invites him for a two-month stay at the Dog Psychology Center.

At the center, Titan gets the full treatment—forty canine friends to teach him the rules and manners of the pack, extensive daily exercise, and quality pool time with Cesar. In addition, Cesar makes a video diary for Bo and Julie, including a how-to (starring his kids and *Dog Whisperer* crew members) showing them the proper way to

Follow-up ❧ ❧ ❧

Julie and Bo are now much more confident in dealing with Titan. They got a puppy recently, an eight-month-old boxer, and the dogs are getting along fine. They tell people no touch, no talk, and no eye contact with Titan until he is calm-submissive. Only then do they allow people to come near.

Behind the scenes

Production assistant Todd Henderson once again became a victim when Titan leaped up and hit Todd hard in the crotch with his paw. Todd is relentlessly teased about this incident by the *DW* crew and they consider Todd the show's "stunt crotch."

introduce Titan to strangers. In the tape, Cesar points out how to spot the split second Titan begins to think about a strike, and how to stop one before it occurs. He even gets a field trip to Long Beach All-Breed Herding, where he can call up the herding instincts in his rottweiler genes and use this breed-related activity to release his frustrations. Titan is a natural in the herding ring.

Before he returns Titan to his home, Cesar wants to test him at one of the places where his aggression has been the worst—at the vet's. This time, Titan is a model patient, as Cesar illustrates to Bo and Julie how they, the owners, can help the vet by remaining calm and assertive at all times. "You are the source of his energy." By exercising him more, learning how to read his aggression signals, and become less tentative pack leaders, the couple will be able to mold Titan into the perfect pet. "Watching Cesar's tape, we realized we were giving him only a portion of what he needs from us," Julie muses. "The ultimate goal is obviously to just open up Titan's life."

The Not So Merry Kerry Blue Terry

Name: Bodhi

Breed: Kerry blue terrier

(episode 316)

Five-year-old Kerry blue terrier Bodhi was great when he first joined the family of Sarah and Alan Roth, but over the years he has developed an unpredictable aggression. Now their two-and-a-half-year-old son Troy has become an occasional target for Bodhi, and Sarah and Alan are worried for his safety. The Roths hired a professional trainer who used positive reinforcement, but that didn't help at all—Bodhi bit one of the neighbors while trying to "protect" Troy. The Kerry blue terrier has now developed a major problem with visitors when they try to leave the house. They can't even say the word "good-bye" without some sort of aggressive reaction from the dog. The Roths have used shock collars, choke chains, praise methods, and treats, but none have worked.

Early in the consultation, Cesar learns that the Roths don't walk Bodhi and allow him to drain his energy playing rope tug-of-war in the backyard. "That's not good. You actually are helping him to practice the killing part of it, or the dominance part, and releasing the frustration that way." Cesar informs the Roths that Bodhi is clearly a very high-energy guy, and he's extremely frustrated and bored. So he's finding negative ways to release his anxiety. "He's saying, 'You guys don't entertain me. I'm gonna entertain myself by keeping people away,'" Cesar explains. "It's part of the terrier mentality. You know? It's not Bodhi right then. It's the breed in him that says, 'Well, look, this is what Kerry blue terriers do.'"

When Cesar first meets Bodhi, it's clear to him that a lot of Bodhi's aggression also comes from insecurity. And the long hair over the dog's eyes is only intensifying that. Cesar gives Bodhi a little trim, and the improvement in the dog's attitude is immediate. "See, now you can see eyes. See how he's looking at me? That's a conversation right there. If you don't see my eyes, you can't see my soul. You can't see my energy."

Cesar works with the couple at the site of some of Bodhi's worst aggression—their front door—to observe their style with him. Sarah picks up the concept of calm-assertive leadership much faster than Alan. But since Bodhi is aggressive with other dogs and has poor social skills, Cesar wants him to come to the Dog Psychology Center,

Follow-up ❀ ❀ ❀

Bodhi has improved greatly, but whenever he doesn't get enough exercise, Sarah finds it much harder to control him.

where he can learn from the best teachers in the world—other dogs. At the center, Bodhi gets structure, exercise, and the chance to act differently in situations that used to threaten him. "Bodhi did great from day one. He adapted, he adjusted, he became part of my pack. In a matter of minutes he just gave up all the baggage, all the issues, all the insecurities, all the frustration. He gave that up. He said, 'You know what? I want to be a balanced dog.'"

When the Roths return to pick him up, Bodhi is a changed dog—but the Roths have to change, too. Cesar Rollerblades with them through his South L.A. neighborhood, teaching them how to help Bodhi when they encounter strange dogs, off-leash dogs, and other obstacles. The Roths are relieved and grateful. "You know, I was starting to get to where I didn't like him anymore," Sarah admits. "And I didn't want to feel like that. And now I already feel different, and I can see he acts different." "When you transform yourself," Cesar concludes, "you transform everything around you."

Lucy Loves Schroeder

Name: Schroeder

Breed: Lhasa apso mix

Lucy had a perfect Lhasa apso named Charlie Brown and says she almost died of sadness when she had to put him down at the age of eighteen. Shortly thereafter, Lucy scoured the internet for the perfect rescue dog and came upon another irresistible Lhasa apso named Schroeder. The rescue person was hesitant to give Lucy a dog so quickly after Charlie's death, but she ultimately decided to let Lucy adopt Schroeder.

Cesar trains Lucy to walk Schroeder with an assist from Daddy.

Schroeder had been taken from his previous owners because they neglected him, and since the day of his arrival, he's been a handful. Lucy tries to incorporate Cesar's methods and walks her dog for forty-five minutes every day with one of Cesar's Illusion collars, but Schroeder still tries to attack passing people and dogs. "When we go out into the world, it's very embarrassing. I know what people are thinking. They're saying, 'Why doesn't she go call the Dog Whisperer?' I feel like they're saying that, so I did."

The moment Cesar arrives, he gets to witness one of Schroeder's outbursts at the door as Lucy tries to hold him back with the leash. Cesar suggests that Lucy drop the leash, because when Schroeder strains against it, the tension can create even more aggression. Using Daddy and Louis from his pack, Cesar asks Ilusion to walk the two dogs nearby as an exercise to correct Schroeder's charging behavior. "Charging is an antisocial behavior, sniffing is a social behavior," says Cesar, giving Schroeder a quick correction with the leash just as he starts to lunge. When Schroeder calms down and starts to smell Louis, Cesar turns Louis around so Schroeder can sniff his rear. "You don't put them face to face, you put the rear in front. When they're face to face, they're more

Follow-up ❁ ❁ ❁

Lucy had a brief setback when Schroeder was attacked by a larger dog while on a walk. Fortunately, the thickness of the Illusion collar prevented Schroeder from receiving any puncture wounds when the dog bit his neck. Lucy believes the Illusion collar saved Schroeder's life. As she continues to work with Schroeder, her dog is becoming better and better behaved.

likely to create eye contact. So instead we're telling the brain, "Look, brain, this is how you meet dogs."

Lucy learns quickly and is able to give Schroeder quick and properly timed corrections after just a few tries. According to Cesar, "She knew a lot, she just didn't know how to put it into practice. And when she put it into practice, she wasn't paying attention to her timing and to her energy, and that's what I focused on today."

Lucy is thrilled by the results. "There's nothing like having Cesar right here showing you exactly what you're doing wrong. And I've never had Schroeder so close to other dogs as we did. We had a whole little pack going there."

Chapter 15

Aggression Toward Dogs and Other Animals

Cesar corrects Sophie in front of Gayle, John, and Crystal's dad.

Dueling Basset Hounds

(episode 306)

Names: Riley and Sophie

Breed: basset hound

In December of 2004, Crystal and John Klooz welcomed two basset hounds into their home—Riley, an eight-week-old pup, and Sophie, a three-year-old rescue dog just days away from euthanasia. From the time they brought Sophie home, there were problems. Sophie attacks and bites Riley over food, treats, or any attention from Crystal and John. "There've been so many times that Sophie's gone after Riley and bitten her and drawn blood, I can't count. I'm afraid that Sophie will get hold of Riley and take an eye out, take her life, just hurt her so bad that we couldn't save her," says Crystal.

Follow-up ❀ ❀ ❀

Crystal was dedicated to helping Sophie, so she went to work changing herself first. She changed her eating habits and began a boot camp workout program. As Crystal's anxiety level went down, she was able to be more patient and calm-assertive with the dogs. After Cesar's visit, Sophie went seven weeks without attacking Riley, then four months without an attack. Crystal says that Cesar's philosophy is helping her as well as the dogs.

Behind the scenes

Crystal's dad works as Santa Claus, and he now uses Cesar's calm-assertive techniques to calm kids when they're afraid or acting up.

Key Cesar Tip

By worrying that a dog attack might happen, you can actually contribute to creating a dog attack. Remember to live in the moment and trust that you can handle any situation that occurs.

Crystal's parents have their own pack of dogs, and when Riley and Sophie visit, Sophie fights and bites those dogs as well. As avid watchers of *Dog Whisperer*, the Kloozes tried using Cesar's techniques, but so far they have not been successful. When Cesar first talks to the couple, Crystal admits to being a generally anxious person. "I'm nervous, tense even when I'm not around them. I'm nervous at work, I'm nervous going to somebody's house." Cesar replies, "You're being very honest, which I like. You're nervous and you get anxious, and pack leaders are not anxious or nervous."

Cesar's toughest challenge in this case is to teach Crystal how to access her own calm-assertive energy. First, he demonstrates how to correct Sophie by "biting" her on the neck with his fingers even when she just gives Riley an intense look. The first time she gets a correction, Sophie rolls right onto her back into a submission position. Next, Cesar teaches Crystal and John how to remove Riley's fear by showing Riley they are in-control pack leaders. Cesar gives Riley a bone and lets him chew it while Sophie watches from a few feet away. Sophie stays calm, so Cesar rewards her with a bone, too.

They all travel to Crystal's parents' nearby house to try to teach Sophie how to get along with the two Labs and three dachshunds that make up John and Gayle Raida's pack. Cesar notices potential trouble right away. "It was a very chaotic situation, and then Sophie comes into this chaotic situation. She's not going to get the benefit of being with a pack because the pack is not balanced." Sure enough, Sophie attacks one of the dogs and Cesar makes the bassett hound lie on her side and then brings the dog she attacked right next to her. "When a dog is going to teach another dog a lesson, he pins it on the ground and keeps it there, so that's what we did. We grabbed Sophie and made her stay there. She had to finish in a surrendering mode."

Cesar's message comes through loud and clear for Crystal. "Cesar is amazing. When he had some problems, he worked through them and kept on going. He didn't lose his cool, he stayed calm and assertive, and that's my goal. I want to be like that."

No Peace in the House

Name/Breed: Lulu/poodle mix

Name/Breed: Sasha/Maltese

Name/Breed: Bebe/Pomeranian-Chihuahua mix

Lulu is the "first child" of Jeffery Palmer and Ace Champion, but she acts like the baby. Lulu is continuously possessive of Jeffery—and the addition of Sasha and Bebe into the family has seemed to make matters worse. Lulu is often aggressive toward the other two dogs. She won't share her toys and gets upset if Sasha or Bebe sits on Jeffery's lap. The family can't even make it through one quiet night at home without a dogfight or a barkfest. "It just gets so loud, and then I've had enough and I'm like, 'Quiet! Shut up, everybody!' So I would like to have a little bit more calmness," Jeffery laments. Ace is a little concerned about Cesar's visit, saying, "I just don't know if Jeff will be able to handle it. He might like freak out or something because he's very emotional with those dogs, and I'll have to hold him back."

Cesar believes that since humans and dogs are both pack-oriented species, humans need to take on the role of pack leaders; otherwise a dog may attempt to take that position. But Jeffery is concerned about disciplining the dogs because "it feels like I'm being mean." Cesar tells him, "I totally understand that yelling, that's not a balanced kind of discipline. So if you're disciplining somebody with frustration and anger, it's not a good thing. You can't create quietness with frustration." When Cesar hears that the dogs get walks only once a month, he says, "Now that's mean!"

Follow-up ❁ ❁ ❁

Jeffery and Ace are walking the dogs every day, and their behavior has dramatically improved.

While they sit on the couch, Cesar witnesses a three-dog dustup and splits it up right away, with his attention focused mostly on Lulu. "You can stop her the same way I did. Anything that you don't like, you go '*tsst.*' Since they don't have rules, it's taking more than two times for them to get the picture. '*Tsst.*' So it's not so much what you're saying, it's the energy behind what you're saying. At the same time, you are not exercising them. So the only activity they have is to fight for you. As soon as you're peaceful, they're going to imitate your energy."

Ace says, "The lightbulb went on for me when I realized that it was actually us, not the dogs. It's all in our attitudes." Cesar prescribes a daily half-hour walk for Jeffery, Ace, and their three dogs, and to calmly and assertively enforce new rules in the house. "They have a very simple case, and I really hope that they embrace the knowledge today, because I like the journey that Jeffery is on. He wants peace. I like that. I think everybody should look for peace."

Key Cesar Tip

Giving firm rules, boundaries, and limitations to a dog will not harm its spirit. As pack animals, dogs look to a leader to set the rules for the pack.

The Life of Riley

Name: Riley

Breed: mastiff

(episode 307)

"*She's on this* earth to be treated like a princess and we're supposed to make her life wonderful and great," Jessica Sitomer says with a laugh, describing her 125-pound mastiff, Riley. Jessica and her boyfriend, Sean Waxman, find that while Riley is a sweetheart inside the house, she turns into a demon when they hit the streets. That's when Riley becomes frighteningly aggressive to mail carriers, skateboarders, and other dogs. Jessica is a professional career coach and Sean trains athletes. But even with their combined professional training, they still can't manage to get control over Riley.

Cesar tells the couple that Riley's size is not the issue. "A Chihuahua can control a bigger dog. So it's not the size of the body, it's the projection of the mind. It doesn't matter if you can bench-press a thousand pounds. If at that moment you are in a weak state of mind, your body means nothing."

Cesar also wonders whether Sean and Jessica's discipline of Riley during her outbursts is actually more like punishment. "When parents discipline children with fear, aggression, or frustration, they're punishing the children, not disciplining them. Discipline comes from a calm-assertive state." Jessica replies, "Oh, then there's no discipline in this house." Cesar wants Sean and Jessica to use their skills as coaches when working with Riley. "Because you are my pack leader when you are my coach, I'm going to follow you. So the best situation you can have is for me to be in an active-submissive state in order for me to do whatever you're saying."

Cesar begins with Jessica because she has the most trouble controlling Riley on walks. One of Jessica's friends agrees to walk by with her dogs to help the rehabilitation process. Cesar teaches Jessica to pick one side of the sidewalk in such situations and make sure to calmly own it. Cesar also recommends that Jessica keep Riley's leash short, which will give her better control over her huge dog. It takes Jessica several attempts, but she is finally able to walk Riley by the other dogs without a struggle.

Once Jessica has experienced walking the new, balanced Riley, Cesar enlists her help in coaching Sean. Jessica observes Sean working with Riley and says, "He shouldn't be repeating the 'sit, sit' so much. It's not so much about the voice as much as his energy, so his voice sounds very frustrated with her." Cesar comments, "Once Jessica went into a coach mode, then she stepped out of the picture. She was able to see why it wasn't working. She wasn't blaming Sean, which I love. She was just showing me and telling me, 'This is why it's not working.'" By calling up his experience as a bouncer in a nightclub, Sean also gets the hang of properly disciplining Riley.

Jessica and Sean realize that with her strength and his energy, they will make the perfect calm-assertive team when walking Riley from now on.

Follow-up ❧ ❧ ❧

Jessica is very happy with her progress with Riley. She has realized her dream of bringing Riley to the park in Manhattan Beach, where she can control Riley despite loud trucks, skateboards, and people with other dogs. Riley remains well behaved and they have accomplished what Jessica used to think was impossible.

Break-Up Dogs

Names: Chip, Hope, and JoyJoy

Breed: Jack Russell terrier

Jack Russell terriers Hope, JoyJoy, and Chip.

Nurse Shelby Ahrling is the proud owner of three Jack Russell terriers, collecting them one at a time after a series of three romantic breakups. Shelby is now in a happy relationship with Dr. Greg Suelzle, but life with her dogs is anything but stable. After she was attacked at the dog park, female Hope—her second dog—suddenly developed an uncontrollable aggression toward other dogs. Then JoyJoy—the third dog and Hope and Chip's offspring—seemed to pick up Hope's newly aggressive behavior. If Shelby pets any of the dogs, they will fight each other, vying for Shelby's attention. They are extremely dog aggressive, barking with insane fury at dogs that pass outside the window. After Greg brought his Italian greyhound Kobe into this wild pack, that previously calm canine also started lunging at other dogs.

After listening to Shelby's story, Cesar tells her, "JoyJoy is dominant, Chip is territorial, Hope is aggressive. So all those things are really bad; it only leads them into fights." Cesar is pleased that Shelby Rollerblades with her dogs on her days off, but he's concerned that the dogs are not getting proper discipline. During the consultation, the dogs start to fight and Cesar breaks up the ruckus by giving Hope a "bite" on her neck with his fingers and giving a firm "*tsst.*"

Cesar demonstrates a way to handle the dogs when they misbehave—he picks two of them up by the scruff of the neck. "This is what works for me. I grab just the way the mother would grab them in the beginning. By my lifting them from their neck, touching them with a calm-assertive energy, this makes them surrender. Especially with little dogs—you can't do this with rottweilers and German shepherds!"

When Cesar tests Shelby's dogs by having two neighborhood canines walk by the window in plain view, he notices that Hope is the main troublemaker. Cesar touches

Hope on the neck and makes her back away from the window. "Discipline is two steps: you address and then you follow through. I used Hope as an example to the rest of the pack. I used her, their pack leader, to let the others know that I am now their pack leader." Greg remarks, "I've never seen calm like this, looking at dogs through the window."

Next, Cesar happily takes everyone out for a skating session. "Here is the first client on the show that actually Rollerblades. And that was a nice thing. That was actually the best thing that could happen for me today."

Shelby learns an important lesson from Cesar's visit. "I have come to see now that it is Hope who is more of the problem. So I will be taking Hope out to walk by herself and help her learn techniques to be calm just with me first so she'll be a better leader for them."

Follow-up

Shelby is Rollerblading with her pack four times a week and is now able to keep her Jack Russell pack under control. Hope, Chip, and JoyJoy get along well these days, with only occasional issues cropping up. On long walks, Shelby is able to stop and make the pack sit and obey her. She is very happy with what she has learned; in fact, Shelby has become such a good Dog Whisperer that she is now helping friends and family with their dogs.

Key Cesar Tip

If you have more than one dog that is out of control, address yourself first to the dog that's creating the unwanted behavior.

Day Care Nightmare

Name: Fondue

Breed: French bulldog

(episode 308)

Ben Sutor and Michelle Le Doux have serious day care issues. According to Ben, "We both work in the entertainment industry, so we both have to travel and we have very unpredictable schedules and very long hours. So we need to be able to board our dogs and for them to be healthy enough to do that." Their Lab mix Jasper isn't a problem, but the newest addition to their family, Fondue, doesn't play well with others, especially at the first doggie day care they tested. After the staff member let Fondue roam with just one other dog for a short test, Ben recalls, "He brought out Fondue and he said, 'Your dog wants to eat other dogs. He really wants to kill other dogs.'" The couple has actually turned down work while struggling—unsuccessfully—to get Fondue's behavior under control. "My first feature film that I worked on is premiering in a film festival, and I don't think I can go," says Ben.

Ben admits to Cesar that he gets frustrated and angry when Fondue tries to attack other dogs. Cesar tells him, "You can't correct your dog's behavior until you correct your own behavior. It's impossible to motivate or inspire somebody when you're in an equal state of mind. So anger is not going block or redirect a red-zone dog."

Cesar starts the couple with a simple walk through the neighborhood to evaluate Fondue's level of aggression and Ben's correction techniques. When they come across a barking dog behind a fence, Fondue starts to explode. Cesar takes over, walking Fondue closer to the fence and making him sit calmly with his back to the barking dog. "The thing is, he has to be sitting down, relaxing, looking away. Not sitting down looking at the dog." It takes Cesar about four minutes before he has Fondue lying calmly near the other dog and looking away. Ben repeats the exercise eight times before he can walk Fondue up to the fence and make him sit down facing away from the dog without any kind of negative reaction. Ben says, "I realized that what I was doing was trying to project calm-assertiveness without actually feeling calm or assertive at all."

Over the next seven weeks, Ben and Michelle work hard to change Fondue's behavior, though they suffer another setback when Fondue gets into a fight at a different doggie day care. To boost Ben's confidence, Cesar invites him to the Dog Psychology Center to watch Fondue interact with a calm-submissive pack. Cesar notes, "Ben says that Fondue failed, but when dogs sometimes "fail" at a day care center, it's not always the dogs. A lot of day care centers, they have this very excited state of mind environment. So dogs like Fondue would not be able to be in there with that pack. So it's very important that a calm-submissive state of mind is there when a new dog comes into the picture."

When Fondue meets Cesar's pack, there are no fights, just a bunch of calm-submissive dogs sniffing each other. Cesar tells Ben, "It's important for a new dog to be welcomed with different energy." Ben is happy to see that peace with other dogs is possible, "That's so terrific to see, because when we started this whole thing, we didn't think he was capable of that."

The Case of Cat vs. Dog

(episode 314)

Name/Breed: Bella/terrier mix

Name/Breed: FoFo/Birman (cat)

Soap star and director Michael Damian and his producer wife, Janeen, have both had a quiet home life with their cat, FoFo. But when they added a five-month-old puppy, Bella, to the mix, the household descended into chaos. When the rambunctious puppy sees the fluffy feline, she tears after her, stopping at nothing until she reaches the cat. It's been two months, and fearful FoFo has retreated to the back of her kitty condo.

Cesar arrives to help the couple get past the age-old rivalry of cat vs. dog. He sees right away that Michael and Janeen are trying to "love" both cat and dog into a more peaceful situation, but in this case, love isn't enough. "When a dog goes into a prey mode, a cat is prey. In order for you to block that behavior, you have to be authority figures. You can't just be 'dog lovers.' Dog lovers cannot block instinctual behavior."

Observing the cat and dog together, Cesar notes that when cornered into a confrontation, FoFo exerts her own kind of dominance—a hostile, hissing behavior that sends Bella into avoidance mode. When they're actually together, it's Bella who becomes the follower. Cesar puts them both together on the couch, using his calm-assertive energy to help calm both cat and dog and turn them into a "pack." Part of the Damians' problem is that they have been separating the two animals, never allowing them to work out their differences. "I'm blocking the cat from fighting, and I'm blocking the dog from ignoring," Cesar explains. "My goal is for them to relax right here in front of me. But if I don't ever put them together, how can I correct this behavior?" The Damians are thrilled and amazed at how quickly Cesar effects this change.

Finally, taking a page from his power of the pack dog psychology and applying it to the cat, Cesar brings in a pink cat stroller and takes the family for a walk—dog and cat together. "We make sure the cat is part of the family. I think that's the most important part: we put a cat and a dog together, we make the humans become pack leaders. And I think it's a great ending."

Follow-up ❖ ❖ ❖

Michael and Janeen report that Bella is so improved that FoFo now comes out of her cat condo. They have walked the dog with the cat in the stroller regularly, which they believe has helped bring about the change.

The Food Bully

Name/Breed: Bojo/bloodhound-Catahoula mix

Name/Breed: Tippy/border collie

(episode 316)

Donna Moss and her son Gabriel's two dogs—Bojo, a male bloodhound-Catahoula mix, and Tippy, a rescued female border collie—are the best of pals. That is, until food comes into the picture. At mealtime, the normally mellow Bojo morphs into Cujo and lunges at Tippy or any other dog. Donna now feeds Tippy in the front yard and Bojo in the back, separating them with a fence and a house. Tippy is afraid to take a treat, play with a ball, or do anything that would cause Bojo to attack her. She even leaves a little bit of her food in her bowl for Bojo.

During the consultation, Donna reveals that normally Bojo is a fearful dog, and she's never done anything to help him overcome that state of mind. Instead, she's inadvertently nurtured it. Cesar senses that Donna's spoiling of Bojo and her high anxiety level may have something to do with his abrupt personality changes. He removes her from the backyard when he decides to see whether Bojo can be "snapped out of it" when he's in his aggressive state. Once Donna is gone, Bojo responds instantly. When Cesar places steak in front of him as a temptation, he ignores it completely and allows Tippy to be fed. Once Tippy sees that Bojo's not going to explode, Tippy eagerly relaxes and takes food. Cesar tells Gabriel that it's all about the timing and intention of the correction. Bojo, a generally passive fellow in most other situations, is happy to oblige when corrected.

Gabriel is amazed at how instantly Cesar is able to transform their bad food bully into a mealtime model citizen. But when Bojo gets a glimpse of an anxious Donna inside the house, he immediately starts to whimper. Cesar tells mom and son that Bojo's rehabilitation is going to take teamwork from both of them to pull it off. "Whenever they're ready to feed, it should be like a project between mom and son to rehabilitate dogs. And it's gonna be a win-win situation. Mom is gonna get rid of anxiety and fear, and Gabriel is just gonna become more assertive."

Follow-up ❀ ❀ ❀

Bojo is doing great, letting Tippy eat first and not bothering her during chowtime. Donna still has the leash on when he eats, just to be on the safe side. As long as she's vigilant, there's peace in their household.

Canine Complex

Name/Breed: Rune/pit bull-pointer mix

Name/Breed: Kasha/husky mix

Name/Breed: Emma/mastiff-pit bull mix

Name/Breed: Mac/pit bull-boxer mix

Name/Breed: Sadie/American Staffordshire mix

(episode 318)

Marni Hills, Jacy Crawford, Audrey Fox, and Mary Ricketts all moved into the same pet-friendly apartment building in North Hollywood, assuming everyone would have friendly pets. They were wrong. Jacy's mastiff-pit mix Emma began developing dog aggression after the death of Jacy's other pet. Mac, Audrey's pit-boxer mix, is aggressive to humans whether inside or outside the apartment. Mary's American Staffordshire mix Sadie is randomly aggressive on leash toward other dogs. Pit-pointer mix Rune and husky mix Kasha belong to Marni. Rune has severe dog aggression to unfamiliar dogs, but when Rune can't get the other dogs, he turns on Kasha, and sometimes even on Marni. Cesar is called in to restore some peace to this dog-friendly building.

Cesar decides to begin the rehab with the worst case—Marni's dog, Rune. Cesar has Jacy and his dog, Emma, pass by the apartment door, where Rune usually goes crazy. Having only limited success with his usual corrections, Cesar takes advantage of Rune's great fondness for cheese and uses it as a positive incentive that distracts Rune and keeps him from becoming aggressive when other dogs pass by. The cheese works, and the next step is to see if the dog's behavior improves outside the apartment, on the street while passing by Audrey's dogs, Lulu and Mac.

Out on the street, Rune explodes almost immediately. Cesar points out to Marni that her own tension is transmitted to her dogs—who immediately send that same energy to all the dogs on the street. "I guess I really was tensing up more than I realized," Marni admits. "I was mentally preparing for the disaster that was to come, and obviously he feels that, so he takes it right off of me."

Since Mary's dog Sadie is more of a hyperactive case, Cesar focuses his next effort on Emma, who has become overprotective of her owner, Jacy, since his other dog passed away. "The human's still grieving, and the dog is imitating the feeling. Grieving a dog is a beautiful thing, but you do have to move on." Cesar teaches Jacy how to recognize Emma's warning signals in her body language, so he can correct her before she lashes out. Finally, Cesar ends the session by getting the whole group to walk together as a pack. The tenants are amazed that they can have all their dogs in one place and still have peace. And as Marni comes to realize, working together is the key. "I'm feeling great, I feel confident," she says. "I feel our problems might be fixed if we only stick to it."

Follow-up

Marni reports over 80 percent improvement with Rune when walking and passing other dogs, though Rune still sometimes charges the door when the neighboring dogs pass. The other dogs in the building continue to improve. All the residents of the apartment building who participated in *Dog Whisperer* report that they are better friends, better neighbors, and more informed and cooperative dog owners. The show was a "bonding experience" for them.

Not So Goodfellas

Name/Breed: Chuy/Chihuahua

Name/Breed: Carmine/Chihuahua

Name/Breed: Jack/Jack Russell terrier

Daniel and Rebecca Diaz own multiple businesses and are on their way to opening another one, yet they can't seem to multitask when it comes to their three little dogs—Chuy and Carmine, both Chihuahuas, and Jack, a Jack Russell terrier. The dogs got along beautifully until the day Jack and Carmine got into a terrible brawl, and ever since then the two have been mortal enemies. Daniel even got a chunk taken out of his arm

Cesar helps Rebecca and Daniel walk Jack, Carmine, and Chuy.

when he tried to break up a fight. Daniel is making the mistake of favoring Jack and blaming Carmine, while Rebecca forgives Carmine everything and focuses instead on how "cute" he is.

When Cesar arrives, he recommends an immediate intervention. "You have two dogs who have gone to red zone," he says. "They have to start this life brand-new somewhere else. It's like detox; they are so addicted to trying to kill each other, just changing the environment will change the state of mind." Daniel and Rebecca agree to bring Jack and Carmine to the Dog Psychology Center, to see if they can be influenced by the power of the pack. Arriving at the center, however, it's Daniel and Rebecca who get an immediate shock. Right before their eyes. both Carmine and Jack adapt fairly quickly to their new environment and begin to act like normal dogs. "His whole problem was us," Daniel marvels. "They come with you for two seconds, I mean, it almost like they didn't even have an aggression problem."

Two weeks at the center do wonders for the not so goodfellas, Carmine and Jack. Going on treadmill runs, bike riding, and Rollerblading together with Cesar force them to work on teamwork as a pack, instead of working against each other. And the Dog Psychology Center pack shows them by example that calm-submissive energy goes a long way toward maintaining a more peaceful way of life. Cesar returns the dogs to the Diazes, accompanied by his pack of calm-submissive dogs—Daddy, Louis, and Sid, Carmine and Jack's new friends. When he arrives, he sees that Rebecca and Daniel have made as many changes as their dogs have. "We just started to realize, you know what? If we just let them go and then they come back without doing any work, it was all for nothing. It became a rehabilitation center for us." But there's one wrinkle in the plan—Chuy, the supposed "good guy" of the family. The moment his brothers return home, Chuy starts trying to goad Carmine and Jack into returning to their bad boy ways.

Sure enough, after Cesar leaves, Chuy's troublemaking causes the dogs' aggressive behavior to return, and it's back to square one. Cesar asks Rebecca to bring all three dogs back to boot camp—but this time, she's got to attend a full three-day session alongside her pack. "It was very important that Rebecca become a pack leader, not just with her dogs, but with the pits, with the rottweilers, and for her to be seen as a queen." Though Cesar decides to keep the higher-energy Jack at the center for a little while longer, Chuy and Carmine return home to a fully rehabbed household. "This has been more than trying to get a couple of dogs to behave," says a newly enlightened Daniel. "This is a whole way to look at life. This was more for us, and we needed this probably a thousand times more than our dogs needed this. So they actually keep us grounded now. This is a new way of life for us."

Follow-up 🐾 🐾 🐾

Daniel and Becky have transformed their home from a nightmare to a place of balance. Daniel walks the dogs daily, at least three to four miles in the morning and four to five miles at night. The dogs are doing great, and Daniel has lost so much weight that every time he goes to the dry cleaner, he asks them to take his suits in a little. They are seeing continual improvements in the dogs' behaviors and can bring them to work every day now. They've also smoothly added another dog—Rocky, a pit bull mix—to the pack. Jack has remained at the Dog Psychology Center, where he is currently a beloved member of the pack and even has helped rehabilitate other dogs. Recently, Daniel and Becky visited the center, and Daniel was able to walk nine dogs at once! Cesar is immensely proud of how they have grown as pack leaders.

Ricky on the Outs

Name/Breed: Ricky/Shiba Inu

Name/Breed: Jordan/corgi

Amy Kneupper and her roommate, Stefanie Santangelo, are two cheery twenty-somethings. Two-and-a-half-year-old Ricky, a Shiba Inu, never barked when people came to the door and always got along great with other dogs. But when Stefanie brought home a five-month-old corgi named Jordan, Ricky's aggression began to emerge. Ricky gets protective and extremely jealous around Jordan. Ricky and Jordan will play all day long, but if another dog comes near the corgi pup, peaceful Ricky becomes red-zone aggressive. Amy claps her hands and makes loud noises, but nothing seems to deter the ferocious canine.

Right away, Cesar sees that the young women have no experience being pack leaders. "There is nothing wrong with the dog. The dog is only exhibiting dominant and territorial behavior. And you guys, no human took that position. And then he took it. You can have that position back."

Cesar begins the session by observing how Ricky acts when faced with his nightmare situation—his former best friend, golden retriever Jasper, who would now rather play with corgi Jordan than the pushy, dominating Ricky. From the moment Jasper arrives, Ricky begins to act his worst, howling the high-pitched, wailing Shiba Inu cry. "We have a dog who potentially can attack another dog that is close to the toys or close to the other dog because he feels that that's his position, that's his job."

Follow-up 🐾 🐾 🐾

Ricky has calmed down and is now less aggressive with strange dogs. He also lets other dogs play with puppy Jordan.

Cesar moves the session outside, where he works on teaching Ricky some calm-submissive manners, but more important, teaching the young women how to incorporate calm-assertive energy into their lives. "I think they were so sweet, and because of the sweetness, it took a while, it took repetitions of reminding, 'Okay, it's not that we don't want to love them, it's just we can't treat them as humans because they're doing dog behavior right now.' So today I think

I was like a friend who came and gave them a reality check." After showing them how to properly walk the two dogs together and how to respond to Ricky's aggression on the walk, Amy and Stefanie begin seeing an enormous difference. Cesar predicts they will need months of hard, consistent work to permanently turn the situation around, but he's thrilled by their willingness and motivation. "We have a lot of homework with Ricky," says Amy. "Now we know to treat him like a dog and not like a kid."

Brawling Boxers

Names: Duke and Lila

Breed: boxer

Cesar introduces Duke and Lila to Lotus.

Shortly after John and Jeri Wehrle moved from Colorado to Los Angeles with their two boxers, Duke and Daisy, tragedy struck. While playing outside, Daisy ran into the street and was hit by a car and killed. John and Jeri decided to get a new playmate for Duke, another boxer, named Lila. Everything was going well until one day at the dog park, a dog came out of nowhere and attacked her. Since then, Lila has taken on the mantra, "Kill or be killed." Vet bills have been piling up due to Lila's attacks on other dogs. Duke, on the other hand, used to be friendly with other dogs but has now taken up Lila's aggressive behaviors. Jeri walks the dogs a half hour every morning and they have a long run for about an hour every night, but the neighborhood has become a danger zone.

Upon his arrival, Cesar discovers that most of the mishaps have occurred when John is walking the dogs. "There're two packs in this house. Definitely the girls and the boys," Cesar observes. He starts his exercise with the girls—Jeri and the trouble-maker, Lila. Repeatedly passing by two dogs that are among Lila's worst enemies, Cesar shows Jeri how to time corrections and what body language to look for to make sure she stops Lila before her aggression escalates. It's clear that Jeri understands the concept from the very start. "I learned how to handle her so that my fears didn't trickle down through the leash and into her," Jeri says of the session.

Working with John and both dogs, Cesar sees a different scenario. John, describing himself as "nonchalant," allows the dogs to walk in front of him, doing whatever they want. "Mr. Johnny's hiding, he just doesn't want to be responsible for anything," Cesar observes. He gives John the hard truth—the dogs won't change unless both he and Jeri follow the same program. After several repetitions, walking the gauntlet of the Wehrles' dog-saturated neighborhood, Cesar sees huge improvement from Jeri but feels that John isn't fully getting the pack leader concept. He assigns him the homework of working with the dogs every day for the next several weeks.

When Cesar returns five weeks later, he is amazed by John's progress. "I'm proud of this man! He totally turned it around!" But Cesar's arranged a final exam— he's brought five dogs from the Dog Psychology Center to test Duke and Lila's reactions. The Wehrles not only pass with flying colors, the two boxers shine as the best-behaved dogs in the neighborhood! "How do you like that?" Cesar crows. "The most powerful breed in this neighborhood was the role model. It's an amazing, wonderful, balanced experience. Everybody participated." The Wehrles are just as happy. "It was a very positive experience from beginning to end," says John. "Every bit of it."

Follow-up ✿ ✿ ✿

Although Lila still sometimes responds to other dogs on walks, Jeri is able to correct her before things escalate. Their walks together continue to improve.

Behind the scenes

There was one member of the Wehrles' pack that didn't need Cesar's help. Buttercup, a giant green iguana, weighing eight pounds, hangs out in the trees and shrubs in the yard, sleeps on the couch, and comes and goes in the house like another dog.

Snoopy Unplugged

Name: Snoopy

Breed: bearded collie

(episode 320)

Veronique Munro thought she found the perfect match when she spotted Snoopy in a pet store window. But it took only a few months before Snoopy was terrorizing the neighborhood and trying to attack other dogs. Veronique's relationship with composer Andrew Ross hit a sour note when Snoopy began expressing his distaste for Andrew's music by barking, howling, and scratching incessantly. It is impossible for Andrew to compose on his piano or for Veronique to join him on her guitar when the dog is around.

When they first meet Cesar, the couple tells him that they find some of Snoopy's bad behavior amusing and they think he whines for attention. Cesar quickly determines that Snoopy's behavior problems are directly related to the inconsistent energy and lack of discipline in the household. "There's a big confusion going on in this environment. There's confusion, there's nervousness, there's anxiety, there's dominance. It's really bad."

Cesar puts a leash on Snoopy, then picks up the guitar and starts strumming. He gives Snoopy a quick tug on the leash or a "*tsst*" every time the dog starts to move because of the music. "What we are doing is we are blocking him from becoming powerful just by moving. If he moves, he gets excited. If he doesn't move, he gets calm." Next, Andrew plays guitar and Veronique attempts to correct Snoopy, but when Snoopy doesn't respond, she says, "It's not working." Cesar believes that Snoopy is actually a mild case, and his concern is more focused on the human side of the equation. Cesar notes, "Veronique was very draining to me."

They go to a nearby park and meet up with a vizsla that Snoopy tries to attack. Cesar has no problem keeping Snoopy under control—until Veronique decides to disobey Cesar's instructions and sit down on the bench next to him. "My goal is always to help the dogs and empower the humans. But when a human being is resistant, and is certain with all her heart and all her mind that these dogs are going to kill each other, it's a really hard energy to compete with."

When Cesar is quickly successful with both Snoopy and Andrew, even getting Snoopy to walk calmly next to the vizsla, a lightbulb finally goes on for Veronique. "I was very, very nervous. Once I became aware of how my energy was impacting Snoopy's behavior, I think it made something shift in me. You don't think about it impacting your dog. But it became very clear today that that was the case."

Follow-up ❄ ❄ ❄

Veronique now knows how to stop Snoopy from barking, and Andrew can play the guitar in peace. Snoopy is getting along well with his former arch-enemy, the vizsla. They actually can walk next to each without any problem.

The Beers' Bitter Brew

Name: Amber

Breed: golden retriever mix

(episode 320)

On the surface, Amber seemed like the perfect dog for a laid-back retired couple like Barbara and Peter Beers. "She's warm and fluffy, she does tricks, she answers commands, and is well behaved, really," claims Peter. The problem is that she wants to attack any dog in sight, even if she sees it through the picture window of the Beers' house. Walks with the high-energy Amber are so out of control that Peter broke his ankle the first week they had her.

When Cesar meets with the couple he learns that Barbara likes to quilt and Peter enjoys quiz shows and games with mental challenges. "When I was in front of Pete and Barbara, I felt that I was having a wonderful conversation but it was at a low-level energy. And in the world of nature, assertiveness is what leads the pack. That's the only way we are going to lead Amber into the balance that they are looking for."

Observing Peter trying to walk Amber, Cesar notices that Peter gets tense when attempting to correct his dog. Cesar works with Amber in the backyard with the help of some neighborhood kids and their dog, and away from Peter and Barbara's energies. "Because Amber has built so much resistance to any kind of discipline, we needed to match that intensity she has built and to start touching part of her body so we can start softening the body." Cesar corrects Amber both with the leash and tapping her on her hindquarters with his foot to redirect her attention. "Every time I give her a correction, I lower the intensity. I never give a correction that is going to infuriate her or make her more immune to corrections."

Next, Cesar tries to work on Amber's aggression when she sees a dog through the picture window. During those moments, Peter tries to distract Amber with a ball. Cesar warns Peter, "If she's in an aggressive state of mind, and you give her a toy, you are actually helping her to accomplish killing the object or killing the target. It only made it real to Amber. 'I am chewing on the dog. I know I'm not close to him, but in my mind, I'm chewing on that dog.'"

During their first session, Cesar demonstrates that Amber's behavior can be corrected, and he asks the Beers to walk her every day for at least thirty minutes. Four weeks later, Cesar returns with several members of his pack and surprises the Beers and Amber by bringing them all into the backyard. Amazingly, Amber shows no aggression at all when the pack arrives. Peter remarks, "You know, you see that on the show, but you know that there's a possibility of cutting and pasting and all that. But it really happened like that. And it was amazing."

Follow-up

Peter and Barbara continued to have trouble walking Amber. After working with the Beers twice at their house, Cesar invited them and Amber to the Dog Psychology Center on two separate occasions to give them additional tips and suggestions to improve their walks. They have reported that they are finally making progress after their most recent Cesar sessions.

Key Cesar Tip

It's harder to be a successful pack leader if your dog has more energy than you do.

Chapter 16

Territorial/Possessive

Maltese Kisses—pretty in pink?

Not So Pretty in Pink

(episode 301)

Name: Little Miss Kisses

Breed: Maltese

Judging by her name, Kitten K. Sera sounds like she'd be a cat person, but it was a cute Maltese named Kisses that won her heart. When Kitten walks Kisses, it's not uncommon for people to stop and take their picture—because Kitten's dyed her tiny dog cotton-candy pink. Kisses may be memorable, but she's also high maintenance. She snaps at her owner's heels as she walks around the all-pink apartment and becomes aggressive and tries to bite when chewing on her favorite toys.

Cesar likes to approach each case with a fresh outlook so he rarely

Kitten reports that Kisses is behaving well. She is not biting Kitten's feet anymore and has stopped wetting in the apartment. Kitten admits that Kisses still gets growly sometimes, but she now knows how to correct her.

Behind the scenes

Kitten related an incident where she was stopped on the street by the actress Sandra Bullock, who exclaimed that she had seen Kitten and Kisses on *Dog Whisperer*. Kitten thought that was ironic, considering how famous Sandra is.

knows anything about his clients or their dogs before he comes to call. In the case of Kitten and Kisses, Cesar gets a shock . . . in pink. "I always evaluate the energy at the moment I walk in, and this is a wonderful pink palace. Wonderful energy." When Cesar learns that Kitten has a very difficult time reprimanding Kisses when she's bad, he tells her, "It has to be the difference between punishing a dog and disciplining a dog—discipline is good, punishing is bad. Discipline is when you're in a calm-assertive state. Punishing is when you are frustrated or nervous or care about what other people say. You are in a negative state, and that's why the dog doesn't listen."

Cesar helps Kitten bring out her calm-assertive side when he asks her how she would respond to a boyfriend who wanted her to wear blue jeans instead of her signature pink. She firmly declares, "Not on your life!" Cesar tells her that's the energy she needs to have when disciplining Kisses.

Cesar demonstrates how to move in on a bone that Kisses is chewing and then get her to drop the bone. "Don't forget that the energy is very important. If you touch the bone hesitantly, then she feels that you are hesitant about what you are doing." Cesar instructs Kitten to hold her hand out in a fist position when confronting Kisses. This way, Kisses won't be able to nip at her fingers . . . while at the same time this helps Kitten to feel more empowered.

Kitten will always remember how to reconnect with her calm-assertive side. "The blue jean analogy that Cesar gave me is really going to help because it's something that I can go back to every single time."

Biker Dog

Name: Holli

Breed: American Staffordshire terrier

(episode 302)

On Labor Day several years ago, Renee Raley was jogging when she felt something bump into her leg—a stray American Staffordshire terrier. Renee and her boyfriend, Craig Pasetta, adopted her and named her Holli. Eight months later, Renee and Craig's happy life with Holli took a horrific turn when Holli bolted away from Renee during a run and was hit by a school bus. The bus ran over one of Holli's front legs, but to avoid amputating it, Craig and Renee chose to have experimental surgery done. With an unconventional skin graft and months of physical therapy, Holli's leg was restored but not quite to its former glory. "I ended up taking off three or four months from work to stay here with Holli, do bandage changes, physical therapy, back and forth to the vets. It was my life. I believe if Holli was able, she would do the same for me," Craig says tearfully.

Renee and Craig on motorcycles with Holli riding shotgun.

Craig even went so far as to build a sidecar to his motorcycle for his dog. Holli is a perfect companion when she is riding shotgun. But whenever they take a walk, Holli turns into an uncontrollable rebel. Holli pulls relentlessly on her leash and hops on one of her good legs. Holli's vet has noticed early signs of tendinitis in that leg, which will eventually lead to premature degeneration.

Craig tells Cesar he believes his emotional connection and feelings of guilt about Holli might be why he can't change her behavior. Cesar agrees. "Animals live in the moment. So if you change what you project, they change how they react to you. Animals first connect instinctually, then emotionally, then spiritually. You're following the spirit and emotions, but no instinct. You have to have instincts to drive a motorcycle; it can't just be emotions and spirituality."

When Cesar notices how tense Craig is while walking Holli, Cesar tells him Holli is

Follow-up 🐾 🐾 🐾

Holli is doing great. Before Cesar's visit, Holli used her leg 20 to 25 percent of the time. Now she uses it 80 to 90 percent of the time. If she's on the grass, she uses her leg all the time. Craig walks Holli twice a day for forty-five minutes each time. Craig takes Holli in her sidecar almost daily after he takes her out for a walk.

picking up that tense energy through the leash. "My arm might be stuck that way," Craig admits. Cesar replies, "It's not your arm, it's your brain."

Cesar wants Craig and Renee to walk Holli as a team, so Renee can help out whenever Craig gets tense. Craig marvels at the nearly instant change in both Holli and himself. "Without the tension that I've been creating with this thing [the leash], and this thing [his brain], she's not fighting with me. I'm amazed at how deceptively simple it was. I didn't anticipate it would be a complex solution, but now I have the insight to see where to go."

Four-Alarm Firedog

Name: Wilshire

Breed: Dalmatian

(episode 304)

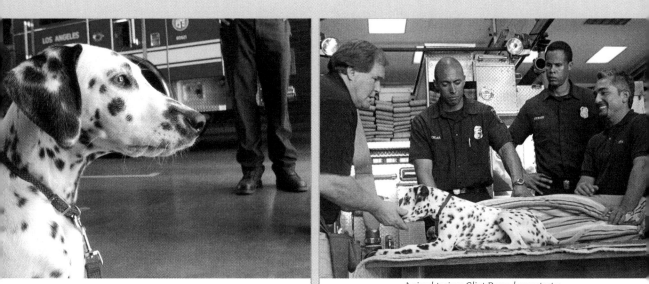

Wilshire the fire dog.

Animal trainer Clint Rowe demonstrates
how to train Wilshire to stop, drop, and roll.

Firehouse 29 on Wilshire Boulevard in Los Angeles is a city landmark and home to a crack team of firefighters. However, one summer these heroes faced a natural disaster even L.A.'s finest had no idea how to overcome—a three-month-old Dalmatian puppy they named Wilshire. The Firehouse 29 members recently rescued Wilshire from near death at a pound and had good intentions when they took in the spotted pup, but it wasn't long before the hyperactive Dalmatian was running the firehouse—bolting out the door whenever there was a call, jumping on children who come to visit, and stealing the firemen's grub.

   If the men can't teach Wilshire to behave like a proper firehouse dog, it's certain the city attorney will have him taken away. The firemen place an emergency call to Cesar, who has always admired these rescuers for their calm and assertive behavior in life-or-death situations. How could all these brave American heroes have allowed a puppy to take over their lives?

Cesar quickly discovers that the firemen aren't consistent in establishing rules for Wilshire, and they are giving Wilshire affection when he is acting out of control or trying to dominate them. Cesar recommends that they come up with a consistent plan for Wilshire and to leave messages all over the firehouse so everyone can enforce the rules the same way.

But even before their initial consultation is over, an emergency call comes in and half the firefighters hurry to leave. During the commotion, Wilshire slips out the door and heads straight for six-lane Wilshire Boulevard and certain disaster. Luckily, Cesar is able to get the puppy and bring him back to the firehouse garage. There Cesar gives Captain Gilbert Reyna and the remaining firefighters a lesson on how to keep Wilshire from going past the boundary of the garage door. "The exercise at the garage door is very important, because it's a life-and-death situation here," says Cesar. Whenever Wilshire tries to move past Cesar, he taps the dog on the neck and makes him move back and sit inside the garage. Captain Reyna notes, "It was amazing where he stopped right at the door; Cesar was able to control him in a minimal amount of time, whereas we would have been chasing Wilshire down Wilshire."

Next, Cesar has the perfect plan to help the firefighters drain some of Wilshire's high-level energy. There are two treadmills in the firehouse garage, so Cesar shows the firemen how to get Wilshire walking on a treadmill. Captain Reyna says, "Every morning it's a requirement of the Los Angeles City Fire Department that their members exercise. So why we don't have Wilshire out there is our fault. It won't happen again, though."

In a few weeks, the fireman have worked together to give both exercise and discipline to Wilshire, and the change in the pup is dramatic. Then Captain Reyna has one more request: he would like to train Wilshire to "stop, drop, and roll" so they can have him demonstrate this lifesaving technique to kids at school assemblies. Cesar rehabilitates dogs and trains people, not the other way around. To help teach Wilshire these new behaviors, he calls in Clint Rowe, who has more than forty years' experience training animals to star in major Hollywood movies. Using positive reinforcement

Follow-up ❧ ❧ ❧

Wilshire is a huge success story and, with the help of Clint Rowe and firefighter Penrod, he continues to be an ambassador of goodwill for Firehouse 29 and the entire Los Angeles Fire Department, teaching fire safety at schools all over Los Angeles County. Wilshire has become so famous that he now has his own web page at www.wilshirethefiredog.org.

and clicker training—which includes rewarding the dog every time he performs a desired behavior— Clint teaches firefighter Ryan Penrod and a few others the basic way to get a dog to sit ("stop"), lie down ("drop"), and roll over ("roll").

Several weeks and many practice sessions later, Wilshire makes his debut at a Los Angeles school. On cue, Wilshire executes a perfect stop, drop, and roll maneuver to a room filled with delighted first graders. "I don't think this would have been imaginable a couple of months ago," Captain Reyna comments. "This is exactly why we wanted a dog. I can't thank Cesar enough. He wasn't training the dog; he was training us." Cesar says, "Not to help a dog that has so much potential like Wilshire, that would be a bad story. Now everybody is cooperating for the welfare of Wilshire and Wilshire is going to pay them back a thousand times."

Maya Madness

(episode 305)

Name: Maya

Breed: border collie-springer spaniel mix

Diana Kleinman adopted Maya the day before she was scheduled to be euthanized and took her home to her husband, Lou. Maya gets plenty of exercise; she and Diana go on a three- to five-mile walk every day. It's on these walks that Maya's pulling problem arises. If any small animal happens to be nearby, Maya bolts toward the animal, causing a whiplash motion for Diana. Diana recently had major neck surgery resulting from a car accident, and doctors warned her that she could still become paralyzed from any further neck trauma. "It's a potential hazard for me. I've already been head-butted by Maya and had a mild concussion. And when I go hiking, out of nowhere, she just pulls me and bolts. I'm in that motion that I'm not supposed to have," says Diana.

First, Cesar shows the couple how to stop Maya from jumping up on Diana. Cesar gives Maya a quick tap on her hindquarters with his foot and the dog stops jumping up. Diana is amazed. "The minute he kind of tapped her, she immediately stopped and it was like, 'Wow, how did he get that kind of response so quickly?'" Cesar tells them, "You have to claim the area. The reason she stopped is that somebody owned the place. And jumping was not allowed." Diana realizes, "My tendency was to move away from her because of fear that she's gonna hurt me, then Cesar showed me that when you step in she doesn't like that. She moves back. And then she sits very obediently."

Next, they head to Griffith Park to work on Maya's pulling problems. Cesar decides to put Maya's leash around her shoulders, making it more like the harness on a Seeing Eye dog. "It makes sense for me to take your leash and make it a tool used by dogs that assist people. Maya has never been asked to be an assistant. It took only seconds for Maya to understand

Follow-up ❀ ❀ ❀

Although she is still a challenge, Maya is doing much better. The Kleinmans can get her to stop jumping and she is much better behaved on walks.

the concept. It's just a matter of being patient and using repetition." Using the leash this way, Diana is easily able to walk and control Maya.

Even though Diana is thrilled to see a different Maya, Cesar is thrilled to see a different Diana. "I saw Diana changing right in front of my eyes. But I don't think she saw herself changing. It was real to me. It was very clear to me that she did transform herself into a calm-assertive state."

Pushy Poodle

Name: Lilly

Breed: standard poodle

Tami and Adam Kusleika are an outgoing young couple in Bennington, Nebraska, with a large extended family of siblings, cousins, nieces, and nephews whom they love to entertain. There's only one speed bump to their busy social life—a pushy poodle named Lilly. If guests dare to come through the front door, Lilly is all over them, jumping, nipping, and nudging them for attention. When small children come over, Lilly pushes the kids around and tries to herd them.

The problems with Lilly escalated after Tami gave birth to their first child, Miles, a year and a half after the Kusleikas brought Lilly into their home. "Lilly has to continuously be in his face. We push her back to try to tell her to give us our space, but it doesn't always work," Tami says with a sigh.

When Cesar arrives, Tami tells him that they've asked guests to try to follow Cesar's rule of "no touch, no talk, no eye contact" when they first arrive. When they do, Lilly seems to calm down fairly quickly. But many kids can't grasp the idea of not approaching and petting a dog that comes up to them. Cesar says, "That's why you have to have the highest level of leadership in order for you to control situations when other people are not following the rules. The human gets excited—we can even scream when we see somebody else, and we see that as happiness. But if you greet a dog like a human, you're just going to keep him bouncing, especially circus dogs—like poodles, like schnauzers, like Jack Russells, they bounce."

Cesar asks to hold baby Miles so he can show Tami how to control Lilly even with Miles in her arms. When Cesar has someone ring the bell at the front door, he turns to Lilly, snaps his fingers and makes a firm "*tsst*" until she calmly sits down. Then he opens the door and brings the guest inside without further incident. "And Miles is feeling the energy. That's how we learn to be pack leaders or followers at that early age," Cesar tells them.

Cesar believes there are several similarities between raising balanced dogs and balanced children. "I have two kids of my own and I tell them the rules, the boundaries, the limitations." When a bunch of the Kusleikas' nephews and nieces come over to play, Cesar tells the children, "Let's pretend for the first ten minutes when you come into the house that Lilly is not here. Okay? Then you can play with her when she's calmed down." Cesar also teaches the kids how to calm Lilly down with a "*tsst*" and a snap of the fingers. When Cesar says, "Show me the Dog Whisperer move!" little pack leaders start to emerge. Tami says, "It's gonna take a lot of energy and work and determination from both Adam and me every day, so that she will remain the dog that we want her to be, and that she wants to be." "Until Miles is old enough to do it for us," adds Adam.

Follow-up ❧ ❧ ❧

Lilly's manners at the door have improved, and she's now showing consistent respect to Tami, Adam, and Miles. In fact, fifteen-month-old Miles knows how to be a pack leader—calming Lilly down with the "tsst" sound! The Kusleikas' nieces and nephews are also learning how to control Lilly and interact with her safely.

Key Cesar Tip

You are never too young or too old to become a calm-assertive pack leader.

Dingo Dilemma

Name: Aussi

Breed: dingo mix

(episode 306)

The wild dingo is one of the most famous—and infamous—breeds of dogs in Australia. Like wolves, these pack-oriented predators hunt everything from rodents to kangaroos to unsuspecting sheep on Australian ranches. Over the years, dingoes have been bred with all kinds of domesticated dogs, and their descendants can now be found on several continents.

Seven years ago, seventy-year-old Betty McVay brought home a malnourished and neglected three-month-old dingo mix named Aussi and nursed her back to health. Aussi became a constant companion for Betty, bringing comfort throughout Betty's two successful bouts with cancer. But when Aussi needs her own routine medical care, she is a defiant patient. Aussi's fierce and uncontrollable behavior in the examining room has kept her from having virtually any kind of medical treatment or checkup for eight years. According to Betty's current veterinarian, Dr. Gail Renehan, "I'd love to do a blood draw on the dog. There's no way we can even restrain her for that at this point in time."

When Cesar meets with Betty, he asks her how she survived cancer twice. "I was a fighter. You have a certain amount of fear when they tell you that you have cancer. But I said, 'I'm not going to die, I'm going to live.'" Cesar responds, "Dog aggression is like cancer, but you don't need chemo to cure it. You just need energy. So instead of using fear energy to cure that problem, you need calm-assertive energy to cure the problem. Avoidance is not going to cure the problem."

Cesar's goal is to try to make the vet visits as positive as possible. First Cesar recommends taking the dog on a long walk before they visit the vet to help drain her physical energy. After a good walk, Cesar brings Aussi into the clinic and is ready to play the role of vet tech. But the moment Cesar puts Aussi on the examination table, the dog starts fighting uncontrollably and squealing. "She created a sound that said you're killing her. It's important to see where she is. She was not in an aggressive state; she was in a panicked state. And if that overwhelms you and you stop the exercise, from that point on they know how to manipulate their human." After the initial struggle, Aussi calms down enough so that Dr. Renehan can examine her. Moments later, Aussi fights again, and in the process scratches Cesar and draws blood. Then Cesar gets Aussi lying down calmly on the table while Dr. Renehan takes a rectal temperature, draws some blood, and even clips her toenails. At the end, Cesar gives Aussi a massage as a reward for getting through the entire exam. Then when the dog is fully relaxed, he lets her down from the table.

For future visits, Cesar recommends that Betty bring her son, Lewis, who has good pack leadership skills with Aussi. Betty is thrilled to see Aussi make it through an exam and tells Cesar she is ready to do the work necessary to make all of Aussi's vet visits more positive. Cesar says, "Betty's taken the responsibility of being the pack leader, not just the dog lover. So it's only going to get better."

Follow-up 🐾 🐾 🐾

Aussi is doing great. Before Cesar, Betty couldn't walk her at all. Now she can walk her past a gauntlet of barking dogs, and she passes right by them. Betty bought a backpack for Aussi and walks her twice a day now. Every two weeks, they go to the vet's for practice "friendly" visits. Even her vet says Aussi is not the same dog.

Key Cesar Tip

To get your dogs to associate the vet's office with a positive experience, take them on a long walk before you arrive. Then, try bringing them into the office on a day when no treatment is scheduled and just let them relax in the waiting room and maybe even get a treat from a staff member.

Demonic Dasher

Name: Dasher

Breed: Italian greyhound mix

Shannon Benecke loves animals so much that she quit her job as a teacher and is now a dog groomer, although her ultimate goal is to start an animal shelter. Shannon and her husband, Greg, currently share their home with cats, birds, a Chihuahua mix named Radar, and the newest addition to the family, a rescued greyhound mix named Dasher.

As time went by, the couple discovered that Dasher became possessive over toys and bones. In the beginning, Shannon tried to take the toys away with her hands and ended up being bitten. The only way to pry his toys away from him is to use barbeque tongs. Greg worries that even Cesar won't be able to rehabilitate Dasher, because Dasher is thirteen years old.

Cesar believes that you can rehabilitate unwanted behavior, even when a dog is thirteen years old. But first, both Greg and Shannon have to stop living in fear of Dasher. "Fear is weakness. And he can sense that. Mother Nature attacks weak energy, so he's not going to be compassionate to you just because you rescued him. He's going to take advantage of you."

When Cesar puts his feet near one of Dasher's bones, the dog starts to attack and bite Cesar's shoes relentlessly. "Brand-new shoes. Don't worry about it. I just want to claim the bone; I don't want to hurt him." As Cesar steps on Dasher's bone, he continues, "This is like arm wrestling. The only way he can get the bone is if I *give* it to him. This way I control the situation." Greg notices, "Dasher's outbursts kept coming, but the intensity was a little bit less every time."

Cesar suggests that Shannon and Greg use an unusual tool—a broom—to help them get the upper hand with Dasher without getting bitten. They can use the broom to gently push Dasher away from his bone (or toy) and claim the bone by putting the broom over it, then picking it up with Dasher on the other side of the broom. After Greg and Shannon both successfully make Dasher back quickly away from the bone with the broom, Shannon exclaims, "I just felt a lot of positive energy and a lot of control over him. To be able to take something away from Dasher and not get bit was the best feeling I could possibly feel."

Their work with Cesar is only step one of Dasher's rehabilitation. Greg and Shannon will need to work with Dasher every day in order to change the balance of power in their house. Now we're going to have a happier home," says Greg. "Cesar gave us the greatest gift," adds Shannon.

Follow-up 🐾 🐾 🐾

Shannon has not been bitten by Dasher since the day she worked with Cesar, and she's looking forward to continuing Dasher's rehabilitation.

The Howling

Name: Elmer

Breed: beagle

(episode 308)

Cesar helps Henry learn to master the walk with Elmer.

Henry Griffith and Brian Donahue were living happily with their nine-year-old beagle Jake in a suburb of Atlanta. As a favor, they agreed to take in a friend's beagle, five-year-old Elmer. A month and half after Elmer's arrival, he began howling incessantly during their walks. Whenever they encounter another dog, Elmer erupts into his painful performance. "Oh, it's ear shattering, piercing, and sounds as if he'd been hit by a car sometimes. It's that loud," Brian says. Henry adds, "One of these days I'm afraid somebody is going to haul off and hit us because they'll think we're injuring the dog."

After their initial consultation, Cesar asks the two men to demonstrate how they prepare to take Elmer and Jake on a walk. After Henry puts a leash on Elmer, he wraps the leash around his hand several times. Cesar asks him why. "Because once I didn't do that and he broke my finger. And that's to keep him from getting too far in front of me," Henry tells him. When Brian opens the door, the two beagles scurry to get through while the two men call out, "Us first! Us first!" Cesar informs them, "Before you even leave the house, make sure the dog is not excited. I think that's number one." Cesar notes that wrapping the leash around the hand multiple times and holding it taut can actually add to the feeling of tension.

The two men bring Cesar to their local park, where their lesson continues. When Brian and Henry try to restrain Elmer, they pull back on the leash. Cesar suggests that they make a correction by pulling to the side. "When you pull to the side, you create an out-of-balance experience. When you pull back, they ground themselves even more. So they're stronger." Cesar also relates how beagles were originally bred to howl when they found their quarry during a hunt. Elmer howls primarily to announce that he's found another dog.

The two men watch Cesar as he is able to quickly correct Elmer as soon as he begins to howl. It doesn't completely eliminate the howl, but it is certainly no longer earth shattering. "You can't stop a beagle from howling. You can only redirect him. So we just have to let him know, "Yes, you found the dog. And you're going to meet that dog. But you're going meet her on my terms." After spending another hour walking Elmer by dogs and giving him corrections, Brian and Henry feel like they know what they need to do. Brian tells Cesar, "I do feel empowered by your suggestions and all your help." Henry adds, "We can do it."

Follow-up ❧ ❧ ❧

Henry and Brian have Elmer under control now, and he is no longer an embarrassment to them. Elmer is walking on the leash without going crazy, and they have to correct his howling much less often. He no longer goes out of control when he sees another dog.

Behind the scenes

Ilusion Millan's birthday was the day of the shooting, so after an exhausting day of working, devoted husband Cesar rushed off to an Atlanta mall to make sure he had a special present for that night's dinner celebration.

Silence Is Golden

Names: Woody and Wally

Breed: Pomeranian

In 2002, Carlos and Katie Warner purchased Woody from a breeder. In the beginning, Woody was easy to walk and very affectionate. His only flaw was a mild separation anxiety that was more of an annoyance than a problem. Katie and Carlos purchased Wally, another Pomeranian, from the same breeder, with hopes that Wally would help fix Woody's separation anxiety, but Katie says, "Wally just immediately took on Woody's negative behaviors, and then Woody's got worse and Wally's got worse, so it's this cycle of madness. It is hard to leave them because they flip out when we leave. Wally turns into a whirling dervish. He just runs around in circles, throws himself at the window, at the wall."

The Warners also have problems with the dogs in the car. If Carlos or Katie leaves the car to pump gas, the dogs bark and spin and attack each other. After living with the behavior for five years, Carlos and Katie now have a new baby and are desperate to fix this situation.

During their initial meeting, Katie tells Cesar, "I get very frustrated and nervous and anxious. The more they bark, the more it grates on my nerves, and then the more I feel that way the more they bark." After observing Katie's nervous energy at the door, Cesar decides to let Daddy and Coco from his pack act as calm-assertive role models. "I brought Daddy not to help the dogs but to show Katie and Carlos how a dog will control a situation when he's in front of unstable dogs. How he's going to deal with the behavior, how he's going to claim that little space, even though he's being bothered by their energy." Daddy simply walks into the house wagging his tail and ignoring the barking and spinning Poms. Cesar continues, "Everyone says pit bulls will kill your little dog, but right now it's a Pomeranian that's misbehaving and trying to act a little tough about it. But when a dog is balanced, he knows how to how to control the situation without aggression. So it's not the breed, it's who's behind the dog."

Cesar tells the couple that they can't let their dogs bark and run away from them, particularly Wally, who is the primary instigator. They need to claim their space at the front door, make the dogs back away from the door and sit quietly when Carlos and

Katie let people in. Cesar shows Carlos how standing proud and erect actually helps transmit calm-assertive energy. Carlos is amazed by the quick transformation. "In the span of a half hour, we went from a horrible experience to them sitting there and behaving."

At the car, Cesar makes the two dogs be completely calm and submissive on the ground. Then, rather than letting the dogs jump in on their own, he lifts them, one at a time, into the car. If either dog starts to act in an excited way, Cesar stops him with a firm "*tsst.*" Katie marvels, "That was amazing. I have never gotten in or out of a car without them attacking me and each other and just going haywire. It was amazing to see how differently they acted with just that amount of training."

Finally Cesar recommends that consistency and teamwork—with Katie in charge of dealing with one dog and Carlos the other—will also help the couple to get the behavior they want in their two Poms.

Follow-up 🐾 🐾 🐾

Carlos and Katie report that things with the Poms were much better for a while after the taping. The couple practiced often and learned how to control the dogs in the house and in the car. "We know that we represent the show when we are out in public," they write, "and thankfully the boys are 90 percent better on walks. Often people say 'are those the dogs from the *Dog Whisperer*?' and we are proud to say yes." However, Carlos and Katie confess that when the demands of their jobs and their new baby overwhelm them, they tend to walk the dogs less, and the bad behavior returns, especially in regard to separation anxiety barking. "Inconsistency will cause their behavior to regress," Carlos admits.

Key Cesar Tip

Improving your dog's behavior is like staying on a diet. You'll see lasting results only if you stick with it for a long time.

Food-Aggressive Swiss Mountain Dog

Name: Kane

Breed: Swiss mountain dog

(episode 310)

It's a long way from Dallas, Texas, to the Swiss Alps. But when Rob Robertson and Diana Starke decided to start a family and get a dog, they wanted one with those mountains in its blood. In their heyday, Swiss mountain dogs were used by farmers for herding and other chores. Because of their ability to pull carts, the breed was sometimes known as "the poor man's horse."

After six months, Rob and Diana noticed that Kane growled whenever they came near or touched him while he ate. Rob says, "He was the smallest in the litter and obviously he was not getting as much nutrition as the other animals. And I think that somewhere in there it was etched in his wee little brain that he has to fight for every morsel of food he gets." Diana adds, "He's still a puppy, but he scares people because he's a big dog. And we imagine that he could bite our kids or do something like that."

When Cesar arrives, Diana and Rob relate the various methods they've tried to deal with the behavior. "One suggested approach was to start off with us feeding him by hand. Once we got to that stage, the next step was to bring in the bowl. Then putting his bowl in the right spot and petting him. Then we tried dominance, where we stand over him when he eats and make him sit, make him do something for his food. When he becomes aggressive, we reprimand him very physically, and when I did that, he bit me."

Follow-up ❖ ❖ ❖

Rob and Diana continued to have difficulties with Kane's food aggression. When Cesar was in Austin, Texas, to give a seminar, he met with the couple and Kane again to try to reinforce his message.

Cesar tells them, "It's not that the strategies or tools are not good; it's that the humans are not providing the energy that is required to *make* it work. By feeling sorry that he was the runt of the litter, he saw that your energy was weaker than his. You can't lead him." Cesar believes that the couple needs to be in control of the entire mealtime process, and that includes making Kane wait for his food, because the dog should receive food only when he is calm and submissive. Then they should bring Kane to his bowl rather than let Kane approach the food on his own. Cesar also suggests keeping a leash on Kane during the feeding process so they can give him corrections whenever he starts to growl or display aggression.

Finally, to help fulfill the Swiss mountain dog part of Kane, Cesar puts together a makeshift cart for Kane to pull. Kane is spooked by the cart noise at first. "Eventually we saw Kane moving forward without a problem. We don't know if the parents of Kane were cart dogs, but we know it's part of his genetics, so it was just a matter of time for us to bring him back," says Cesar.

Key Cesar Tip

"I think what Rob and Diana learned today is how to prevent escalation. Kane's going to be hard to control when he's in dominant state, and he's going to be even harder to control when he's in aggressive state."

Free the Frenchies

Names: Tallulah, Bella, Boris, and Groucho

Breed: French bulldog

Lynn Arlt is a New York City psychiatric social worker who can soothe the minds of disturbed human beings but can't handle her own four French bulldogs—Boris, Bella, Tallulah, and Groucho. This pack of bulldogs has begun their own French Revolution. Tallulah is a compulsive jumper. She is very attached to Lynn and gets upset if anyone or anything tries to steal her spotlight—including the vacuum cleaner and mop. Once Tallulah starts, the rest of the clan joins in, and fights often ensue. The dogs are so hyper and unpredictable that Lynn can't find a dog walker who'll agree take them out during the day. Living in a one-bedroom apartment in downtown Manhattan and keeping peace among the four frenzied Frenchies makes Lynn feel like every day she's storming the Bastille.

Cesar immediately notes that Lynn has a very anxious energy and is sabotaging herself. Because of her work with severely mentally ill patients, she admits she's a pro at staying calm at work, but with her bulldogs she's at her wit's end. "I know that she has the experience to deliver this information. She just has to be the doctor to herself."

Since Lynn hasn't been able to vacuum or mop her dusty apartment for weeks, Cesar begins by teaching her to claim these items with a more powerful energy. If she can learn how to address the dog that instigates the troublemaking behavior, the rest of the dogs will fall in line. She must also make sure the dogs never circle behind her, because that is the classic warning sign of a pack attack. Lynn is a slow learner, but finally she experiences a revelation. "That's the first time that any of them, let alone Tallulah, has ever let me vacuum without attacking it, or biting me."

Cesar then shows Lynn how to keep the dogs calm and submissive while leaving the building and in an orderly formation during the walk. He coaches her to

Follow-up ❖ ❖ ❖

Lynn moved to Minneapolis and is counseling soldiers who have post-traumatic stress disorder. Lynn and the dogs have made a lot of progress since their move.

stand up straight and express her leadership through her body language. Lynn is able to experience walking along the spectacular New York harbor for the first time, noticing inspiring sights like the Statue of Liberty instead of obsessing over her badly behaving dogs. Her friend and former dog walker, Jeane, marvels at the transformation—not just the dogs' but also Lynn's: "I saw her get her self-confidence back." "I felt a true sense of freedom," Lynn says. Cesar too is satisfied. "So we create freedom. We embrace the spirit of New York, a beautiful, magical city."

Behind the scenes

Lynn Arlt's four Frenchies are all survivors of the September 11, 2001, World Trade Center attack. Her apartment in Battery Park City is directly across the street from Ground Zero. While she was at work, the entire apartment complex was evacuated just before the World Trade Center buildings collapsed, but her friend and dog walker, Jeane Marie, was able to get all the Frenchies out just in time.

Sweet and Sour Candy

Name: Candy

Breed: Yorkshire terrier

(episode 314)

Four years ago, MTV personality "Downtown" Julie Brown and her husband, Martin Schuermann, bought Candy, a Yorkshire terrier, for their twelve-year-old daughter, Gianna. The family spoiled Candy with toys and affection, letting her get away with everything. Today, Candy doesn't like walking on a leash; she simply sits down and refuses to move. More disturbing, Candy has started trying to bite and attack Gianna. When Julie is in the kitchen and Gianna comes in, Candy goes after her. When Gianna tries to sit or lie next to Julie, Candy bites and attacks her. When Julie picks up her daughter from school each day, the minute Gianna gets in the car, Candy tries to bite her.

When Cesar arrives, he immediately sees that because the family has been treating Candy's bad behaviors as "cute," those behaviors have been allowed to escalate to dangerous levels. "The myth that little dogs should not be disciplined creates instability not just in the dog but in the whole environment," Cesar tells them. "A dog can create unity, or a dog can create separation. And in this case, the dog was creating separation—between mother and daughter." In fact, Cesar is shocked to learn that Julie is more likely to tell her daughter to leave the room than to discipline Candy for biting her! "I think Julie's priorities got lost. Gianna's becoming an adolescent; she's no longer a little girl. So the dog can fulfill Julie's dream of having this eternal baby, but it's beneficial only to the human. So these two sisters are fighting for the attention of the mom. One of them bites, the other one doesn't."

Cesar's job is to get Julie back on track in her pack-leader priorities and to empower Gianna not only to correct Candy but also to create her own special bond with the dog by walking with her. Because Candy is so small, all it takes is a calm-assertive touch to her neck to stop her aggression in its tracks. By the

Follow-up ❀ ❀ ❀ ❀

Shortly before the show's airing, Julie and her family finally started implementing Cesar's techniques, and Candy made a tremendous turnaround. Julie was able to stop Candy from attacking Gianna.

end of the session, Gianna is getting the picture, and Candy is sitting peacefully on her lap—something that hasn't happened in years. Cesar reminds Gianna that if she can handle a yappy Yorkie, she can apply the same techniques to boyfriends down the line! Julie is thrilled and proud of her daughter. "It seems like a little problem, but it has been a big problem for me, because I basically have been pushing Gianna away just to keep the peace, which isn't fair."

"What I feel I did today is, I brought mother and daughter together as a pack," says Cesar at the end of a perfect day. "So I am glad that I am here because I brought back peace and I brought back unity."

Key Cesar Tip

Even though it may seem cute at first, never let a little dog get away with anything you wouldn't let a big dog get away with. Remember, dogs are dogs first, before breed and name.

Dominating Doggies

Name: Penny

Breed: beagle mix

(episode 315)

Supporting players: Rico, Roxy, Lou, and Solomon

Tim Russell and Laura Hildebrandt live in a restored loft in the up-and-coming "artist" area of downtown Los Angeles. Over the past three years, twenty-five foster dogs have been in their care. They currently care for five dogs—Rico, Roxy, Lou, Solomon, and Penny. Beagle mix Penny has proved to be more of a problem than they've ever had to deal with before. Lashing out and barking at any passerby, her anxiety spreads to the rest of the pack, creating dog hysteria on the bustling downtown L.A. streets. Tim describes an outing with Penny as like "walking a cobra." But Penny's aggression isn't a laughing matter. "My fear for Penny is that someday she's going to bite someone and it's gonna be bad and I'm going to have to put her down," says Tim. "And she's my little angel."

From the moment he arrives, Cesar realizes the problem isn't with Penny—it's with Tim. Though Laura had once been the disciplinarian in the multidog household, her chronic lupus has recently made her a less effective boss. But Tim's been unwilling to pick up the baton. "I just can't look in those eyes and get mad for more than a second," Tim admits. Cesar observes Tim get ready to take Penny for a walk. "Tim had a good start. He put the on leash right, he made the approach, he waited till Penny settled down." But once they hit the outside world, Tim's leadership immediately fell apart. "That's when he let Penny in front of him. And from that point on, he was already getting fearful about just getting close to the gate." Now Penny was the aggressive leader and Tim was the terrified follower—a recipe for disaster on the chaotic, bustling streets of downtown L.A.

Cesar takes charge and shows Tim how simple it is to redirect Penny when she begins focusing on a person or another dog and to correct in a to-the-point, nonemotional way. "The correction is just to snap her away from where she is. It's not to hurt her feelings." Cesar brings in his faithful sidekick, Daddy, to test Penny's reaction around another dog that means her no harm. The moment she begins to fixate, Cesar corrects.

When Tim takes the leash, he's still living in fear of an explosion, so his corrections are too tense. Cesar explains, "When you give physical touch and you stay tense, the brain never understands what's the point of it. That's not a correction, that's a punishment." Once Tim begins to understand the difference, Penny's response is remarkable. It's like she's been waiting for this kind of discipline all her life. Tim marvels, "I had no idea I was being so tense and that I was sending it down the leash to Penny. I had no idea that I had so much to do with how she was behaving on the leash out there."

Finally, the group takes a pack power walk through downtown L.A.—a veritable smorgasbord of scents and the perfect testing ground to keep a dog calm and submissive. For Laura and Tim, the day has been a revelation—and a powerful lesson in what true leadership is. "I always thought it was the loudest, the most aggressive, the firmest one who was the top dog," Tim muses. "But it's really the one that is showing control and confidence and is just relaxed about the whole thing."

Follow-up ❀ ❀ ❀

The dogs are doing very well. Tim can walk all six dogs at a time now—including Penny!—with them all staying by his side. All the dogs are less anxious and more obedient.

The Terrible Two

Names: Mollie and Maggie

Breed: Maltese

(episode 316)

Kathleen Kane's two adorable Maltese, Mollie and Maggie, are like her children and like grandkids to her elderly parents, who live in the nearby Fair Oaks Retirement Hotel. Harriet and Wally Kane love having Maggie and Mollie to care for while Kathleen is at work, but the terrible two have become the terrors of the retirement hotel. Maggie has even bitten a couple of the workers there, and the manager said that if the dogs bite one more person, they will have to be banned from the residence. Kathleen doesn't want to deprive Wally and Harriet of having the dogs around, so something has to be done.

When Cesar meets with Kathleen and her parents, Kathleen admits that she's never treated her dogs as dogs but as the children she never had. She actually dropped out of obedience classes because Maggie didn't like them, and she doesn't walk the dogs much because of the ruckus they cause. Because Kathleen never gives her dogs boundaries at home, Cesar is concerned that she's bringing two very unstable minds into a place that requires peace in order to function. "This is as bad as it gets," he tells Kathleen. "This could be very detrimental to the environment, to the parents, and anybody around. The dogs should come to places like this to intensify peace, not to create war."

Cesar asks a volunteer to come to the door, to gauge Mollie and Maggie's response. As usual, they begin to bark and rush the door. Cesar shows Kathleen and her parents how to "own" the space around the door and how to use leadership energy to make the dogs become submissive before the guest enters. Cesar points out to Harriet and Wally that they can use their canes the way emperors of old used staffs and walking sticks—to empower themselves and make themselves bigger in the eyes of the little dogs. "Now you are the emperor of this place!" he tells Wally. But true rehabilitation of the dogs can't take place until Cesar trains Kathleen how to become the pack leader in her own home.

Two days later, Cesar arrives at Kathleen's home to see that she's already taken his first day's lessons to heart by owning the space in front of her door when visitors come to call. But by her own admission, Kathleen is at a loss for what to do about the walk. Mollie and Maggie pull her in opposite directions—they are completely in control. Cesar notes that the harnesses the dogs are wearing work fine with the more submissive Mollie, but Maggie needs a stronger form of control. He has Kathleen place the leash higher up on Maggie's neck, so she'll respond better to corrections. Kathleen is amazed at the changes, and once she learns how to handle the leash without tension, she's walking the dogs together beautifully. Even adding pit bull Daddy to the mix does nothing to mar the delightful experience. Kathleen promises Cesar that walking will be her new routine before she brings the dogs to the nursing home in the mornings.

"I can still love them the way I love them, but first I have to make sure that they know I'm the leader," Kathleen summarizes. "And they're going to be much happier."

Follow-up 🐾 🐾 🐾

Mollie and Maggie are doing so well that the retirement home staff members can now pet them regularly. Peace has been restored to Fair Oaks.

Behind the scenes

Dog Whisperer producers learned about this story from Abbie Jaye Shrewsbury, who was featured with her dog Sparky in Season Two. Abbie Jaye volunteers at Fair Oaks and thought Mollie and Maggie—not to mention Kathleen—could use Cesar's help.

Maureen's Gift

Names: Chloe and Uncle Sam (Sammy)

Breed: cocker spaniel

Maureen walks with new "service" dogs Chloe and Uncle Sam, as Wendy, John, John Sr., and Cesar look on.

Born with cerebral palsy, Maureen Lovetro formed a special bond with her grandfather John during her many months in the hospital. When she was four, Maureen's grandfather promised to buy her a dog when she got older, with the hope that by walking the dog, her legs would grow stronger. Now that Maureen is seventeen, her "gift dog," cocker spaniel Chloe, is eight . . . and things haven't exactly turned out as planned. Maureen's mother, Wendy, never felt that Chloe respected Maureen but instead treated Maureen like her own puppy. Chloe often takes things from Maureen's hands and "taunts" her. While on walks with Maureen, Chloe goes where she wants and pulls on the leash, often knocking Maureen from her walker. If people try to greet Maureen in the house or on the street, Chloe barks and nips at them. Wendy would like Cesar to teach Maureen how to gain Chloe's respect, so she can become a real service dog, as intended.

When Cesar meets the Lovetro family at their Brooklyn, New York, home, he immediately notices the Lovetros' other dog, a shy, peaceful spaniel named Uncle Sam, Sammy for short. The Lovetros had always thought of Sammy as more looks than brains, but Cesar suggests that they've been stuck thinking of Chloe as Maureen's gift and haven't allowed Sammy to try out for the role of Maureen's service dog. "When you ride horses, you don't ride the untamed horse. You ride the tame horse. Right? Because that's a horse that already knows how to be with any human being." Cesar advises Maureen to call up her experience learning to ride horses and draw on the leadership skills she learned there. "We want you to stay in that state. You know, what makes you strong, what makes you unique, what makes you a leader? So it has nothing to do with disability, it has to do with state of mind."

Cesar, Maureen, and Sammy take to the streets of Brooklyn, aided by Maureen's father, John. Sammy is a natural follower, but he keeps bumping into Maureen's walker. So Cesar decides to make the walker into a tool that Maureen can use to guide Sammy. By attaching the leash to the walker, he is able to create a physical boundary that Sammy can't cross—and also give Maureen the ability to use her walker as the leash in order to give corrections. As they move forward, Maureen becomes a more assured leader, and formerly timid Sammy begins to gain confidence. "Slowly Maureen is using all the tools that we have.

And slowly the dog understands that what he's supposed to do is just to stay right there moving forward without being distracted." Next, Cesar puts a backpack on Sammy to intensify the working experience for him. With the backpack on, Sammy transforms into a natural service dog. "Sammy was just looking for a job. We put that backpack on and he feels like a million dollars, you know. He felt good about himself. Working for Maureen is the ultimate state of mind you can give him."

Maureen and Sammy are doing so well that Cesar decides it's time to try to bring Chloe into the mix. But after so many years of running the show, this stubborn spaniel is not eager to become a follower. Wendy has to bring Chloe's haltie training collar to help calm her down. "One thing they forgot to tell Chloe, she was just going to be a gift, not the queen of Brooklyn," Cesar jokes. Cesar wants to condition Chloe to become more of a follower by walking her himself, behind Maureen and Sammy. But as Chloe gets into the flow, he decides to let Maureen try to handle Sammy and the rebellious "queen" together as a pack. Surprisingly, Chloe falls right into line, taking her cues from Sammy! Even Cesar is amazed as Maureen masterfully handles them both by herself!

It's been more than a year since John Lovetro has seen his granddaughter. The family has secretly flown him in from Florida. On the way back to the house with her newly obedient pack of dogs, Maureen looks up to see her grandpa come out from behind a tree. He and Maureen share hugs and tears of amazement. His gift to his granddaughter has finally come to fruition. "I would just say thank you so much to Cesar," Maureen marvels. "It's kind of like a dream come true because it makes me so happy and my grandpa so happy, and I never thought I would be able to control my dogs this well and walk them this well and have them listen to me."

Raw Cotton

Name: Cotton

Breed: American Eskimo dog

(episode 319)

Three years ago, Diane and Eliot Krieger adopted Cotton, an American Eskimo dog, and brought the dog home to their two children, Seth and Adam. In the beginning, Diane liked the fact that Cotton was a bit of watchdog, but it wasn't long before he had taken that role too far. Cotton lunges at guests and attacks windows and doors when people pass by outside. But the real trouble comes when the car pool arrives to pick the children up for school: Cotton attacks their backpacks and chases them around the driveway, scaring the car pool driver and the other kids.

On the morning Cesar comes to meet with the Kriegers and Cotton, Cotton has already bitten two people, including neighbor Terence Duffy, his mortal enemy. Yet Diane is still in a little denial about Cotton's dominant behavior. "One little dog is creating a really uncomfortable way of living. These people have become antisocial because this thirty-five-pound dog is creating this chaos."

Cotton is waiting for Cesar in the garage, in his crate. While Cotton acts aggressively at first, Cesar holds his ground and uses the crate to tower over him, like a bigger dog would do. Without even a touch from Cesar—only his energy—it's just a matter of minutes before Cotton has calmed down and is acting submissive. Next, Cesar brings Cotton into the kitchen to show the Kriegers how to keep him calm during the chaotic mornings and the rush to the car pool. Cesar shows the family— especially harried mom Diane—how to keep Cotton in a calm-submissive position, even with all the activity swirling around him. "We are blocking him and putting him in a follower position, so he can deal with the situation."

When friend and neighbor Terence Duffy came over earlier in the day, Cotton went on the attack. Cesar is determined to prove to the Kriegers and Terence that all Cotton needs is some firm leadership and consistent rules. By Cesar "owning" the area around the door, an amazed Terence passes Cotton

Follow-up ❀ ❀ ❀

The Kriegers have not been able to successfully implement Cesar's techniques.

several times without incident. Now it's up to Cesar to train Diane, Eliot, and the kids to duplicate his efforts. The Kriegers seem to be excellent students—they learn that good leadership has everything to do with projecting the right energy. "The energy you project is the attitude that you have," Eliot observes. Diane too has learned her lesson well. "It's an easy fix. It's so idiot simple that it sort of boggles the mind that we didn't hit on it earlier."

Fears and Phobias

Banjo.

Banjo Runs Scared

Name: **Banjo**

Breed: coonhound

At two years of age, black and tan coonhound Banjo had lived a good portion of his life in an animal testing lab; an isolated, sterile environment where his only human contact was a technician with a syringe who came to draw his blood. Rescued by the Humane Society of Nebraska, Banjo was deemed "too fearful" to be adopted and was only hours away from being euthanized when he caught the eye of Humane Society volunteer Beverly Lachney. "As a matter of fact, that day I could've been a few hours late. It just so happens, I wasn't. So I got him home and let him go in the yard with our other dogs. He loved

Beverly and Bruce work with Banjo every day, and he is far along on his way to trusting humans and becoming a balanced dog.

Behind the scenes

When Cesar decided he needed coon urine to help Banjo, the thankless task of finding a bottle of it on a moment's notice in Nebraska fell to *DW* series coordinating producer Christina Lublin.

my other dogs, but he didn't want anything to do with me or my husband, Bruce."

Four years later, Banjo is still terrified of all people. Although another vet told them Banjo was a lost cause and should be put down, the retired couple is committed to Banjo and contacts Cesar for help. When Cesar learns of the dog's time in the animal testing lab, he says, "They were just using him as an object, as an experiment. So that blocks his whole being: the dignity, the integrity, the honesty, the loyalty are all squashed."

Cesar prepares to meet Banjo in the Lachneys' basement, where all the dogs sleep. He opens the latch to Banjo's kennel and, keeping his back to the dog, slowly slides in. "I'm just letting him feel my energy. This is actually better than talking to the dog. I'm not talking to him, I'm not hugging the dog, or feeling bad about what happened in the past."

Once Cesar feels that Banjo is ready, he slips a collar on the dog and gently leads him outside the kennel. "What is going to create the real trust and real respect is a walk with the pack." Cesar brings the Lachneys along for the walk with all four dogs currently in their care. Although Banjo seems a tad skittish, he appears to have no problem with all the people leading the pack walk. Beverly says, "I am just in shock. I have never seen this before, ever. I'm just amazed."

Next, Cesar wants to appeal to the breed in Banjo. Coonhounds are trackers, so Cesar asks a crew member to find a bottle of raccoon urine (Cesar pronounces it "your-eene"). It is an unbelievably foul-smelling concoction. As Cesar rubs some of the urine across the ground, he explains, "What we're doing is creating a scenario where we can bring more self-esteem. We want the nose to pick up the scent. Automatically the scent tells the brain what to do with it." Within seconds, Banjo picks up the scent and starts following the trail. Beverly is thrilled to see this, because "he's never sniffed anything."

Cesar has one more exercise for Beverly. While in her yard, he wants her to walk Banjo on the leash for a short distance, then drop the leash and walk away from the dog. "That simple exercise is just letting him know that he is not running away from us, *we* move away, which eventually creates the behavior, 'I must follow.'" As if on cue, Banjo walks back over and sniffs Beverly. Overcome with emotion, she exclaims, "I waited four years to see this."

Cesar is hopeful for Banjo's future. "As bad as this case is, a dog that was traumatized by humans recovered. We saw the dog move forward in a matter of a day, and that means a lot."

Imaginary Walls (episode 303)

Name: Jane

Breed: American Eskimo dog–border collie mix

Cesar, on his LandRollers, cruises around Chicago with Jane.

Carolyn Gordon and Giuseppe Scurato got Jane from a rescue group when she was six months old. The dog is now seven and a half years old and she still refuses to walk outside. It seems that anything can frighten her, including wind. Carolyn says, "When Jane doesn't want to go somewhere, she puts her tail between her legs and it looks like she's just paralyzed with fear." According to Giuseppe, "At some point she sees an invisible wall and she doesn't want to cross that wall and she actually runs back home really afraid."

When Cesar makes the journey to Chicago to lend a hand, he tells Carolyn and Giuseppe, "The most important part that we have to focus on right now is just to help her to jump over that obstacle that she's been living with for the past seven years."

Before they head outside, Cesar addresses the fact that Jane barks relentlessly whenever anyone comes to the door. But Carolyn seems unsure, saying, "I'm feeling very unassertive right now because I have this dog I can't control, and it's been for so long that I'm afraid that I'll never be able to do it right." Cesar responds, "But that's just a conversation in your mind." Cesar doesn't want Carolyn's fear of failure to become an insurmountable obstacle to Jane's rehabilitation.

When Cesar decides to walk with Jane to assess the level of her fear, he discovers that after only a few temper tantrums of resistance, the dog is ready to walk right next to him. Next, Cesar slaps on his LandRoller skates and takes Jane for a roll around the neighborhood, with Jane leading him like a sled dog for much of the time. With Jane's energy drained, Cesar has Carolyn walk with Jane on one side and Daddy on the other. "When Carolyn met Daddy, Daddy changed the whole energy. She wasn't thinking anymore. She was just being."

Carolyn is stunned by the change in Jane . . . and in herself. "When we first started walking, I absolutely felt that I had a wall around me—not one that I knew about, and it turned out it wasn't a very hard wall to crumble. That lesson that Cesar taught me about being in the moment—about the stories that we make in our brain—has implications for every area of my life. That was just really powerful."

Follow-up

Jane's fear of leaving the house is completely gone and she now loves her walks.

Behind the scenes

At the time of filming, Giuseppe Scurato, Carolyn's husband, was an executive chef at Boka, a top Chicago restaurant. He treated the crew to a magnificent gourmet dinner the night after filming.

Genoa's Nightmare

Name: Genoa

Breed: golden retriever

In more than twenty years of working with canines, Cesar has discovered that a dog's behavior issues are more about the human than the canine.

Dan and Lori Hall were high school sweethearts who married, raised a family, then adopted golden retriever Genoa. Genoa is a dream dog. She keeps Lori company while she does laundry in the garage, but when Dan comes home and begins using his air compressor in the garage, Genoa's anxiety escalates to the point of panic. Lately, Dan merely has to enter the garage to send Genoa rampaging through the house trying to find a place to hide. Dan says, "It's like a panic attack." Lori adds, "The vet prescribed phenobarbital. We did that and that doesn't even faze her."

Early in the consultation, Cesar asks Lori about her feelings for the garage. After some gentle probing, she admits that she is jealous and sometimes angry about how much time Dan spends out there working on his cars. Cesar tells them, "It really goes back to energy. So if a dog spends a lot of time with a certain human being, and that human being doesn't like a certain area, the dog learns not to like that area."

When they go into the garage, Cesar keeps Lori distracted with a conversation, and he keeps Genoa distracted with some food while Dan turns the air compressor on and off. Although Genoa acts up a bit, he asks Lori to ignore the behavior. "The food is just to soothe the mind for that second. If the dog takes the food, it works only for that second, but at the same time, you're blocking the mind from escalating."

Follow-up 🐾 🐾 🐾

Lori says Dan can turn on the air compressor now and Genoa will not run away. They have a new puppy that does not find the air compressor frightening, which also helps Genoa's peace of mind.

Key Cesar Tip

Dogs live in the moment. That's why they can quickly overcome years of behavioral issues with the proper guidance.

Within sixteen minutes, Genoa is lying on the garage floor showing no signs of panic while the air compressor goes on and off. Cesar believes that Genoa's panic attacks will completely go away if Dan—and especially Lori—create a positive experience for Genoa whenever she's in the garage. A delighted Lori says, "I feel like I have tools now that I can practice with her. I know what to do and how to practice and how to think about it when I'm practicing."

Regarding Howie

Name: Howie

Breed: Lab-chow-shepherd mix

Howie.

In 2004, police officers in Cherokee County, Georgia, discovered the worst case of animal abuse they had ever seen. Officers found Howie, a Lab-chow-shepherd mix, with a leash tied so tightly around his neck that it had grown into his skin. The leash had to be surgically removed. The owner was fined and given a year's probation, but it took six months for Howie to heal. For two years, Howie has resided at the Animal Hospital of Towne Lake and exhibited aggressive behavior toward new people. He is sweet and loving with the staff of the vet's office, but if clients walk by his room, he responds with fierce growls and warning barks. His caretakers despair that he'll remain fearful and unadoptable for the rest of his life.

After speaking with the vets, Cesar is shocked to hear that Howie has not been for a walk in the outside world since he arrived at the hospital two years earlier. Vet techs Kate Barth and Kathy Strickland admit that—even though he's completely physically healed—they are afraid of putting a collar around his neck and traumatizing him more by exposing him to things that might scare him. Cesar sees right away that the women's protective love and attachment to Howie is actually thwarting his growth. "I know that Howie has a horrible story, and I feel for him. But to help somebody psychologically, to help somebody to move forward, we have to live in the moment. It's not about hurting him now; it's about helping him."

When Cesar goes to meet the defensive Howie, he is able to make putting on a leash a pleasant experience for him by associating it with Howie's favorite toy plus affection. The staff looks on in amazement as Cesar takes him for his first trip into the outside world. Howie responds immediately—his body language is good and his timidity disappears almost instantly. "I'm very happy, 'cause he's not a bad case. Come on, Mr. Howie. He did really good!" Cesar shows Kate and Kathy the correct way to walk their former patient to help increase his self-confidence.

While he has been living at the hospital, Howie has become a hero in his own right—by donating blood, he has already saved several animals' lives. But he is afraid of the scale he must be weighed on. After many repetitions and using treats to create some positive associations on the scale, Cesar shows every staff member how easily Howie can come to the location that once spooked him—providing his human pack leaders bring him there with calm-assertive energy.

"I can see a light in the future that I didn't see before," Kathy proclaims. "As Cesar said, this is a new birth for him. This is the day Howie becomes Howie the dog and not Howie the victim that we knew him as."

"I really want to see the whole cycle of a rescue dog," Cesar explains. "We took him away from abusive humans. We already rehabilitated the body. Now we're on the way to rehabilitating him psychologically, so he can eventually find a responsible, loving home."

Follow-up

Howie has been adopted into a wonderful new home, and he frequently returns to the vet's office to visit his old friends. He is behaving well and the new owners do not have any problems with him. They even gave the vet center a painting of Howie as a gift.

Key Cesar Tip

Feeling sorry for a dog that has been abused can actually have negative repercussions for the very animal you want to help. In the animal world, sympathy is a weak energy. The best thing we humans can do for abused animals is to provide them with the kind of confident, calm-assertive leadership they can trust, and to give them room to regain their natural peace of mind.

The Amazing Calvin

Name: Calvin

Breed: Rhodesian ridgeback mix

(episode 313)

After losing his left front leg in a car accident, Calvin, a ridgeback mix, found a loving adoptive family with Tony and Teri Nuss and their young sons, Bennett and Bodie. "Having only three legs doesn't hold Calvin back at all," Tony observes. "I think he thinks other dogs have one too many." But a few weeks after he'd settled in to his new home, the Nusses learned that Calvin had a few tricks up his three paws that would put Houdini

Ridgeback mix Calvin.

to shame—he's an escape artist extraordinaire. When his fearful separation anxiety rears its head, there isn't a door or window he can't open in order to make a dramatic disappearance. When the Nusses started wiring doors and windows shut, Calvin almost killed himself jumping through a glass window to find his owners. He is terrified of strangers, particularly males, and the Nusses fear his next escape may be a fatal one.

After observing Calvin in action, Cesar notes that he's an insecure dog that is also curious. "This kind of dog requires another dog to help him to come out. He will become curious and want to copy the normal dog's behavior." The Nusses eagerly agree to have Cesar help them choose a friend for Calvin that will join their pack.

First, however, Cesar invites Calvin for a short stay at the Dog Psychology Center, to use the power of the pack to help him come out of his shell. In order to get him there, Cesar has to get Calvin to trust him and a leash, without traumatizing him, so he will see strangers in a positive new light. But once at the center, the formally skittish Calvin begins behaving like a new dog. The relaxing influence of the pack inspires him to act more comfortably, even around human strangers, including the Dog Whisperer film crew, which he'd originally found terrifying.

Meanwhile, Cesar makes a visit to L.A.'s North Central Animal Shelter to find Calvin the perfect pal. "We can't be emotional right now. We can't bring an excited dog, anxious dog, nervous dog, tense dog, aggressive dog, or dominant dog into Calvin's life because it's only going to intensify his instability. So the most important thing is to stay focused on what is best for the whole family, which is to bring a calm-submissive dog." Cesar finds that dog in Lucy, a one-year-old female spaniel mix with a sweet, outgoing personality. When Cesar brings Lucy to meet the pack, all the dogs—including Calvin—enthusiastically approve of his selection.

The only obstacle left to overcome is to introduce Lucy and the rehabbed Calvin to Calvin's home environment, where he temporarily reverts to his nervous temperament. When Calvin gets spooked by the camera, Cesar sees a perfect opportunity to teach the Nusses to help Calvin overcome his fears without nurturing them. "So it's your job to bring him to face what made him a little nervous." Only after Calvin relaxes does Cesar reward him. "This is a perfect time to give affection because he's dealing with it."

The Nusses are thrilled with Lucy as a new addition to their pack and are hopeful for Calvin's future. "I think we've finally learned how to treat a dog so that you get the most out of him and he gets the most out of life," Tony summarizes.

Follow-up 🐾 🐾 🐾

Calvin and Lucy are inseparable, and the family is grateful to Cesar for all of his help.

The Stubborn Italian Mastiff

Name: Promise

Breed: Italian mastiff

Paul and Pamela Stockwell's Italian mastiff Promise is a wonderful dog in many ways, but the one-year-old big beauty is simply terrified of cars—both getting into them and riding in them. At ninety pounds, it's nearly impossible to hoist her up. Once in the car, she'll shake and her bowels will literally explode all over the backseat. Unfortunately, Promise must make regular visits to the vet due to her bad hips.

"I knew that the only way I could help Promise," Cesar observes, "was if I made the right promise, which is you can move forward with me." Seeing forward momentum as the key to overcoming Promise's phobia, Cesar uses a food reward plus the neighbor's yard to create an "obstacle" course for the horse-sized dog to condition her to plow ahead against all barriers. Surprisingly, Promise takes to the obstacle course, so much that it becomes "Disneyland" to her—she doesn't even care about the food reward! Using this as incentive, Cesar makes getting in and out of the car a part of the course, and Promise follows him right in. "It was just a matter of unlocking the brain from hesitating for so long and from having traumatic experiences in the car."

Follow-up 🐾 🐾 🐾

Promise is doing wonderfully in the car. Pamela says they have bought a new SUV with more room for her, which has also helped. While they need to coax her into the car, she is not frightened anymore. Promise goes to the vet and to the park in the car without incident.

Now it's Paul and Pamela's turn to try. At first, their hesitation sends Promise right back to her old mind-set. But once they relax, they too are able to get her into the once-hated vehicle. Cesar shows them how to make Promise wait inside the car until she relaxes—an exercise in patience—and gives them the homework of constantly repeating these exercises before the next trip to the vet. "Increase the amount of time the dog stays in the car—five minutes, ten, fifteen minutes. Feed the dog in the car. Give water in the car. Create positive associations in the car," Cesar orders. "You just gotta go and do it again, in a calm-assertive way, a thousand times."

Obsessions

The Farmer and the Dog

Name: Molly

Breed: blue heeler

Molly has some big paws to fill, being the latest in a series of farm dogs to work the fields with three generations of the Eggers family farmers. Mark and his daughter, Lesha Eggers, got Molly when she was a few months old and trained her to be the herding dog her breed prepared her to be—but they also fell in love with her. "There's a strict division between a working dog and a pet. Molly has completely combined those roles. She's more than just a working dog to us. She's a sweetheart and she's my dad's best friend," claims Lesha.

After six months of happy puppydom, Molly began exhibiting a life-threatening obsession. First, she started biting at the tires on Mark's pickup

Follow-up

Since Cesar's visit, Molly's had no more injuries or accidents from compulsively chasing tires. Though she still sometimes has the desire to chase them, the Eggerses can control her when they are consistent about corrections.

Behind the scenes

At the time of filming, Lesha Eggers was a recent graduate of the University of Nebraska, Lincoln, and was about to begin veterinary school in Ames, Iowa.

Key Cesar Tip

Cesar strongly urges seeking the help of a professional whenever considering the use of an e-collar.

truck. Then Molly would chase the truck down the driveway, snapping at the tires, until the day she caught a tire, her teeth stuck, and she flipped over. But losing some teeth didn't faze Molly; she progressed to the bigger tires on the farm's tractors and combines, with tragic results that damaged her jaw and cost her an eye. The Eggers' vet has warned that Molly's life is in danger if she chases tires again.

Because this is a life-and-death situation, Cesar recommends the use of an electronic collar, or e-collar, a device the family had tried a few times and then abandoned. Cesar says, "This is an extreme case, so we really have no choice. We have to come up with a tool that can help to keep her alive." As he puts the e-collar on Molly, Cesar gives her an affectionate rub and tells the Eggerses, "We want her to associate the tool with something positive, something that she enjoys, and that has implications for every area of her life. She will definitely enjoy affection and massages."

Cesar sets the collar's remote-control handset at 40 percent, which will not shock Molly but create a feeling like a joy buzzer, which is intended simply to startle her and cause her to stop the unwanted behavior. Molly's first test is on Mark's pickup truck. The moment Cesar sees Molly fixate on the tires, he pushes the button on the e-collar and, although the sensation lasts less than one second, it makes Molly run away from the truck.

Next, Cesar corrects Molly around the treacherous wheels of the tractor. When Cesar sees Molly start to move toward the tire, he hits the button and she immediately backs away. Molly learns fast. After only two corrections with the collar, she's already avoiding the temptation of the tires. After Cesar shows the Eggerses precisely how to use the collar, he says. "Tools like the e-collar are here to help, just like the tools that they use around a farm. Those tools are helping the farmer to stay alive, to keep everything in place, to keep everything balanced."

Ironing Out Fosse

Name: Fosse

Breed: Yorkshire terrier

Six years ago, Daphne Logan purchased four-pound Fosse from a breeder. Named after dancer-choreographer Bob Fosse, this petite pup has completely taken over Daphne's morning routine. Not only does he hate Daphne's deodorant and hair dryer, he goes completely out of control around the iron and ironing board. "It has escalated over the years. He attacks the legs, the cover, everything. Now he's gotten past the ironing board itself and attacks the actual iron cord, which of course is dangerous."

Pit bull Daddy meets Yorkshire Fosse.

Cesar has contended with a wide variety of vicious little dogs over the years, but he's never met one that has an issue with ironing boards! "I think this is one of those cases of a little dog gone bad. Little dogs get away with a lot of unwanted behavior because they're cute, and people think they should not be disciplined because their feelings might get hurt." Cesar informs Daphne that when little dogs get carried everywhere, they can develop a Napoleon complex because they tower over every other dog while in their owner's arms. "But even if he's just two inches big, a dog needs exercise, discipline, and then affection."

They head to Daphne's bedroom for an iron showdown. When Cesar starts to remove the ironing board from the closet, Fosse starts to charge. Cesar gives the terrier a tap on the neck and the dog backs away. After that, Cesar is able to use "*tsst*" to make Fosse back off. "The less he gets to his target, the less powerful he becomes." But when Daphne tries, it's not easy for the nearly six-foot-tall woman to bend down quickly to give tiny Fosse a correction. "One of the assets of the little dog is how fast he can move. And a lot of people become defeated by the speed and by the ability to run and disappear." Cesar recommends that Daphne keep Fosse on a leash when

Follow-up ✻ ✻ ✻

Daphne can now stop Fosse's behavior when he attempts to go after the ironing board.

Key Cesar Tip

It's best not to use a dog's name when disciplining it, so as not to have the dog associate its own name with unwanted behaviors. Also, Cesar advises clients not to use a dog's name when its mind is in any way unstable.

she works with the ironing board. That way she can step on his leash whenever he tries to run away.

When Cesar suggests that Daphne channel the energy of someone powerful in her life, she selects her mom, a former school principal. In less than thirty minutes, Daphne is able to make Fosse back away from the ironing board and iron. Daphne is impressed. "I've seen the show on TV many times and knew that it was fast, but I didn't know that it was *that* fast. You have to see it to believe it, I guess."

Gracie and Me

Name: Gracie

Breed: Labrador retriever

(episode 309)

After the death of Marley, hero of the best-selling book *Marley & Me*, author John Grogan and his wife, Jenny Vogt, brought home Gracie, a yellow Lab, just like Marley. The Grogans were happy to learn that unlike the clumsy, hyperactive Marley, Gracie was peaceful and sedate. But it soon became apparent that Gracie had her own very different issues in the bad behavior department. Marley always wanted to be in the middle of family affairs, but Gracie is aloof and refuses to come when called. She is also obsessed with stalking and hunting animals and birds in the Grogans' expansive backyard. Gracie has wined and dined on one of the Grogans' favorite chickens, Liberace, and would clearly like nothing more than a few more of the family pets for coffee and dessert. The formerly free-ranging chickens are now bunkered down in a coop outside the perimeter of the Grogans' electronic fence, where Gracie continues to stare at them and drool.

A devoted fan of *Marley & Me*, Cesar is thrilled at the opportunity to meet the family of the "world's worst dog." But while the Grogans seem to believe that Marley's and Gracie's issues are worlds apart, Cesar sees an immediate similarity. "I got from your book that you were able to create trust and loyalty but not respect with Marley." Cesar explains that this is exactly the

Cesar, the Grogans, and Gracie.

A chicken aids Cesar with Gracie's rehabilitation.

same situation that exists with Gracie. "If they respect you when you say, 'Come,' they come. Boom. No questions asked, no hesitations. There can be a rabbit right in front of her and she will come." The difference with Gracie is, she's a purebred dog from a long line of hunting stock. Because she's bored, because she doesn't respect her owners, she is practicing the "calling" of her breed on her own. "Once you buy a purebred dog, expect more intensity," says Cesar. "Now if you don't fulfill the needs of that breed, the dog is going to give you problems."

Cesar starts the exercise by "claiming" the Grogans' chickens and correcting Gracie when she begins to fixate on them. Little by little, Gracie begins to become desensitized to the chickens. The chicken in Cesar's arm is so relaxed at one point that she lays an egg. "Oh, my God!" Cesar exclaims. "I'm a dad."

Cesar also instructs the Grogans to take advantage of the hunting professionals in their community to help teach them how to control Gracie's powerful instincts instead of being controlled by them. The Grogans contact local obedience trainer Missy Lemoi, who also helps prepare retrievers for field trials. Missy is an expert in harnessing the natural instincts of these intelligent animals.

Five weeks later, Cesar returns to check on Gracie's progress. Jenny and Gracie have been working with Missy, and they demonstrate a game called "runaway" that will help Gracie come when called. "It's like a giant game of hide-and-seek with the dogs," Missy explains. "Gracie needs to use her nose in a hunting mode, and what better than to have her go hunting for her family?" To demonstrate a more advanced exercise that she hopes Gracie will be able to complete someday, Missy brings in a Labrador named Hawkeye—a champion retriever that can respond to hand signals from Missy in searching for hidden objects. "You know, the Labrador is a retriever. They don't kill, they retrieve," Cesar points out. "But because nobody used that part of Gracie's breed she went into predator mode. So we are going to block the predator and bring out the retriever."

The Grogans are hopeful and optimistic when they bid good-bye to Cesar. "If we had you to help us with Marley," Jenny jokes, "we wouldn't have had a book." Cesar smiles. "You know, Marley made a lot of people laugh. Marley made a lot of people cry. I feel like he guided me here today to help John and Jenny to get the respect they needed and Gracie the balanced life she deserves."

Follow-up ❀ ❀ ❀ 🐾

The Grogans report that Gracie is becoming more and more obedient and that Jenny and Gracie are starting an intermediate training class together. They also plan to get more animals, including chickens! All of their hard work is a great tribute to Marley.

My Three Schnauzers

Names: Cassie, Skyler, and Tori

Breed: miniature schnauzer

Jim and Marcia Sasser's miniature schnauzer Tori is obsessed with spinning in circles. After about a year, the Sassers decided to try to solve the problem with some playmates for Tori, two more miniature schnauzers—littermates Cassie and Skyler. However, Tori's spinning didn't sit well with the new additions to the family. Whenever Tori begins her whirling routine, Cassie and Skyler attack her. When Jim and Marcia try to pick up Tori, Cassie and Skyler bite at Tori's feet. Tori has been spinning for five years, and the attacks have been escalating and are now drawing blood. "I got these dogs for Tori to play with, and instead they torment her. It's gotten so bad that I really think that they're going to kill her," says Marcia, who is wracked with guilt.

When Cesar arrives, he immediately pinpoints the cause of the Sassers' home warfare. Since the spinning Tori is so obviously unstable, the two other schnauzers are doing for the pack what the Sassers have not done for five long years—they are trying to correct the erratic behavior! It's time to teach the humans how to become leaders of this three-dog pack.

Since the ringing doorbell is often an instigator of the household mayhem, Cesar demonstrates how to put a leash on Tori and simply step on it to stop her before she begins to spin. In a very short time, Cesar has her remaining calm and submissive, even after repeated doorbell rings. What's most interesting is the reaction of the other dogs. When they see that Tori's not going to spin, there's nothing for them to get upset about. So they stay calm as well. "Because she is not misbehaving, they're living in the moment. That's what I want you to understand. Live in the moment."

Jim and Marcia Sasser each practice correcting the dogs, always addressing themselves first to the dog that is instigating the problem. When Cesar asks Jim, a supervisor of a large department, how he would react to an employee who was displaying

Follow-up ❀ ❀ ❀

Jim and Marcia report tremendous improvements, and although Tori still spins occasionally and Cassie can attack, they are much better at controlling the situation.

When the *Dog Whisperer* crew arrived at the Sassers' Atlanta home, they could hear the three schnauzers' high-pitched barking from far down the block. The Sassers themselves were so accustomed to the chaos that they didn't even seem to notice the annoying racket. During the consultation, Cesar learned that the couple had owned miniature schnauzers for years yet had never once walked them! The Sassers attributed the bedlam and the barking to the breed. Once they learned how to master the walk, they discovered that one of Cesar's frequent axioms is true: it's not the breed, it's the owners!

neurotic behavior, Jim answers readily: "Generally I go ahead and take them off to the side first and clear the air: 'Okay, there's not going to be any of this, you know, going on.'" "So there's no negotiation?" Cesar observes. Suddenly, the lightbulb goes off for Jim. "So that's what I need to be doing here."

The couple must also learn how to prevent Cassie and Skyler from attacking Tori when they go to pick her up. "Picking up Tori is not allowed by Cassie and Skyler; that is just a big no-no in this house." Cesar describes what the dogs were trying to communicate when they attacked. "'You do not touch Tori. She is an unstable creature. She is gonna give you the cooties if you pick her up.'" By owning their space and creating an invisible boundary around Tori, Marcia can communicate to the other dogs that everything's all right.

"It amazed me,"Marcia says at the end of the day. "Just that it can happen that fast, that the dogs are smart, and they're wanting to make the correction. We just never did it before."

Motor Mouth

Name: Rudy

Breed: Jack Russell terrier

When Mary and Mark Bursack took up the hobby of motorcycle riding, trouble began to brew with their Jack Russell terrier, Rudy. Rudy's a mama's boy—very attached to Mary. The moment her sees her putting on her leathers to get ready to ride, he starts to get agitated and begins barking incessantly. Rudy also attacks the muffler of the motorcycle, which can be dangerous when the muffler gets hot. Mary and Mark would really like to take Rudy with them when they ride their motorcycles; they even bought a special bag to carry him in. Riding Harleys is a big part of their lives and they want to share it with him.

Being a Jack Russell, Rudy already has high spirits in his genes—yet Cesar notes that the Bursacks are contributing to his overly excited nature by yelling at him when he acts up. "The escalation of excitement, anxiety, and dominance creates an explosion," says Cesar. "He's anxious about the motorcycle, he's nervous about it, he's fearful about it—so that's the weakness. And he covers that with strength by attacking the motorcycle." It takes only two physical corrections before Rudy gets the picture, responding to Cesar's calm-assertive energy alone and relaxing in the presence of the Harley.

Because Mary is the pack leader of the family, Cesar first works to empower weak-link Mark with Rudy. Showing Mark how to employ the same techniques he used with Rudy, Cesar teaches Mark to reduce the dog's anxiety and then to invite Rudy aboard the bike when he's calm-submissive. Next, it's Mary's turn. Cesar shows her how not to let Rudy's excitement escalate when she puts on her leathers and to gently correct him when he gets anxious, instead of nurturing his anxiety. By the end of the session, Rudy is aboard a bike ready to rumble, and the Bursacks see clearly how their behavior had inadvertently contributed to the problem. "It was more for us; we made *us* feel good reinforcing that bad behavior because we thought it was the right thing to do. We got him all excited, and basically he was able to take control and we lost control."

Follow-up ❀ ❀ ❀

Mary and Mark really tried to get Rudy used to the motorcycle but were ultimately unsuccessful. Mary wishes Rudy could ride on the back of the motorcycle with her, but she accepts him and loves him for who he is.

Before he leaves, Cesar counsels the Bursacks to go on a vigorous walk or run with Rudy before they invite him to go biking with them. He's a high-energy dog and needs an outlet for his frustration that doesn't have two wheels. The Bursacks are pleased. Mary says, "I totally believe that within a short period of time, being consistent, that Rudy can enjoy the motorcycle with us and be a part of what we like to do."

Collie without Borders

Name: Milo

Breed: border collie

(episode 313)

Living on a working ranch with horses, Tanii and Charles Carr wanted border collie Milo to accompany them when riding and walking. But at six months old, Milo stopped obeying his owners. He began chasing the horses; he's been kicked by them more than once and taken to the vet, but even pain hasn't stopped him. Now, at sixteen months, Milo's herding instincts have expanded from herding horses to herding cars. Tanii can't walk him by the street without fearing for his life. The Carrs want him to remain a working dog, but most of all, they want him to be safe.

Cesar arrives at the Carrs' ranch, hoping to corral this errant border collie. First, he has to teach Tanii and Charles that they need to control Milo before they even leave the house for a walk. Making him calm-submissive to the leash, leaving the house before him, and leading, not following him on the walk itself are all new skills that the Carrs have to master. By keeping Milo's attention focused on the pack leader, and by picking up the pace of the walk, Cesar prevents him from fixating on the cars going past.

Finally, it's time to tackle Milo's issues in the horse ring. Cesar starts by making sure Milo is calm-submissive before approaching the horses. Cesar has Milo wait outside the ring, and corrects him only when he begins to fixate on the horses. Because Cesar and Milo already bonded on the walk, Cesar is able to influence him from far away, using just sound, eye contact, and energy. Milo gets the message instantly. When the exercise is over, Cesar tells the Carrs to make sure to reward the behavior.

"The lesson is, you need to learn how to stop your dog from becoming too excited early on," Cesar summarizes. "Don't wait until he's already out of control."

Follow-up ❀ ❀ ❀

Milo is definitely better since doing the show. He walks better when Tanii is being the leader and doesn't pull her around cars. He's much better behaved around the horses too. He still has some issues, but Tanii says it has to do with her finding the time to work with Milo—she knows it's not Milo's fault.

Actress Virginia Madsen with Jack and their dog Spike.

Family Decisions

Name/Breed: Spike/French bulldog

Name/Breed: Belle/Chihuahua mix

Academy Award nominee Virginia Madsen and her eleven-year-old son Jack suffered a loss in their family—Dixie, a thirteen-year-old shepherd mix. When Dixie became ill with pancreatitis, the time came to make a difficult decision. Virginia called Cesar, who had helped her with Dixie six years earlier. Virginia recalls Cesar's advice, "You can keep giving her medication and it's going to hide the symptoms, but the illness is still there. You can sense it if it's time. The dog will let you know if it's time." Jack agreed with Cesar's assessment. "Dixie looked at me in a way that I've never seen. She looked at me like, spiritually, and I knew it was time for her to go, because I could tell she was in pain."

When they decided to put Dixie to sleep, it was a tragedy for both the family and their ten-year-old French bulldog, Spike. After Dixie's death, Spike was depressed and lethargic, but recently he has been acting like his old self again. Virginia calls on Cesar to help them adopt a pet that's a good match for Spike.

Cesar tells Virginia and Jack how dogs deal with the loss of a pack member. "They do grieve, and then they move on. Everything is a process—being born, living, and dying. Spike let us know what would be the right process. Let's go through it, let's embrace it, and let's move on."

Rescue group United Hope for Animals brings over an array of small dogs recently rescued from Mexico for the family to choose from. Jack is attracted to Foxy, a two-year-old Pomeranian-papillon mix who bears a resemblance to Dixie. Virginia selects Belle, a vocal four-month-old female Chihuahua mix. The group heads out to the backyard where they can observe both candidates off leash. Foxy immediately starts marking his territory around the bushes. Although Jack is leaning toward Foxy, Cesar makes an important observation about Foxy's dominant behavior. "Jack went into a little emotional state instead of a psychological state about it. If you focus only on how cute the dog is, you pay the consequences."

Cesar suggests removing Foxy for a little while, so Jack can see how Belle behaves on her own. Jack ultimately decides that Belle should become part of their family. Cesar is pleased and says, "There's a lot of wisdom in this house. That's why I didn't give them any instructions today." After making their decision, they learn that Belle was about to be electrocuted in a Mexican pound just before she was rescued by United Hope for Animals.

Even though Jack is excited about Belle, there will always be a place in his heart for Dixie. "Even if you lose a dog, and you can't see it, or you can't feel it, that doesn't mean that it's not there. It's always with you, there's always a little piece of him in your heart. If you think about it, they're always with you."

Follow-up ❧ ❧ ❧

Virginia and Jack loved their new life with Spike and Belle. Unfortunately, several months after they adopted Belle, she ran into the street and was killed when she was hit by a car.

Key Cesar Tip

If you are getting a dog to replace a recently departed pet, make sure you have gone through the grieving process, so your new dog doesn't pick up weak energy from your state of mind.

Cesar's Special Delivery

Name: various

Breed: various

(episode 310)

It is said that "neither snow nor rain nor heat nor gloom of night stays these couriers from the swift completion of their appointed rounds." But nobody said anything about dogs. According to the U.S. Postal Service, approximately two thousand letter carriers each year are the victims of dog bites. One of them is Bonnie Moon of Atlanta, Georgia. On Bonnie's route, she faces lunging dogs, growling dogs, barking dogs, and the infamous "Don't worry, he doesn't bite" dogs that every mail carrier fears. "I walked up to a customer's house, she had a certified letter. I was getting ready to have her sign it, and one of her dogs bit me and punctured the skin. I've never been afraid of animals, but after that bite, I still am apprehensive about going to any door."

Cesar with USPS letter carrier Bonnie.

Cesar travels to Atlanta to teach Bonnie and her coworkers how to handle the dogs on their routes. After giving a miniseminar and answering questions for a group of letter carriers, Cesar heads out with Bonnie on her rounds. They arrive at the house where Bonnie's recent dog bite took place. The two dogs in residence like to charge the front door. Bonnie's assailant was a high-strung miniature pinscher. Cesar says, "It's very important that letter carriers and dog owners work together. Dog owners have to exercise their dogs and they have to learn how to create boundaries so the letter carrier won't feel challenged by the dog." Cesar has the dogs' owner, Courtney, put them on a leash for the exercise. But when Courtney moves to answer the front door, her dogs go ahead of her and Cesar says, "What you just did right now, you just empowered them, because you were following them. You were holding the leash, but you were not in front of them."

Bonnie and Cesar head for another problem house where one day a dog came

Follow-up ❀ ❀ ❀

Cesar's advice has helped tremendously with the dogs on Bonnie's route. She now keeps a positive attitude and the dogs react very differently. Mr. Ardell, one of the residents on Bonnie's route whom we profiled, has found that Cesar's methods have greatly improved the behavior of his dog, Opie. Opie now sits on command when Bonnie comes to the door with the mail and no longer barks at the postal jeep.

Key Cesar Tip

Many letter carrier–dog conflicts could be avoided if dog owners learn to be responsible, to teach rules, boundaries, and limitations to their dogs and to try to introduce their dogs to their letter carriers. "They have to make the time," says Cesar. "Otherwise, how can the dog learn that this person is a nice person?"

bolting out the door, "and the customer said, 'Well, the dog is okay, he won't bite.' But how do we know that?" When Cesar observes the dog in action, he says, "The owner was right. This dog, in the beginning, would not want to hurt you, but if you move wrong, you can get hurt. Again in this case, we actually saw a dog that had no clear-cut boundaries."

Cesar wants Bonnie to realize that if she displays fear around a dog, that dog will pick up her fearful energy as weak energy, which could trigger an attack. If Bonnie can project a calm and assertive energy while delivering the mail, she can reduce the number of dog incidents.

Bonnie is grateful for her lesson in dog psychology. "I feel that Cesar gave me a sense of power within myself to be able to go up with an assertive energy but yet a calming energy. I'm looking forward to trying that when I meet those dogs that don't necessarily like me."

A Ruff Day at the Office

(episode 309)

Name/Breed: Bella/boxer

Name/Breed: Big Boy/pit bull mix

In keeping with their company's casual, free-spirited image, the owners of Paul Frank Industries allow workers to bring dogs to the office and even provide a private dog park. The majority of the dogs are relatively well behaved, save two—boxer Bella and pit bull mix Big Boy. Bella belongs to co-owner John Oswald, and as the boss's dog, no one wants to tell her what to do. She dominates the entire office, going where she pleases and asserting herself over whomever she wants. Big Boy belongs to Jillian Leeman, the business sales manager. Big Boy fixates on his toys and is aggressive toward other dogs. It's gotten to the point where Jillian can't bring Big Boy to work anymore.

Cesar takes Big Boy for a swim.

Cesar tackles the easier case first. "Bella is a basic case of a dominant dog that has not had regular rules, boundaries, and limitations in her life." Cesar follows Bella through the offices that house the dogs Bella is used to terrorizing and shows the dog owners how to snap Bella out of it. Despite the fact that Bella belongs to the boss, he wants all the employees to become Bella's pack leader. "At the moment she switches from being calm-submissive to assertive, we have to do something about it. If everybody participates that way, she stays calm-submissive."

Big Boy, however, is another story. "This is one of those typical cases that go to the center," Cesar tells Jillian. "This is not a case where you can help at home." Once Jillian arrives at the center with Big Boy, she learns that it won't be only Big Boy undergoing treatment. Cesar perceives Jillian's anxiety and unsure demeanor as the weak link in the relationship. "I also want you to practice leadership with my pack before you leave him here," cautions Cesar. "I want you to leave with that state of mind in your own internal self. So it's really about empowering you that creates balance in him."

Jillian returns home, realizing that she's got a lot of work to do on herself before she can help Big Boy.

Meanwhile, Big Boy adjusts well to the pack and welcomes the opportunity for them to teach him doggie social skills. "What he's doing is really good because he's allowing other dogs to smell him, and that makes him the submissive one, that makes him the respectful one. This is why the pack becomes so vital to the rehabilitation. Big Boy is doing absolutely great."

Twenty-three days later, Jillian returns to show that she too has been rehabilitated. When she handles Big Boy in front of Cesar and the pack this time, she's firm and confident in her demeanor. Cesar is genuinely impressed. "I didn't tell her what to do. She just did it on her own. She's really doing a 180."

Finally, Cesar gathers together all the Paul Frank Industries employees and congratulates them on their new pack-leading skills. Now, former troublemakers Bella and Big Boy are the role models for the rest of the dogs. And the whole company is participating. Says one employee, "Everyone's become pack leaders. Everyone is trying their hardest to keep peace among all the dogs."

Baseball Dog

Name: Joe

Breed: Australian shepherd

The first time Debbie Meymarian took her one-year-old Australian Shepherd Joe to watch one of her softball games, it was a disaster. Debbie tried leaving Joe behind the fence with her friend and softball teammate, Shelye Potter, but whenever Debbie came up to bat, he started to panic and bark. He's broken free of his leash and run onto the field twice, chasing Debbie around the bases and disrupting the game. In the gym that Debbie and Shelye own together, Joe also acts up if anyone—including Shelye—tries to take him away from Debbie.

Joe learns to walk on a treadmill.

Cesar and Debbie strike out with each other at their first consultation on the ball field. Cesar notices that Debbie won't make eye contact with him, doesn't smile, and will not admit that her behavior has any part in Joe's problems. Cesar asks Debbie if Joe is "dominant," and Debbie replies, "No. He's 'willful.'" It remains to be seen who the willful animal really is.

When Cesar first takes Joe away from Debbie, the dog protests wildly, but within minutes he is happily walking around the field with Cesar. But Shelye gets upset watching Joe struggle, and Debbie is tense and defensive. "I didn't feel that either woman was behind what I was trying to accomplish. The negative energy they were both practicing was being transferred to Joe." After two more strikeouts, Cesar decides to take the unusual step of calling off the rest of the day's game. Although he takes pride in never giving up on a dog, he feels he is not getting his message through to Debbie and Shelye. He agrees to meet them at their gym the following week.

Surprisingly, when Cesar arrives at the gym, he sees a huge improvement in attitude—not just Joe's, but Debbie's and Shelye's as well. Debbie has been giving Joe limits for the first time in his life, and Shelye's relieved that Debbie is finally admit-

Follow-up ❀ ❀ ❀

Joe no longer barks at clients and Shelye can walk him without any problems. They've yet to take him back out to the baseball diamond, though.

ting that she is a part of the problem. Cesar's goal today is a come-from-behind victory—getting Joe to walk on the treadmill, which will help keep him calm at the gym while Debbie is working. At first, Debbie is in "mommy mode," and her overprotectiveness only fuels Joe's panic. But when Cesar coaches her to go into "personal trainer mode" with Joe, everything changes, and she sees how an inner shift in her own energy can transform Joe almost instantly. Debbie and Shelye are overjoyed, but it's Cesar who's the most surprised at today's upset victory. "I got to see a totally different side of Debbie today. I never give up on dogs, but from today on, I will not give up on people as long as they don't give up on themselves."

Hope Has No Borders

United Hope for Animals

(episode 317)

United Hope for Animals is a nonprofit organization committed to ending the suffering and mistreatment of dogs and cats in Tijuana and Southern California. Composed entirely of volunteers, United Hope makes innumerable trips to Tijuana, offering free spaying and neutering clinics, as well as humane euthanasia as an alternative to electrocution. The volunteers, including founder Laura Sandoval, rescue the dogs that have a good chance of getting a new home in the States, spay or neuter them, and bring them back to the United States.

Cesar adopts Molly, one of the dogs rescued by United Hope for Animals.

In this episode, Cesar Millan joins the brave volunteers of United Hope in their mission to rescue these stray pets and to educate the citizens of Tijuana about the serious problem of overpopulation of dogs and cats in Mexico. He begins by showing Laura and her coworkers the correct way to rescue the dogs from the Tijuana pound, in order to bring them to freedom with the calmest state of mind. Next, the group visits the volunteer spaying and neutering clinic. Since one female dog and her offspring can potentially produce as many as sixty-seven thousand dogs in just six years, spaying and neutering is a vital part of improving the lives of Mexico's dog population.

Back in Southern California, Cesar meets the selfless volunteers who foster rescued dogs from California and Mexico until they can be placed in permanent homes. "Dogs that are kept in kennels become less and less adoptable," says a volunteer. "Within weeks they become frustrated and angry. A foster person that has a dog in his home, he's observing the dog, interacting with the dog." Cesar works with these volunteers, giving them pointers to help the dogs they foster with some of their issues. At the same time, he falls in love with one of rescued pups, a female dachshund named

Follow-up ❧ ❧ ❧

Little Lilly was diagnosed with advanced liver disease and has since passed away. However, Cesar's visits to Mexico and to Southern California for this United Hope for Animals segment resulted in several successful adoptions.

Molly. "I always wanted to own a dachshund, and I guess I came here to help these wonderful ladies with a little knowledge, but they're going to help me to fulfill my dream."

Finally, Cesar brings an invalid Chinese crested mix named Lilly to the Dog Psychology Center where, despite her many health issues, the pack shows her how to join in with the group and simply enjoy being a dog for the first time in her short life.

DOG WHISPERER WITH CESAR MILLAN
Staff and Crew Credits

Executive Producers
Jim Milio
Melissa Jo Peltier
Mark Hufnail

Producers
Sheila Possner Emery
Kay Bachman Sumner

Series Producer
SueAnn Fincke

Directors
Mark Cole
SueAnn Fincke
Mark Hufnail
Jim Milio
Melissa Jo Peltier

Written by
Jim Milio
&
Melissa Jo Peltier

Editors
Mark Baum
Steven Centracchio

George Copanas
Diana Friedberg
Vicki Hammel
Edick Hossepian
Janelle Neilson
Nena Olwage

Coordinating Producer
Christina Lublin

Associate Producer
Ilusion Millan

Directors of Photography
Bryan Duggan
Christopher Komives

Sound
Miles Ghormley
Percy Urgena

Associate Producer
Nicholas Bunker

Location Manager
Rojo

Post-Production Supervisors
Todd Carney
John Gengl
Beth Jones

Post-Production Coordinator
Aaron Kraft

Assistant Editors
Anouk Erni
Joe Espina
Treyva Estler
Tony Nigro

Script Assistant
Nicholas Ellingsworth

Production Assistants
Bill Parks
Nicholas Ellingsworth
Todd Henderson
Michael St. John
Nicholas Kober
K. C. Duggan

Vice President, Finance
Catherine Stribling

Production Accountants
Bonnie Haner
Amy Higgins
Chris Zerwas

Original Music
Andrew Keresztes
Anouk Erni

Additional Music
Killer Tracks, a unit of BMG Entertainment

Additional Music
String Fever Music/Gregg C. Miner

Special Thanks to
Hadler Public Relations

Executive in Charge of Production
Bonnie Peterson

For National Geographic Channel

Senior Executive Producers
Colette Beaudry
Char Serwa

Senior Vice President, Production
Juliet Blake

Senior Vice President, Production
Michael Cascio

Executive in Charge of Production
John B. Ford

Produced for National Geographic Channel by
MPH Entertainment

in association with
Emery/Sumner Productions

RESOURCES

How and where can I adopt a pet?

Petfinder. www.petfinder.com. Listing over two hundred thousand adoptable animals in shelters across the United States.

PETS 911. www.pets911.com. Listing thousands of adoptable pets, as well as local veterinarians, spay/neuter resources and locations, and local volunteer opportunities.

What do I need to consider before I adopt a pet?

Humane Society of the United States.   http://hsus.org/pets/pet_adoption_information/

Where can I donate to help shelter pets?

The Cesar and Ilusion Millan Foundation.   www.millanfoundation.org

Where can I volunteer for shelter and rescue pets?

www.networkforgood.org

Where can I find information on spaying or neutering my pet?

SPAY/USA.   www.spayusa.org   1-800-248-7729.

Where can I find a canine professional in my area?

We recommend the International Association of Canine Professionals.   www.dogpro.org

Other great animal welfare resources, covering a wide variety of topics

The Humane Society of the United States.   www.hsus.org

ASPCA.   www.aspca.org

Best Friends Animal Society.   www.bestfriends.org

DOG BREED INDEX

DOG NAME INDEX